People
and Cultures
of Hawaii

People and Cultures of Hawaii

A Psychocultural Profile

Edited by
John F. McDermott, Jr.
Wen-Shing Tseng
Thomas W. Maretzki

John A. Burns School of Medicine
and University of Hawaii Press
Honolulu

COPYRIGHT © 1980 BY THE UNIVERSITY PRESS OF HAWAII
ALL RIGHTS RESERVED
MANUFACTURED IN THE UNITED STATES OF AMERICA

92 91 90 89 88 87   8 7 6 5 4

Library of Congress Cataloging in Publication Data

Main entry under title:

People and cultures of Hawaii.

  Includes bibliographies and index.
  1. Personality and culture—Hawaii. 2. Psychiatry,
Transcultural—Hawaii. 3. Hawaii—Social conditions.
I. McDermott, John F., 1929–   II. Tseng, Wen-shing,
1935–   III. Maretzki, Thomas.
BF698.9.C8P46   155.8'2'09969   80–11959
ISBN 0-8248-0706-5

Contents

Editors' Note

Since the publication in 1974 of *People and Cultures in Hawaii: An Introduction for Mental Health Workers,* we have heard and read many thoughtful assessments of that small volume which indicated to us that we had achieved our intended purpose: to provide a means for greater understanding of Hawaii's cultures for all those who seek to work effectively with its people. We noted, however, that the use of the book went far beyond mental health professionals. Teachers found it a readily available source book for the education of their students. As time passed, our colleagues indicated that, although they continued to refer to the book themselves and assign it to their students, they would appreciate an expanded volume that included fewer of the technical aspects of mental health, for example, epidemiology, and more of the psychocultural dimensions of each chapter. They believed it would fit more appropriately the audience it had appealed to—sociologists, educators, psychologists, political scientists, public officials, business people, union officials, journalists, and others.

In order to make this shift in emphasis we have brought together the information, experience, and insights of a number of new authors, consultants, and resource persons. Basically, however, this new volume continues to represent the group effort of the faculty of the Department of Psychiatry of the John A. Burns School of Medicine, University of Hawaii, a department that concerns itself with a broad view of the people it serves and the future physicians it trains. While this book does not pretend to be an exhaustive study of all the ethnic groups of Hawaii, it attempts to provide a practical guide which answers many of the questions asked by those who deal daily with different ethnic groups and their common problems experienced while living in this multicultural society. It is hoped also that this volume will serve to heighten the alertness and sharpen the awareness of readers throughout the United States about the issues and problems seen in such sharp relief in the transcultural laboratory Hawaii provides.

Following an introduction in which the concept of culture in its various aspects is defined, the main body of the book deals with each of the ethnic groups in the order of their arrival in Hawaii: Hawaiian, Caucasian, Chinese, Japanese, Portuguese, Okinawan, Korean, Filipino, Samoan, and the people from Indochina. A final chapter summarizes and synthesizes the main themes of earlier chapters.

The story of each ethnic group is organized along similar lines for ease in reading and comparison:

> History of immigration;
> Traditional culture;
> Stereotypes or myths that need clarification;
> The group's contemporary situation in Hawaii and, in some instances, the homeland;
> Mental health issues—potential psychological problems, the nature of individual and group dysfunction, and appropriate approaches and interventions in understandable, nontechnical language.

In addition to the faculty and close associates of the Department of Psychiatry who are responsible for this work, we are most indebted to Theresa Bryant, our department editor at the time the book was written. Joy Ashton, assisted by Kathryn Braun, provided background data and help with final editorial tasks. Kathleen Awakuni, Carolee Fujii, and Gail Kuroiwa were instrumental in final manuscript preparation. We appreciate all of their time and energy.

Chronology

The following brief chronology of migration should help clarify the peopling of Hawaii since the arrival of Captain Cook and the subsequent development of what is now the Fiftieth State.

750 A.D.	Probable migration from Tahiti
1778	Arrival of Captain Cook in Hawaii
1820	Missionaries arrive from New England on board the *Thaddeus*
1823	Skilled Chinese workers arrive to help set up sugar mills
1852	Second group of Chinese arrive
1853	Smallpox epidemic among the Hawaiian population
1868	First small group of Japanese arrive
1878	First Portuguese arrive from Madeira
1881	A group of German Caucasians arrive
1884–1886	Five shiploads of Portuguese arrive
1885	Main Japanese immigration begins
1887	"Bayonet" treaty
1893	Hawaiian monarchy overthrown
1894	Sanford Ballard Dole elected president of Republic of Hawaii
1898	Annexation of Hawaii by the United States
1900	Okinawan immigration begins
1900	Chinese Exclusion Act
1903	Korean immigration begins
1906	Immigration of Filipinos begins
1907	Presidential executive order banning further immigration

1920–1930	Sharp rise in Caucasian immigration—members of the US armed forces
1921–1925	Korean brides arrive
1924	Oriental Exclusion Act closes door on free entry of laborers to the United States
1924	English Standard school established
1931	Massie murder case
1934	Tydings-McDuffie Act restricts annual immigration of Filipinos to quota of 50
1924–1936	Continued Japanese immigration (about 100 per year)
1941–1945	World War II
1945	Governor of Hawaii reopens immigration, citing labor shortage
1945	Samoan immigration begins
1945	Second wave of Filipino immigration—workers, wives, and children
1946	Postwar immigration of Okinawans
1946	Unionization of plantation workers
1953	Workers offered opportunity to purchase plantation homes
1959	Hawaii becomes the Fiftieth State
1965	President Lyndon Johnson signs new immigration bill, increasing quota to 20,000 (not including spouses and children of US citizens)
1965	Third wave of Filipino immigration
1969	War brides arrive (wives of American servicemen in Korea)
1970	Second Chinese immigration, from Taiwan and Hong Kong
1975	Vietnamese refugees arrive
1975	Hmong refugees arrive
1978	Laotian and Cambodian refugees arrive

CHAPTER 1

Introduction

John F. McDermott, Jr.

The population of Hawaii consists of an exceptional array of different cultural and ethnic groups. Each arrived at a different time. Most came originally to feed the appetite of plantations for low-cost field labor and to escape a dead-end existence in the homeland.

Through the years there has been a remarkable degree of blending among them. Various groups have adapted to and become a part of the American scene. Yet, at the same time, they have managed to retain much of their original identity and culture and through it make unexpected and modifying contributions to the total society. The result has been the evolution of a new and unusual community. There are and have been, of course, other such societies but perhaps none so rich and varied; and, because of the relatively small size of an island community, none perhaps in which the component groups interact with such continuing effect upon one another.

The philosophical framework needed to describe this society considers human behavior as an interweaving of biological, sociocultural, and psychological factors. Only during the past few decades has the sociocultural factor been given equal importance with the biological and psychological. Therefore, we will emphasize the sociocultural, and especially the cultural, factor in human behavior, while always remembering the critical importance of its interaction with biological and psychological elements.

A fundamental question is, Exactly what is culture? Somewhere in between the general makeup of human nature and the specific makeup of each individual lie certain qualities that have been acquired and assimilated. They represent culture—*the values, beliefs, and*

*ideologies held by members of the various ethnic groups as funda-
mental and necessary for effective social functioning.*

Ethnicity is a more specific term than culture. It refers to our identification with others from a common acknowledged heritage. Ethnic
grouping is one of the strongest bonds linking the people in Hawaii's
heterogeneous community. When we acknowledge ethnicity we recognize that certain values, beliefs, and symbolic meanings guide
much of our family life and close personal relations. There are also
common knowledge and behaviors that can be considered subcultur-
al. They guide life in groups that are based on neighborhood, school
experience, and/or work patterns. Overarching all this is the broad
cultural pattern of America to which immigrants become assimilated, beginning with the first generation and continuing as a process, though in varying patterns, rapidly or gradually, through subsequent generations.

If your behavior is consistent with that of your social group you are
no more aware of that behavior than you are of the grammar used
when speaking your own language. But if appropriate questions are
asked, you can reveal much about the rules under which you operate.
You may even become specific about what is desirable and undesirable behavior, something about which cultures may differ significantly. Here, the analogy of a map may be useful. While driving
through a familiar neighborhood, you constantly have a map of the
area in your head. Without giving it much thought, you know how
to get to your destination. So, to an extent, it is culture which serves
as a road map for behavior. On your map there may be a shorter or
less congested route between point A and point B, but you may take
any of several routes, and one of these may be preferable to most persons than the most direct or efficient route. The more different routes
there are to a desired objective, the more variations are culturally
possible. What this means for culture and individual behavior is that
variations have to be kept in mind, and that variations from the norm
may be culturally valid.

To understand cultural rules and how they may govern an individual's behavior is essential for measuring the impact of culture on the
individual. When individuals from different cultures seek help for
emotional problems, it may be appropriate to relate the cultural dimension to the clinical situation; hence a part of each chapter in this
book is devoted to mental health considerations. The clinician

should consider an individual's cultural group as an abstraction, just as a map is an abstraction of a geographical area. The abstraction at the group level serves useful purposes similar to the manner in which map coordinates help locate specific points. Given the coordinates as they appear in the following chapters dealing with the different ethnic groups of Hawaii, the clinician must locate the patient accurately on the cultural map. To interpret accurately the significance of group membership is crucial in assessing the probable impact of culture on behavior.

Precision requires a further word about ethnicity. George DeVos (1972) defines an ethnic group as "some self-perceived group of 'people' that share a past." This definition of ethnicity clearly differs from socially or bureaucratically conceived census definitions. Classification according to descent may or may not be self-perceived. It has been pointed out that linking culture directly with a population group on the basis of race (descent) is racist. Self-perception, therefore, must be considered if the link between behavior and group is to be meaningful.

People in Hawaii do classify themselves ethnically, and where ancestry has been the same for both parents and all grandparents, this may be simple enough. But when intermarriage enters in, the offspring may state a dual ethnic membership, for example, Chinese-Hawaiian, or other mixture. In such cases more direct questioning is indicated: "Do you think of yourself as mostly Chinese or mostly Hawaiian?" or whatever ethnic labels may apply in the individual case. Such questions may yield leads in some cases but not in others. For example, if the individual questioned is sensitive about ethnicity, the answer could easily be, "I think of myself as an American." In the case of persons of Japanese ancestry many may add a generational qualifier to express awareness of being culturally different from their immigrant ancestors, for example, *nisei* ("second generation"). Such a generational qualifier may reveal a cultural orientation closer to that of the Caucasian middle class, in many respects the dominant group in Hawaii and the one understandably identified as most typically American. Questions about language competency and about an individual's awareness of and participation in traditional cultural activities, such as religious or other ceremonies, may also help to identify a person's cultural orientation.

In summary: *First,* to know a person's social group may help one to understand how values and attitudes affect the individual's interaction with others. Early experiences as a member of a social or ethnic group play a significant part in determining behavior, particularly the way in which emotions are organized and expressed and psychological needs met. But, *second,* social and ethnic background alone—especially in multicultural, multiracial Hawaii—are not in themselves sufficient guideposts for therapists. The degree to which social and ethnic background affect behavior needs to be carefully assessed. This applies to conduct both within a group and within the larger society. *Third,* different cultures have different views of what constitutes right and wrong behavior. For example, exaggerated male self-esteem may be a pronounced characteristic of a given group; insults to that self-esteem may produce in an individual from one group reactions which would be considered excessive and abnormal by the standards of another group. *Finally,* although we are tied psychologically to the social group in which we are reared, and in which we function and communicate most comfortably and easily, only part of our behavior can be understood through these factors. Other important factors are one's self-perceptions and the impact of life in a multicultural society, influencing one's cognition along with one's emotions and the manner of their expression. The foregoing qualifications—consideration of the factors inherent in an individual's ethnic identity and membership in a cultural group—are likely to provide an important key to therapeutic strategies.

Reference

DeVos, George. Social stratification and ethnic plurism: An overview from the perspective of psychological anthropology. *Race,* 1972, 13:435–460.

CHAPTER 2

The Hawaiians

Benjamin B. C. Young

History of Immigration and Society

The beginnings of Hawaiian history are shrouded in the mists of time. In chants, legends, and *mele* ("vocal music") handed down from the ancient past, Hawaiians trace their origins to daring seafarers who discovered and colonized these islands. Most anthropologists agree that ancestors of the Polynesians began an emigration several thousand years ago reaching from the Malay Archipelago to the numerous islands of the Pacific and eventually culminating in the great landfall discovery of Hawaii (Suggs, 1960). Many legends describe two-way voyages on magnificent double-hulled canoes between the Society Islands, in particular Tahiti and Raiatea, and Hawaii. The channel between the islet of Kahoolawe and the island of Lanai retains the ancient name of Ke-ala-i-Kahiki, most often interpreted as "The Way to Tahiti." Sometime around A.D. 1000, the voyages ceased and a culture sprang up in Hawaii, which was totally isolated and provided conditions that resulted in the emergence of a society both highly unique and isolated from outside influence.

The societal structure was stratified in a manner reminiscent of medieval Europe with its classes of ruler, priest, knight, and commoner. At the time of European contact in 1778, Hawaii's society was composed of the *ali'i* ("ruling class"), the *kahuna* ("priests" or "experts"), the *maka'āinana* ("commoners"), and the *kauwā* ("slaves"). Social status was determined at birth by hereditary ascription. This society, stumbled upon by Captain James Cook, was highly rigid and regimented under a strict *kapu* ("restriction," "consecration," "separation," or "forbidden") system which dictated daily activity between and among the classes, between the people and the gods, and between the people and nature. The *kapu* had many benefits. Roles were never confused. There were even periods for environmental control that provided for a balance in nature and the maintenance of a subsistence economy. The culture thereby also remained intact. In many ways, Cook observed a people whose habits were in superb harmony with the land upon which they dwelt.

Significant Events of Post-European Contact

Certain significant events and the introduction of certain items had profound effects upon the people. A review of these events will clarify their importance and influence in subsequent years upon the personality and mental health of the modern Hawaiian.

First, the introduction of explosives and iron implements (knives, nails, and especially cannons) had considerable impact on the neolithic culture. Explosives dramatically assisted the young Kamehameha in gaining full control of all the islands. (The island of Kauai came under his control later and without force, uniting all Hawaiians under one rule.) Iron implements catalyzed a shift of the economic base from one of subsistence to one based on trade between foreigners and natives. The change from a subsistence economy to a barter, then money, economy had far-reaching results for a people whose economic concepts for hundreds of years had been based not on acquisition of material goods but on supplying daily needs. Ships' owners were anxious to receive their portions of the highly profitable sandalwood trade with China. The chiefs ordered the natives to cut and haul the sandalwood; no longer did they tend the taro patches or fish ponds. Sandalwood was exchanged by the chiefs for status items, such as iron implements, which boosted the chiefs' prestige considerably. The whaling and sugar industries intensified the confusion among a people who could not understand profit as a motive for living. Thus, the introduction of new items shifted the economic system and brought about changes alien to the mind of the Hawaiians, changes which are still felt and seen today among the people.

Second, the introduction of new diseases devastated a people who, isolated for centuries, had no immunity to many common ailments, such as chicken pox and measles. Venereal diseases also took their toll; though Cook tried to isolate his crew from the natives, his efforts were in vain, and venereal disease spread rapidly throughout the islands. The introduction of small pox, influenza, and plague decimated thousands of Hawaiians whose usual recourse during illness had been to rely upon the expertise of the *kahuna hāhā* ("diagnostician") or *kahuna lapa'au* ("medical practitioner") (Greer, 1965). In the face of new diseases, the power and influence of these *kahuna* were rendered useless and impotent.

Leprosy was especially destructive psychologically to the Hawaiians. In an attempt to stem the surging tide of Hansen's Disease, a desperate isolation measure was tried, which gave birth to the sad and tragic events of the early years of the settlements of Kalawao and Kalaupapa on the island of Molokai (Daws, 1973; Bushnell, 1975). The ostracizing of a few natives whose *'ohā* ("roots") were ensconced within an extended family system destroyed the spirit of many Hawaiians. Family members, including young children, were literally snatched from loved ones and isolated on the so-called anarchic "isle of death" where the motto was often heard, *'A 'ole kānāwai ma kēia wahi,* "In this place, there is no law."

Third, in 1820 the first company of missionaries under the auspices of the American Board of Commissioners for Foreign Missions began the groundwork for "raising the heathen of Owhyhee." Ironically, it was a young Hawaiian whose cries on the steps of Yale University about the "sordid and barbaric" practices of his people provided the catalyst for the conversion of these islands to Christianity (Dwight, 1968). This Christian invasion had considerable impact on the emerging nation: in religion, the church replaced the old system; in finance and economics, many of the descendants of the missionaries eventually dominated the business community; in education, the missionaries put the Hawaiian language into print, setting the stage for the education of the nobility (the Royal School, established in 1839 for children of *ali'i*) and eventually the masses; in music, many Hawaiian songs reflect a hymnal quality, with a very common 4/4 beat to most modern tunes. The well-known song "Hawaii Aloha" was written by the beloved missionary to the Waianae region, Lorenzo Lyons, who was inspired by the old hymn "I Left It All With Jesus." Today, though dogmatism is rare and liberality in doctrine very common, covertly and overtly, religion permeates the lives of all Hawaiians.

Fourth, in 1819 a silent iconoclastic revolution occurred which was to produce an upheaval that sealed the doom of the ancient way. This event was the overturning of the *kapu* system. The importance of the *kapu* as the foundation of Hawaiian life warrants further explanation. Ralph Kuykendall, in *The Hawaiian Kingdom* (1968), explains:

> As a substantive, the word kapu means a prohibition or restriction.
>
> Anything associated with the gods acquired sacredness; hence there were kapus relating to the priests, heiaus, and all other things dedicated to the gods. The alii (chiefs) were believed to be descended from the gods, hence there were many kapus referring to them; there were, however, degrees of sacredness among the alii; the highest of all, the *alii-kapu*, was thought of as being, in some sense, an actual god, through him the nation was kept in rapport with the supernatural realm; hence he was surrounded with many and very rigid kapus, in order to prevent any interruption of good relationship between the people collectively and the gods; in this manner the interests of all were deeply involved and there was little likelihood of these kapus being voluntarily violated. In the fundamental conception noted above can be discovered, likewise, the reasons for the eating kapus and the restrictive kapus affecting women.
>
> Besides the permanent kapus, there were kapus of a periodical character; and the chiefs and priests might impose special and temporary ones. Penalties for violation of kapu were severe, death being a common one. A person might violate a kapu without being aware of the fact, but that did not save him from the penalty. As might be expected, the kapu system was most hampering, if not actually oppressive, in its effect upon the common people and upon women of all classes. It was, moreover, susceptible of great abuse and unquestionably was abused at times.

The *kapu* system was still intact under Kamehameha the Great. Upon his death his favorite wife, Kaahumanu, exerted considerable pressure on Liholiho, Kamehameha II, to end the *kapu*. Although Kaahumanu sought only the abolition of the eating *kapu* (i.e., separation of sexes during meals and the prohibition of eating certain foods, such as bananas and turtle flesh, for women), the elimination of this particular *kapu* had far-reaching effects for the entire societal structure. Few realized that the removal of the *kapu* created the beginning of the end of an era. With its eradication threatening clouds began to appear on the horizon, clouds which would wipe out a way of life for a people who had few resources at that time to cope with the many changes to come. Unfortunately, no satisfactory substitutions were provided and the Hawaiians, after centuries of living under a system of submission to the gods and to nature, wandered in a confused state for decades, a state which for many still exists today. The impact of new ways, new peoples, new religions, has not worn off; some native Hawaiians are still struggling to find ways of dealing and coping with cultural conflicts, while at the same time attempting to discover their ties with the past. With the emphasis on change, and the overwhelming advantages of a more "civilized" culture, Hawaii of precontact times was destined to extinction. Unfortunately, few had the insight to see the value of the indigenous culture. Kuykendall writes sadly that:

> Unfortunately, none of the foreigners who came to Hawaii in the early period, or the missionaries who followed soon after, had any adequate understanding or appreciation of the native culture or considered it, or any important part of it, worth preserving. None of them had the knowledge or the training that would have fitted them to help the natives find a new way of life based upon the old culture but reconciled with the new. The strange new ideas and practices broke the force of the old kapus, weakened the relationship between the common people and the alii (their leaders from time immemorial) and set the Hawaiians adrift on a competitive sea whose winds and currents baffled them for many years.

Fifth, the overthrow of the monarchy in 1893 was a sad day in the history of Hawaii. Stories still abound from *kūpuna* ("elders") who were present when the Hawaiian flag was lowered at Iolani Palace. Beginning with Kamehameha III and continuing with all the remaining monarchs, events occurred that had a dominant effect, leading to the dethronement of Queen Liliuokalani. Hawaii was a tiny kingdom and could not defend itself against world powers like America, France, England, Germany, and Russia. The power of the native rulers had been wrested out of their hands and control was gained by entrepreneurs. Thus, a people were left with figurehead kings and queens who were virtually impotent against the *haole* ("foreigners"). Though most of the monarchs sought to create methods of survival, the attempts were futile. The sad fate of a king who strove valiantly to save his people cannot be more poignantly expressed than in King Kalakaua's dying words, "Tell my people I tried to restore our gods, our way of life." The events following

Queen Liliuokalani's dethronement left the people, then with over one hundred years of exposure to the Western world, in a state of utter confusion. Relieved of their leaders, yet clinging to some of the finest aspects of their heritage, they seemed destined to lose the race for economic supremacy in their homeland. Unable to deal with the introduced concepts of land ownership and taxes, and faced with the continued bombardment of denigrative terms for the native culture, the Hawaiians were poorly prepared to enter the twentieth century.

Sixth, a study of statistical data from 1778 to 1930 (Larsen, 1965) shows that the Hawaiians began to disappear from the face of the earth. With the loss of identity, loss of prestige, and cultural confusion, the Hawaiians had no will to live and began to die at an alarming rate. Estimates are that approximately three hundred thousand Hawaiians were present in Hawaii in 1778. The number of Hawaiians was reduced to sixty thousand by 1930. Disease alone cannot account for the rapid decline. The emotional impact of the data can be felt in the Hawaiian saying *Na kanaka 'oku'u wale aku no i kau 'uhane,* "The people dismissed freely their souls and died." The Hawaiians had lost all the cultural elements that gave interest and meaning to their lives. The disastrous rate of decrease still existed in the first quarter of the twentieth century. At that time, out of every thousand Hawaiian births, there were 212 infant deaths. For all other races, the rate was 40 infant deaths per thousand births. These figures may be further misleading, for, due to the negative connotations of being Hawaiian, many individuals of part-Hawaiian ancestry refused to identify themselves as Hawaiians (Larsen, 1965). The trend has been reversed and at the last census taken in 1970, the number of Hawaiians (including part-Hawaiians) has significantly increased.

Thus, the modern Hawaiian is the product of many events and circumstances which occurred over the past two hundred years. The events and introduction of certain elements previously described led to a way of life very different from that before 1778 and necessitated the development of coping mechanisms and value systems unique to the twentieth century. These may be practical for some of today's Hawaiians, but for many others they are totally inadequate and contribute to the problems faced by Hawaiians. Thus has evolved what is commonly called "the Hawaiian way," a value system that at times is considered quite nebulous and vague, probably in reaction to the reversed acculturation they have undergone, while at others it is the basis for much of the love and warmth found in the dealings of Hawaiians, one with another.

Value System of the Modern Hawaiian

Most Hawaiians today are offspring of intermarriages. There are probably less than three thousand pure Hawaiians. The most common combinations are Hawaiian Caucasian and Hawaiian Asian (Chinese, Japanese, Filipino). To assign a value system based on the combination of ethnic mixture would probably result in erroneous, if not hazardous, conclusions. The Hawaiian way is more accurately Hawaiian ways which have come about through the intricate and delicate mixture and synthesis of many factors and forces, including intermarriage, acculturation, introduction of new concepts, preservation of old concepts, and the tenacious clinging to roots and ties of the past. Given the diverse backgrounds of today's Hawaiians, one must look at a cultural system and lifestyle that varies from locale to locale and from community to community. For example, lifestyles and coping strategies could vary considerably from Ka'u to Keanae to Kapaa. There are major lifestyle similarities, however, throughout the islands of Hawaii, and these will be discussed in terms of the *'ohana* ("extended family") affiliative values, group versus individual pursuits, and coping and resolution of problems.

Many words in the Hawaiian language convey strong emotional feeling, such as *aloha* ("love"), *'āina* ("land"), and *kūkū* ("grandparents," usually pronounced *tūtū*). One of these words, *'ohana,* is derived from *'ohā,* the rootlet of the taro plant, one of the many plants and animals the early Polynesians brought to Hawaii to help start their new lives here. This taro, which survived fierce tropical storms, intense equatorial heat, and devastating effects of salt air and water, was and still is the staple in the diet of most Hawaiians. Very similar to the potato and strawberry plants, the taro plant sends out tiny rootlets from which new plants develop, hence the word *'ohana,* or "extended family," emerging from the parent plant, and yet still connected by genetic ties (Pukui, 1972).

To the Hawaiian the family is the center of all relationships. Here is to be found the core values of the Hawaiian way. In the past, the *'ohana* was the extended family bonded by blood and from which any member could expect warmth and support. This support system was not expected or demanded, it was simply there. In the *'ohana* youngsters were taught their duties; behavior was outlined, needs maintained, and respect accorded to the *kūpuna*. Here also was to be found the true meaning of the word *aloha*, the love of one member for another. From birth to death, responsibilities were understood and these were part of a code of ethics shouldered by each *'ohana* member. Though *'ohana* by blood ties is still very strong, the word has taken on additional meaning for groups which share involvement, responsibilities, or unity of purpose. Thus, it is common for organizations to identify themselves as the *'Ohana Wa'a*, "the family of the canoe," *'Ohana Kaho'olawe*, "the family of Kaho'olawe," or *'Ohana o Hokule'a*, "the family of *Hokule'a*." This concept of *'ohana* binds a group together, and in the group is to be found the strength of purpose and meaning of existence. In these postcontact times, almost any organization united and bonded by common ties will refer to themselves commonly as a *hui* ("group"), but often more intensely as an *'ohana*.

From this discussion of the *'ohana* we can proceed to the affiliative values of the Hawaiians. In observing affiliation as a value system for Hawaiians, one is impressed by the degree to which people would commit themselves to maintain and advance relationships. Perhaps the basis for this degree of commitment is to be found in the Hawaiians' feelings toward children. A house without children is a house without life. In any Hawaiian community children are everywhere. They will be found playing in the streets, running around at the *lū'au* ("feast"), taking part in the dancing and singing, and usually, when evening falls, the children will still be seen slumbering in the corner of a living room while the partying of the adults continues. In virtually every home children are coddled, showered with attention, and fondled. Seldom is an infant left alone when crying. There is much contact, touching, and caressing. In children are first seen the strong human bonds that later emerge into the intense affiliative ties which Hawaiians have for each other. Understanding this attitude toward children is important if one is to comprehend the special concepts of illegitimacy and *hānai* ("adoption") in the Hawaiian community.

If viewed from strict observational and epidemiological data, there are exceptionally high rates of adoption and illegitimacy among Hawaiians. This does not necessarily suggest a negative connotation. In fact, quite often the opposite is true. It matters not that the parents of a child are unmarried. What matters is that a child has been brought into the world and must be cared for. Alan Howard describes this love for children in his *Ain't No Big Thing* (1974): "Nearly every household in 'Aina Pumehana' contains a set of encyclopedias, sold by salesmen who have learned that the way to a Hawaiian American's pocketbook is through his heartfelt interest in children's welfare. Few of these books are ever used, but their presence is a symbol of concern."

With this understanding of the Hawaiians' love for children, regardless of legitimacy or illegitimacy, it is easy to comprehend the concept of *hānai*. In old Hawaii the first-born, or *hiapo*, was given to the grandparents. If a boy, the child was given to the paternal grandparents and if a girl, the child was given to the maternal grandparents. (For a more detailed description, refer to *Nana I Ke Kumu*, Pukui, Haertig, and Lee, 1972.) The child was given outright without ill feeling. The saying was *Nāu ke keiki kūkae a na'au*, "I give this child, intestines, contents, and all." Emotions, intelligence, and qualities of character were associated, not with the brain or heart, but with *na'au*, the guts or intestines *(Nana I Ke Kumu)*. Rather than a severing of ties, there was an extension of ties. A child did not lose his parents through *hānai*, but gained a more intimate relationship with his *tūtū*. The purposes of the old system of *hānai* were multiple: the geneaology was kept and committed to memory, skills unique to the *'ohana* were taught, and learning passed from generation to generation. Today, the term *hānai* still carries with it feelings of love and fondness. Though the first-born is no longer given to the grandparents, foster parents or those who have been entrusted with the care and raising of a child are always looked at with feelings of *aloha*. The adoption may or may not be by legal contract. In a study by Howard (1970) it was found that nearly one third of the community surveyed had both legal and informal adoptions. The characteristics of the adoption patterns were very similar to, if not derived from, traditional Polynesian patterns.

From childhood the values of relationships are learned. Human physical contact is maintained into adulthood, and there is much touching, embracing, and kissing when greeting family or friends. Even beyond this obvious constant human contact is the manner in which Hawaiians will extend themselves to affirm warm human relationships. There is also a need to keep relationships conflict free. This is not to say that conflicts do not occur, but it is totally unacceptable to resolve conflicts openly and through confrontation. An exception is *ho'oponopono* ("to correct"), which will be discussed later. Many strategies have emerged that show the extent to which Hawaiians will go to avoid confrontation. Potentially explosive issues are almost always suppressed. It is better to deny the existence of a conflict, for example by displacing energy into producing a *lū'au* and working together, than to bring the issue to a head. It is more acceptable to pay a loan for which one has cosigned to a bank than to confront the friend who requested you to be a cosigner and who subsequently defaults. Various types of avoidance behavior are common. It is unacceptable to ask questions which might embarrass someone. For example, food is commonly laid out, and without overt invitation, eaten. Thus, the guest is not placed in an embarrassing position of needing to ask for any food or beverage which the host might not have available. When inviting someone to a *lū'au* it is discourteous to ask for a response, that is, an RSVP. At the *lū'au* or other type of party it is the height of embarrassment to run out of food and drink, perhaps causing a guest to ask for food and to be embarrassed if it is not available. The extent to which Hawaiians will go to maintain these relationships has ramifications in today's society; this same avoidance of confrontation often necessitates avoidance of individual success and competition for selfish gain. This is an enigma and a problem which has haunted Hawaiians, for it has forced them, on the one hand, to cling tenaciously to those values of human relationships that stress conflict-free group togetherness and yet, on the other hand, has hampered them in facing the competitive demands of our modern society to achieve educational and economic success. This leads to the next topic, group versus individual pursuits.

Individuals within Hawaiian communities are not expected to perform below their abilities. In fact, there is a recognizable dichotomy between performance for individual gain and performance for group gain. When athletes perform exceptionally well, there is reward in the form of accolade and recognition, but the main point is that the entire team has benefited from the outstanding performance of one individual. Individuals are discouraged from making public displays to seek recognition for self. It is very common for Hawaiians to deny the recognition or to humbly announce that it was the group that made the success possible. To flaunt and publicly announce one's credentials tends to produce opposite results from those expected in Western modern culture. For example, in a small community, an individual seeking public office could not be *maha'oi* ("forward, brazen") and advertise personal accomplishments. To do so would be unseemly. So, one has friends go about telling the successes one has had. Then the follow-up is to deny, or state that one's friends exaggerated, the statements. A small community would already know who you are and what you have accomplished. The point is to publish one's accomplishments without doing so in too public a way. To seek personal gain is unacceptable, but to seek gain for the benefit of the group is acceptable.

This value has ramifications in the classroom, where studying for top grades to enhance one's own image is unacceptable. On the other hand, studying hard to help the group is quite acceptable. Kubany's study (1971), which compares the achievement of a Hawaiian student population with a non-Hawaiian population for both individual and group goals, is interesting. Hawaiians performed much better where the rewards were to be used for the benefit of the group, but performance dropped where rewards were for the individual. In the small community of Nanakuli it was found that "commitments are always more firm and productive if the goal is an intensification of human relationships rather than an accumulation of personal wealth or some individual achievement" (Gallimore and Howard, 1968).

Coping Problems of the Traditional Hawaiian*

It is difficult to discuss mental health problems, and the cultural mechanisms that Hawaiians use to cope with or resolve problems, because of the diversity found in the term *Hawaiian*. They are to be found in all strata of society, from the very poorest to the richest; they are also to be found among the best educated (many from some of the most prestigious universities in the nation), as well as among the elementary grade dropouts. The variables are many: politics, education, economics, occupation, and so forth. Thus, coping mechanisms described here may or may not be applicable to all Hawaiians. In addition, there are problems in defining a Hawaiian, since many with a large percentage of Polynesian blood tend to deny their heritage, while others with no Hawaiian blood who were *hānai*'d from the

---

* Section written by the editors.

time of birth are far more culturally Hawaiian. Thus, communication with the Hawaiian community is perhaps more complex than with any other group; it must be a subtle and delicate blending of concern and intimacy tempered with reserve and observation. Nonetheless, a discussion of the problems, especially those of coping mechanisms, is meaningful, because a large majority of Hawaiians still cling to Hawaiian values and have not been able to traverse the bridge of acculturation into twentieth-century society. It should be noted that this special mental health section, which has been prepared by the editors and not by the author of this chapter, places a pronounced emphasis on certain cultural traditions, in particular, the importance of dreams and the process of *ho'oponopono,* because of the power of these forces in Hawaiian life and their potential use today in understanding and dealing with Hawaiians, both personally and professionally.

There are many people actively trying to discover and define their Hawaiian identity; adolescents and young adults are often resentful that their parents, who have lost touch with their cultural roots, have not taught them the Hawaiian language and the rituals of their ancestors. These new Hawaiians may even display their pride by living out the significance of their names. Unfortunately, the discovery by the young that being Hawaiian is sometimes accompanied by a kind of marginal existence as well, that is, by the reality that Hawaiians' cultural worth and richness are not fully recognized by the society in which they live, sometimes may lead to confusion manifested in violence and "acting out" behavior.

The medical practices and beliefs of many Hawaiians, like their social values, are also very closely linked to their culture and to a strong spirituality in their lives. This strong spiritual connection, a delicate balance between natural and supernatural forces, is why so many Hawaiians can be said to live out their religion, in contrast to the "Sunday Christian" whose faith is often forgotten or ignored by Monday. The Christian dictum that "God is everywhere" is put by Hawaiians into concrete symbols encountered in everyday life which have special meaning and elicit special response or behavior. Many Hawaiians (also many Puerto Ricans and Portuguese) will attest to having had some kind of psychic experience; some identify with the Christian tradition, some with the ancient Hawaiian traditions of family gods and spirits *(aumākua),* and some to beliefs which blend these two as well as others. When professional help is sought to sort out what is spiritual and what is illness, the Hawaiian may look to someone who will try to share the patient's experience by a willingness to recognize the possibility of psychic phenomena or at least its validity for the patient.

Many, although not all, Hawaiians of the present day continue to make extensive use of dreams and symbols in everyday life. In this sense, Hawaiians are perhaps in closer communication with their inner or unconscious lives than many other cultural groups, especially if they make active use of dreams as a creative and helpful force on an individual or group basis. In the old Hawaiian tradition, the word for "dream" was literally "spirit sleep"; that is, while the body slept, the spirit wandered, seeing places and persons, encountering others, and passing on important messages from the supernatural world. Thus, there is a tradition of the "wandering spirit of sleep," with daily life and nighttime experiences forming a continuum representing two sides of a person.

In Western thought we accept, to a certain extent, the ability to see the future subconsciously when consciously we may be blind to it. That is, we recognize that intuition is an important force in all of our lives, that things happen not because we dream them, but we dream them because intuition tells us about ourselves and our faults. This may be an explanation of the heavy emphasis on the premonitory meaning of dreams among the Hawaiians. Our subconscious mind has a wider range of vision, more insight to solve problems, as well as foresight to anticipate them, because in sleep we have given up the constraints of waking life. C. G. Jung, a Western psychoanalyst, believed this: that dreams will show where the unconscious is leading us and point to an end. Thus, Hawaiian belief in and work with dreams is more consonant with the psychology and philosophy of Jung than with that of Freud, although we recognize that dreams can both reproduce unsolved problems of the past and anticipate or work toward a solution in the future. Dreams are also a way to make us face a situation we are trying to avoid; they make us aware of a problem and perhaps its cause and solution.

Hawaiians often feel responsible for dreams about others which have a strong premonitory quality; a dream that warns often is followed by some action the next day to prevent harm to the person in the dream. Thus, dreams are not only utilized to solve problems, but also to forecast events and behavior. This is in contrast to the traditional mental health professional's use of dreams almost exclusively to examine past events and emotions. (For more detailed discussion of the use and meaning of dreams, see *Nana I Ke Kumu,* vol. 2, Pukui et al., in press.)

Many symbols in dreams and in daily life are essentially cultural and carry great significance in one group, but not in another. (There are also some that are universal and some that mean a very particular thing to an individual or a family.) Thus, one must beware of transposing Western dream interpretation upon Hawaiian life in which dreams are utilized in a different framework, or of interpreting symbols across cultural lines. For example, the rainbow, shark, or canoe might possibly be viewed very differently if they appeared in dreams in another society, but they may have a customary or general meaning to Hawaiian people.

Mental health professionals often utilize dreams as one would pieces of a picture puzzle; that is, by themselves they have very little meaning, but a series put together can suddenly form a recognizable image. Hawaiians often interpret dreams themselves, especially those about immediate concerns in the family and problems close to home, but they may also look elsewhere for help with more complicated ones. They may seek out a dream interpreter or a mental health professional who, by recognizing the special importance of dreams and the cultural characteristics unique to Hawaiians, can work with them and allow for their special significance. With many Hawaiian patients one should recognize that they will feel there is a moral or lesson in almost every dream which is often self-recognized and which can be a meaningful communication between patient and therapist if the therapist will ask for and accept this direct message as an important consideration. Hawaiians have traditionally been in closer touch with their own preconscious thoughts, wishes, and impulses, and accustomed to relating them to their daily experiences, but in a prospective rather than retrospective fashion.

Indeed, the traditional Hawaiian belief in dreams, which persists with many Hawaiians today, is so powerful that they may be able to dream on demand, giving themselves and others insight into their inner lives and concerns as related to daily conflicts and problems. Thus, the saying "Let's sleep on it" has very special meaning in Hawaiian culture. If one negates the special meaning of dreams, one negates culture and diminishes greatly one's potential effectiveness in working with this or any group and with their problems.

There are certain classes of behavior that psychiatrists might consider as manifestations of emotional or psychiatric disorders. To traditional Hawaiians, however, these behaviors are linked to certain types of possession *(noho)* or visions which are culturally acceptable and valid. As a people, Hawaiians seem to possess a cultural sensor which can distinguish between these culturally relevant experiences and the manifestation of psychosis or mental imbalance (Pukui and Elbert, 1964). The individual who is separated or isolated from his group, however, without access to a Hawaiian minister *(kahuna)* or healer might seek help outside the normal community channels.

Yet, there is often a hesitancy in many Hawaiians to entrust themselves to a physician or other professional who may refer them to a hospital or institutional setting which is unfamiliar; Hawaiians by nature are a communal and familial group and hate to be isolated from the companionship of friends and loved ones.

Given the values discussed earlier, it could be assumed that one major coping mechanism is that of avoidance. When confronted with a conflict it is obvious that for many Hawaiians it is far better to avoid and deny the problem than to confront and resolve it. This, however, extracts a price in our modern society, for it is difficult to avoid and deny indefinitely.

Though healthful outlets are available to some, such as cooperative efforts to work out frustrations, for others the solution is in withdrawal and avoidance, for example, with excessive use of alcohol. Frustration may also find an outlet in behavioral problems among Hawaiians. Often feelings of powerlessness, of being trapped, and of personal inadequacy result in spouse abuse, child abuse, or physical disputes with relatives; this type of behavior is characteristic of other groups at lower socioeconomic levels who frequently are unemployed and cannot provide the standard of life that they desire for their loved ones.

Avoidance of intimate involvement with outsiders is another method of coping with the frustrations of modern living. Any non-Hawaiian will readily attest to the sense of being ostracized when initial attempts are made to become friendly with Hawaiians. The cold professional direct approach sometimes attributed to the *haole* is very likely to elicit a veiled deceptive response. By the same token, the outsider, regardless of his ethnicity, who attempts "local" speech patterns and inflection is likely to get the same response. The avoidance of involvement will assist the Hawaiian in not losing face or "making A" should anything negative result from the relationship. There is, in addition, a sense of possessiveness and distrust, which keeps an outsider from intruding into the inner sanctum of what remains from so rich a past.

An individual interested in working or helping a Hawaiian must, through an easy, low-key sincerity, create a familiarity, a personal contact; this type of icebreaking can often be achieved by starting an ordinary conversation, "talking story" with the unfamiliar person. The relaxed, undirected exchange will often bring forward problems and concerns which are shared with someone who is emphatic and open, but careful not to be *niele* ("nosey"). Thus the professional must be careful to avoid personal questions even in a client-professional setting. Sarcasm or humor, which could be taken as insulting or critical, should never be directed at the client. This mistake often irreparably widens the void in communication.

The mental health worker must also become aware of the special significance of grief in the life of the Hawaiians, and the importance of the grieving ritual to the Hawaiian (Pukui et al., 1972). For example, a significant person lost by death may continue to appear in dreams, advising, warning, scolding, or comforting; often this is a parent.

If problems within an *'ohana* (the immediate or extended family) develop that are unresolvable, it is possible to utilize *ho'oponopono* (Paglinawan, 1972). *Ho'oponopono* is to set things to right, to restore and maintain good relationships. Historically, this process of therapy was limited to the *'ohana* or other small groups. It involves prayer, the definition of the problems, the setting to rights of each problem, the necessity of self-scrutiny for truthfulness and sincerity, the need for a leader to direct the session or sessions, restitution, and finally, forgiveness. *Ho'oponopono* could never be performed unless the leader and the terms of the process are accepted by all. In many households today this is the only method which would be acceptable for the resolution of problems. The leader is often a *kūpuna* ("elder"), Christian prayers are a necessity, and honesty and the making of restitutions a requirement. A non-Hawaiian psychiatrist, social worker, or mental health worker should not apply *ho'oponopono* or any cultural practice in a random manner without consultation with a cultural expert in that area. If the family is to be gathered to discuss the illness or problem of an individual, it is absolutely essential to know whether the individual is still functioning as part of his family and how well the family communicates as a group. The bringing together of extremely hostile family members or relatives can cause increased tensions and complications rather than the intended reconciliation and solutions.

Consequently, the seeking of outside help is rare unless the source is one that is trusted and has ties to a Hawaiian community; thus, the high trust and esteem which many Hawaiians have for the Queen Liliuokalani Children's Center. It is a facility supported by the estate of Queen Liliuokalani and dedicated to serving the needs of orphaned children. It deals with the problems of Hawaiian families who need counseling through the special ethnically valid approaches provided by its professional mental health staff.

Coping mechanisms all relate to the internal struggles that many Hawaiians still face generation after generation following the significant events after 1778. For some the sacrifices have been many and the price high. But the pinnacle of success has been reached by many, albeit at the price of the loss of one's "Hawaiianness." For many others mechanisms have not been successful and the results more drastic than the melancholy of a lost past.

Stereotypes

Hawaiians have suffered from negative and positive stereotypes. It is not uncommon to hear disparaging comments made toward Hawaiians: lazy, shiftless, unmotivated. Likewise, it is also frequently heard that Hawaiians are easy going, expressive, loving, and generous. Though elements of both stereotypes are to be found among Hawaiians, it would be grossly incorrect to apply these descriptions to all Hawaiians. Whenever a culture has been overwhelmed by another, more "advanced" culture (as evidenced in the Chamorros of the Marianas and the native American Indians), it is commonly ascribed to the defeated natives that they are lazy, good-for-nothing, irresponsible, and indolent. Little is said of the loss experienced by the natives of their culture, of their leaders, of their gods, and of a way of life that is no more. Many did adjust and overcame formidable obstacles to achieve upward mobility. Unfortunately, in the case of the Hawaiians, many have struggled and are still struggling to find a place in the new culture. Not until the recent upsurge of cultural pride in being Hawaiian has the shift taken place. The existence of these stereotypes is important in that the labels have hindered many young Hawaiians from seeking high goals. It was not until the middle of this century that the Kamehameha Schools shifted its emphasis of training young people for vocations, that is, blue collar workers and domestics, to training their graduates for the seemingly unattainable professions. Role models have been too few to stimulate young Hawaiians to aspire to high goals. Thus, many have come to truly believe that they are not meant to become physicians, lawyers, businessmen, leaders, and pillars of the community. It is in the hands of those who have attained high goals that the children of the future must find guidance and leadership in retaining cherished Hawaiian values while achieving their full measure of success according to our twentieth century standards.

Contemporary Situation of Hawaiians

Groups advocating different causes have proliferated among the Hawaiians. Causes espoused range from land issues, water rights, and access to the sea, to politics and education. The Hawaiian civic clubs also play an important role in the debate of concerns and the implementation of plans to raise scholarship funds for underprivileged young people. In the Hawaiian civic clubs are also perpetuated many of the arts and skills, such as feather lei making, quilt making, language classes, and athletic events. Amidst the cacophony of Hawaiian groups—that is, Republicans versus Democrats, advocates of land versus the advocates of the military, upper class versus lower class (usually described as *makamaka*, [slang for "snob"] versus *maka'āinana*, ["commoner"]), *hui* arising with differing and opposing views —there have emerged two things, one an event and the second an organization, that have helped to create a resurgence of cultural pride and unification.

The first of these was the voyage of *Hokule'a* in 1976. Though on the surface it was no more than the building of a canoe true to ancient Hawaiian design, and the sailing of the canoe to Tahiti and back, *Hokule'a* became a symbol of the Hawaiian people, a symbol which epitomized the pride of the accomplishments of the early Polynesians. *Hokule'a* represents the indomitable spirit of all people who challenge the unknown and reach forth to discover new landfalls. Since the completion of the voyage in 1976, thousands of miles have been sailed around Hawaiian waters, but the true significance of *Hokule'a* is the stimulation of cultural pride which the canoe has had on the *keiki o ka 'āina,* the "children of the land." A series of books have been published on early voyages, books which are currently used in elementary schools throughout Hawaii and the mainland United States. Numerous workshops have been held, teaching youngsters the rudiments of navigation, food preservation, and the sailing, lashing, and building of canoes. More important, though, is the instilling of a high level of pride in being Hawaiian.

Secondly, in 1975, a small group of individuals incorporated an organization called Alu Like ("working together") and set up goals to identify the Hawaiian people, to identify the needs and priorities of the Hawaiian people, and to methodically pursue ways and means to implement programs to meet their needs. The initial study revealed inordinate needs in the areas of education, housing, land, health, employment, and economics. Since 1975 the progress of Alu Like has been remarkable. Never in the history of Hawaii since 1778 has any organization been able to rally the support of so many of the Hawaiian people. Alu Like has been the rallying point and the catalyst for programs for many of the underprivileged, and under its leadership the needs are being recognized and programs are being implemented.

Since Captain Cook first made contact with these islands, the world has been impressed with the warmth, graciousness, generosity, and *aloha* of the Hawaiian people. Unknowingly, many of these qualities and virtues were unscrupulously exploited, and the Hawaiians faced changes over the next two centuries for which they were totally unprepared. Since the first quarter of this century, however, the pendulum has shifted and the modern Hawaiian has made astonishing strides toward economic and social self-sufficiency. Today, Hawaiians are found at all levels of society in the state and include the Chief Justice of the Supreme Court of Hawaii. There are Hawaiians in important posts in the state legislature and in some of the key positions with financial institutions, unions, schools, and other major businesses. Since the establishment of the John A. Burns School of Medicine and with the first graduating class of 1975, the number of Hawaiian physicians has more than doubled. There are still, however, a disproportionate number of the poor and dispossessed among the Hawaiians. The largest proportion of high school dropouts, the greatest number of those on the welfare rolls, the highest rate of crime—all are also to be found among the Hawaiians. Through leadership and organizations like Alu Like, Queen Liliuokalani Children's Center, and the Hawaiian civic clubs, there is no doubt that upward mobility through education and community support will come about. It will be important that the Hawaiians' quality of life not be compromised in this "strive to reach the summit," *e kūlia ika nu'u,* Queen Kapiolani's motto. The deeply affectionate extended family relationships and the graciousness and *aloha* should not be displaced as they strive for self-sufficiency.

References

Bushnell, Oswald A. *Molokai.* Honolulu: University Press of Hawaii, 1975.

Daws, Gavan. *Holy man: Father Damien of Molokai.* New York: Harper and Row, 1973.

Dwight, Edwin Welles. *Memoirs of Henry Obookiah.* Honolulu: Women's Board of Missions for the Pacific, 1968.

Gallimore, Ronald, and Howard, S. Alan. *Studies in a Hawaiian community: Na makamaka o Nanakuli.* Honolulu: Bernice P. Bishop Museum, 1968.

Greer, Richard A. Oahu's ordeal—The smallpox epidemic of 1853. *Hawaii Historical Review,* 1965, 1(12):221–242.

Howard, S. Alan. *Ain't no big thing: Coping strategies in a Hawaiian-American community.* Honolulu: University Press of Hawaii, 1974.

―――. Traditional and modern adoption patterns in Hawaii. In Vern Carroll (ed.), *Adoption in Eastern Oceania.* Honolulu: University Press of Hawaii, 1970.

Kubany, Edward S. The effects of incentives on the test performance of Hawaiians and Caucasians. Ph.D. thesis, no. 397, University of Hawaii, 1971.

Kuykendall, Ralph S. *The Hawaiian kingdom* (3 vols.). Honolulu: University Press of Hawaii, (1938–1967), 1968.

Larsen, Nils P. Medicine. In E. S. Craighill Handy, Kenneth P. Emory, Edwin H. Bryan, Peter H. Buck, and John H. Wise (eds.), *Ancient Hawaiian civilization.* Rutland, Vermont: Charles E. Tuttle, 1965.

Liliuokalani, Queen of Hawaii. *Hawaii's story by Hawaii's Queen.* Rutland, Vermont: Charles E. Tuttle, 1964.

Malo, David. *[Hawaiian antiquities]* (Nathaniel B. Emerson, trans.). Honolulu: Bishop Museum Press, 1971.

Paglinawan, Richard, and Paglinawan, Lynette. Ho-oponopono project number II: Development and implementation of ho-oponopono practice in a social work agency. Progressive Neighborhood Task Force. Honolulu: Hawaiian Culture Committee, Queen Liliuokalani Children's Center, 1972.

Pukui, Mary Kawena. *The Polynesian family system in Ka'u, Hawaii.* Rutland, Vermont: Charles E. Tuttle, 1972.

Pukui, Mary Kawena, and Elbert, Samuel. *Hawaiian English dictionary.* Honolulu: University Press of Hawaii, 1964.

Pukui, Mary Kawena; Haertig, E. W.; and Lee, Catherine A. *Nana i ke kumu.* Vol. 1. Honolulu: Hui Hanai, 1972. Vol. 2. In press.

Sinclair, Marjorie. *Nahi'ena'ena, sacred daughter of Hawaii.* Honolulu: University Press of Hawaii, 1976.

Suggs, Robert C. *The island civilization of Polynesia.* New York: New American Library, 1960.

CHAPTER 3

The Caucasians

Thomas W. Maretzki
John F. McDermott, Jr.

Caucasians as a Population Category

Caucasians cannot be considered ethnic in the definitional sense, but are a population based on more broadly defined social or folk concepts of race, much as the term *Oriental* or *Asian* reflects the notion of another racial stock. In other parts of the United States individual ethnic groupings and traditions are found among Caucasians which do have social relevance. With the exception of the Portuguese, however, the separate Caucasian ethnic identities do not play a significant part in the social fabric of Hawaii. Nevertheless, if we use the term *ethnic* in referring to all Caucasians, this is done to avoid the controversial term *race* and to acknowledge the broad generalizations which are applied to and hold meaning for Caucasians.

Caucasians have traditionally thought of themselves as the population which serves as the standard of reference for all other groups. Regardless of their particular geographical heritage, they have been viewed as the neutral ground against which all other groups are portrayed, the group whose values and lifestyle offer the background against which the other groups are measured and evaluated. Only during the most recent years of Hawaii's history has the balance shifted in that respect as more and more Americans of different backgrounds have seen their cultural influence become valued as part of an American pattern.

This remarkable shift has taken place during the last two decades, although individual Caucasians may continue to think of themselves as the representatives of a true American cultural pattern. Cosmopolitanism is replacing the cultural styles primarily associated with Caucasians. Today, given the total population profile in Hawaii, it is appropriate to think of Caucasians as one of the several groups that constitute the ethnic mosaic of the islands, though, of course, not in the sense of a disadvantaged minority. As the only state with Caucasians in a minority, this obviously has an effect on and shapes their current behavior. As Caucasian immigration from the mainland exceeds all others, and as the population in other ethnic groups shrinks relative to the phenomenon, it is believed that there will be a Caucasian population majority by the year 2000. This trend need not imply a Caucasian cultural dominance in the future. Our discussion of the past and present situation of Caucasians leads to a projection for the future which implies both distinctiveness of Caucasians and a more balanced cultural position in comparison to other groups.

At the present, in spite of their diverse backgrounds, Caucasians remain ethnically and culturally distinct from the other population groups. Often, the differences between two Caucasian families in Hawaii may be greater in general, as well as in details of lifestyle, than between a Caucasian and a Chinese, Japanese, Filipino or part-Hawaiian family of similar socioeconomic class. The middle-class Caucasian pattern of culture and behavior has indeed heavily influenced upper-middle and upper-class island families of diverse ethnic backgrounds. When local people, those of diverse ethnic and island background, label another person as "*haole*fied," they draw on the Hawaiian term *haole* (literally, "white European," "foreigner," "stranger"), which characterizes Caucasians, to describe this lifestyle adopted by non-Caucasians. Yet what we refer to as the *haole* lifestyle is nothing concrete that can be circumscribed in a few words. The components are elusive and difficult to present in a clear, precise description.

Unlike the other ethnic groups in Hawaii, the Caucasian group is seldom thought to have subgroups possessing different social and psychological characteristics. A brief historical sketch of the infiltration of these various groups into Hawaii may broaden the concept of "Caucasian," especially for the non-Caucasian reader.

History of Immigration

The psychological set of Caucasians toward other populations is reflected in the term *discovery,* which describes in records down to the present time, the British explorer Captain James Cook's first sighting of the islands in 1778, as well as many other first European contacts in various parts of the world. Such ethnocentric bias may be a human phenomenon not limited to Caucasians, but when combined with technological dominance and a certain moral righteousness, the effects on others, as well as on the dominant group itself, are overwhelming. The historian Gavan Daws reports the attitudes of Captain Cook upon first landing in the islands: "It was a sensible primitive who bowed before a superior civilization. Cook had seen more of life in a state of nature than all of the salon philosophers of Europe together, and experience taught him not to follow the London vogue of overrating Noble Savages at the expense of civilized men" (Daws, 1974).

These first civilized men, the explorers, were soon followed by other Caucasians: seafarers, traders, and then the first missionaries. It is the familiar history of colonization, with a special Hawaiian flavor provided by the gentleness of the physical environment, the nature of the Hawaiian culture, and the psychological characteristics, especially the relatively passive accepting attitude, of Hawaii's political and spiritual leaders. These elements left their marks on the Caucasians who first settled in the islands and on their descendants, just as many Caucasian patterns left their indelible effects on Hawaiians. For the student of the history of Hawaiian early contact with Western populations, enough has been written to provide fascinating details of a complementary relationship which developed between the Hawaiian chiefs and leaders and the Caucasians of all backgrounds who had either religious and educational contributions to make or other contributions of desired knowledge and practical skills. Much has been said about the impact of the missionaries who brought Christianity, in its New England Congregational variety, and education to the leaders and interested parties of the Hawaiian population. But it is also important to consider the constantly increasing impact of the various sailors and adventurers who came ashore. A certain kind of mutuality of interests between Caucasians and Hawaiians began with the need of the explorers to find supplies for their continued voyages and with the delight of the natives about their acquisition of materials previously unknown and quickly recognized as valuable. Even before the famous Boston missionary group arrived on the *Thaddeus* in 1820, a pattern of exchange had begun in which Caucasians played the role of the supplier of "superior" skills and knowledge while Ha-

waiians were cast as eager and sometimes not so eager learners. And
right before their eyes, Hawaiians, with the advent of the missionaries, could perceive the paradoxes in the values and the entire cultural
fabric of Western man, who emphasized both the practical and commercial interests of the here-and-now world and the significance of
the spiritual as reflected in Christ's teachings. The specific implications of some of the inherently paradoxical approaches to life, which
were so characteristic of Caucasians, surfaced when some Caucasians
accepted Hawaiian women's sexual favors while, at the same time,
other Caucasians condemned the free expression of sexuality, which,
to Hawaiians, presented no problems. This might suggest that the
apparently wide differences in social class among Hawaiians con-
cealed relatively common values regarding sexuality, while a much
wider diversity of values existed among the *haole,* part of the difficulty in discussing them as a group, then or now.

An organized Christian religion, schools, printing, and books using an Anglicized Hawaiian alphabet were some of the tangible manifestations of this early Caucasian influence. That these activities
would swiftly reduce the use of a tongue that had for centuries only
been spoken, a language which had been the vehicle not only for daily interchange but for the maintenance of a permanent historiogra-
phy of Hawaiian lore and genealogies contained in religious chants
and spoken legends, did not seem to occur to the Caucasians at all. If
it had, it would probably not have concerned them greatly because of
the characteristic righteousness the missionaries all seemed to share.
Thus, the Hawaiian language and the oral lore were almost totally
eliminated by the time Caucasians became aware of the need to preserve a record of past Hawaiian generations. Hawaii, with its benign
climate and rich environment, presented an opportunity, a challenge, a host of personal dreams which the Westerners, Caucasians
all, translated into much more than a missionized community.
Hawaii became a tropical model of Western enterprise and governmental style.

Traditional Culture of the Caucasians

By the second part of the nineteenth century, the pattern of Caucasian influence and enterprise had emerged in the establishment of
business ventures, sugar plantations, trading companies (called factors), and in an increasing number of services desired and needed in a

Western community, and now also important to the acculturating segment of the Hawaiian population. The plantations, in their search for laborers, found not only that Caucasians could not be expected to be attracted to the hard physical demands of this industrial agricultural work, but that Hawaiians showed an equal disinclination to accept work which was little better than temporary enslavement in a relatively benign but exhausting and unrewarding occupation. At this time Caucasians acquired a supervisory and controlling role over the imported laborers from the Orient and an economic advantage that lasted for at least a century. This oligarchy was probably inevitable, for Hawaii was a crossroads, a center of the Pacific, which attracted the interest of several Western powers, any of which, if successful in settling the islands, would have settled it with determined men and women, whether missionary, trader, or military.

Economic domination also required political control. Western principles of government had been introduced to the Hawaiian leadership and were further monitored and developed through the strong influence of Caucasian political advisors who held key positions. But ethnic superiority, based on moral and economic convictions and successes, could not long tolerate vagueness of national sovereignty. In 1898, following a Caucasian-organized revolution that replaced the Hawaiian monarchy, which was making an ill-fated effort to reassert itself with a short-lived republic, Hawaii was annexed to the United States. This development solidified and strengthened the power of a small Caucasian elite. For the next forty years, politics and economy, along with the souls of the Hawaiians and the lives of the imported field hands, were under the firm and pervasive supervision of the Caucasians, or as they came to be known, the *kama'āina.*

The *kama'āina* lifestyle was a mixture of New England values and continental (European) courtliness cultivated in a unique fashion by earlier association with the Hawaiian monarchy, suggesting a kind of purity of ancestral lineage with historical personal roots here in the islands. The *kama'āina* (the word literally means a child, *kama,* of the land, *'āina*) carved a psychological mold very much like that of the American southern gentry in the Antebellum era. The oldest families intermarried and are known to each other as ''the cousins.'' Old women, whether grandmothers or not, are called *tūtū;* whether blood relatives or not, old friends are known to children as ''uncle'' or ''auntie.'' This is much like upper-class family interrelationships on the mainland, but carries a special connotation because of the isolation of the *kama'āina* in Hawaii. They were a very cerebral, closely knit clan, complete with private social clubs, private schools, and special churches, which admitted no outsiders. They became the "local Caucasians" with their own special blending of mainland sophistication and island intimacy.

Although the number of Caucasians in Hawaii increased, the established *kama'āina* elite constituted only a tiny number. Caucasians were brought to Hawaii in small numbers from several European countries for plantation labor but proved, by their insistence on special treatment, to be more troublesome and expensive than Oriental laborers. As plantations grew, some of the *haole* were given preferential treatment in filling new supervisory positions.

Caucasians have worked at all levels in a variety of occupations and represent a range of lifestyles, but in comparison to all the other ethnic groups they have enjoyed distinct social privileges and economic advantages. A few among them, homegrown *haole* rather than college-educated mainlanders, as Fuchs refers to them, were admitted into the inner elite. Others, even though they were bright and successful as professionals, would be kept at a polite distance unless related by blood or marriage to the true *kama'āina* (Fuchs, 1961). A definite class structure had developed among the Caucasians in Hawaii by the early part of this century.

Although the borderlines of *kama'āina* membership appeared fluid, to members of the elite families it was always obvious who belonged and who did not. Only in a more general sense does *kama-'āina* refer to well-established Caucasian families who have lived in the islands for decades, building large homes, sending their children to the same schools as the elite *kama'āina*, and belonging to the same clubs, and who are therefore almost indistinguishable to the outsider because of the established and comfortable positions that are comparable to those of the "true" *kama'āina*.

Today, being a "true" *kama'āina*, or a descendant from early missionary or other prominent families of Caucasian background which often intermarried with Hawaiian nobility, is somewhat akin to being listed in the social register elsewhere. The number of families is relatively small, their lifestyle no longer as expansive as in earlier times. The large houses, servants, beach or mountain bungalows, the memberships in the Pacific Club, Outrigger Club, Oahu Country

Club, and similar distinctions are no longer the hallmark of the exclusive privileges they once were. But a *kama'āina* quality continues. Some have written their own family histories, such as the Cookes of Oahu and Molokai, which are privately circulated. Many have interests in the old business establishments as well as in the largest ranches. Punahou School, a secondary private institution begun by missionaries for children of Caucasian and established families and for children of Hawaiian nobility and those among commoners converted and seen as promising, still carries some of the flavor of the onetime *kama'āina* exclusiveness, even though it has broadened and includes a large number of non-Caucasian students. While some of the older members of *kama'āina* families still maintain the memories and traditions of an earlier era, with values which admit little of the significant changes, the younger generation has almost completely blended with the rest of the population, though economic and social advantages still help to shape their careers. Central Union Church, like Punahou School, the social clubs, and the once exclusive residential sections where *kama'āina* estates were located are now open to everyone, or at least to socially desirable Caucasians, Orientals, and others who are wealthy and influential.

Caucasians in the Recent Past

The proportion of Caucasians rose from 5 percent at the time of annexation in 1898 to 25 percent in 1940. The sharpest rise occurred in the 1920s and 1930s. A considerable part of the Caucasian influx of that time came in the uniform of the United States Armed Forces, particularly the Navy which, since the turn of the century, had firmly established itself as the reigning branch of the military in this maritime setting of great strategic significance. The Army, and eventually, the Air Force established their own bases and roles in the years prior to World War II.

The early influx of the military was made up of mostly single Caucasian men from the farmer and worker classes of American society, many of them away from home for the first time in their lives. Their motives for enlisting in the service ran the gamut from "join the Navy and see the world" to wanting to protect the democratic way of life. During their tours of duty these men were confined to their posts and ships through the week; their only opportunity to come into town was during weekend shore liberty or passes. In the towns and cities from which these young, unsophisticated men came, there were probably few brown or yellow faces besides those of blacks, and often none of those either. Consequently, these soldiers and sailors, armed with only their childhood prejudice and ignorance of anyone "different," probably viewed the unfamiliar Japanese, Chinese, Filipino, and Hawaiian people as dark, exotic natives; even today "local" suggests "foreign" to the same type of military individual. It is not uncommon to hear a GI say he'll be glad to "return to the United States." Merchants and barkeeps of Chinatown and Waikiki were naturally eager to attract as much business and as many American dollars as they could from these lonely, bored young men, though the obsequious facade of acceptance and welcome they often presented masked feelings of hostility and dread of the unbridled and undecorous behavior of "GI Joe."

The officers, during these early decades, were often men from prominent American families with long traditions of being gentlemen soldiers. Unlike their enlisted subordinates, their families often accompanied them on their military assignments. Single or married, however, the military gentry was often entertained by influential *kama'āina* families in Hawaii interested in the benefits of contact with the American military and political structure.

In recent years the composition of the military forces in Hawaii has changed considerably. Families of enlisted men in all the services are now able to accompany their husbands and fathers on assignment. As of 1976, the total number of members of the US military on active duty in Hawaii was 33,846, with 73,239 dependents, the majority Caucasian. To this could be added the Caucasian civilian workers in armed forces facilities and other federal employees whose assignments are made on a rotating basis. This population lives in a relatively closed, self-sufficient system, typical of any military installation, with the usual support services, post exchanges, service clubs, and recreational facilities. There is also a total health system with the largest hospital facilities in the Pacific Basin. Not all these families live on base or in housing developments constructed with military funding; even those who do not are oriented toward the service and social opportunities offered to them exclusively. Yet families with children in the local schools, with wives who work in the private sector, and with opportunities to extend tours of duty or to return for subsequent assignments, relate more to the activities and social interchange in the nonmilitary community. Although once referred to by a series of newspaper articles as Hawaii's hidden community, sheer numbers and the fact that so many retired military personnel have settled in Hawaii help to increase the links of the military to the total community, but there is a continuing segment of quite isolated families who rely on each other in a fashion that tends to reinforce and magnify situations and problems inherent in this type of mobile lifestyle.

Single individuals and those on temporary duty without families are still the least related to the rest of the community. A small portion of this group, especially in the Navy, who seek entertainment and more gregarious stimulation after the weeks of confinement and isolation on submarine and carrier duty, continually frequent the haunts of Hotel Street and Waikiki, sites of occasional disruptions and incidents with locals who still resent the presence of outsiders. But in the context of this discussion it is also worth noting that the Caucasian military are a constant and important source of support of mainland-style culture in popular music, talk shows on radio stations, or special events reflecting the current interests and styles of other states. This aspect of the so-called "melting pot phenomenon" can be seen in the arrival of hamburger and fast food chains which serve saimin, a local food, as well. Although obviously not the only source of such infusion, the constant turnover, frequent travels on leave, and other continuous contacts with the mainland, as well as plain homesickness and desire for the familiar, give the military a strong role in fostering mainland tastes.

An example of the domination of Caucasians and the political influence of the military in the 1930s, especially the Navy, as well as of the beginning of the end of Caucasian rule, was the celebrated Massie Case (Daws, 1968; Wright, 1972).

The case began in an atmosphere of purely local interest. Thalia Massie, the wife of a young naval officer attached to Pearl Harbor, was allegedly picked up and assaulted by five "native boys" after she left an officers' party at the Ala Wai Inn near midnight on 12 September 1931. Five young men—two Hawaiians, one Chinese Hawaiian, one Japanese Hawaiian, and one Japanese *nisei*—were arrested the same night and ultimately brought to trial after being identified by Mrs. Massie. The evidence presented was so thin, however, the jury refused to bring in a verdict.

While the young men were awaiting a retrial, one of them, Joseph Kahahawai, was lured into a car by Mrs. Massie's mother, Grace Fortescue, her husband, and one of his sailors, and was driven to a house in Manoa where he was shot to death. His kidnappers were arrested while trying to dispose of his body in the ocean. The murder of Kahahawai and the subsequent trial of his killers transformed the case from a local incident to one of national interest. The four Caucasian defendants, represented by the great criminal lawyer Clarence Darrow, were convicted of manslaughter and sentenced to ten years in prison. But Republican Governor Lawrence Judd commuted the sentence to one hour, to be spent in the governor's chambers at Iolani Palace; they were then released (Judd, 1971).

The verdict and aftermath created a racial explosion that threatened to tear Hawaii apart, yet the social and political tension working in the encapsulated "pressure cooker" of Hawaii probably resolved many problems for the future because it affected everyone in a lasting way. George Wright, the Caucasian editor of a local newspaper, wrote, "More harm has been done to the cause of Americanization by recent events than can be remedied in many years" (*Hawaii Hochi,* May 10, 1932).

A subsequent investigation of the case concluded that the five young men, one of whom was killed, could not have been involved in the assault—if there was one at all. In short, the entire matter was a miserable miscarriage of justice; however, the investigators' report was never publicly released.

The willingness of territorial politicians to sacrifice the five "native boys" to appease the Navy, rather than insisting on a genuine inquiry into the unsupported allegations of Mrs. Massie, left a scar on the public conscience and also left the Caucasian oligarchy exposed. The consequences of these incidents were the beginning of a swing of all races toward the Democratic Party and the delay of statehood for Hawaii—the Massie case being cited in 1935 as evidence of Hawaiians' unreadiness. (Paradoxically, the case could have been used as an example of the injustice of the ruling oligarchy and the need for statehood to escape the arbitrariness of military rule.) Thus, guilt, shame, and indignation resulting from this case were enormous. In a closely knit multiracial population, it probably marked the beginning of the end of overt racism and catalyzed the development of the image of Hawaii as a melting pot.

In summary, a profile of Caucasians of the '20s and '30s shows the *kama'āina* families well settled in large homes in choice locations on Oahu—Nuuanu and Manoa valleys, and the hillsides of Pacific Heights and Makiki Heights—and on the other islands. It shows the military in their enclaves at Pearl Harbor, Fort Shafter, Schofield, and Hickam Air Force Base, and it points to a rising population of the *haole*—those who represented the federal government, university faculty, technical experts, those in specialized service industries, and, of course, those in the shipping and trading firms, or with the leading "Big Five" Caucasian companies of Hawaii and the many smaller and more recently established firms having head offices or branches in Honolulu. Additional professionals, physicians, lawyers, and other specialists came in small but steady trickles. And by this time also, a few wealthy retirees, some artists, writers, musicians, painters, and others came to settle in the islands, adding to the increasing Caucasian population and their cultural, educational, economic, and political dominance in island life. The two major newspapers were under full Caucasian control, and, if there was any doubt, one glance at political as well as society news revealed it all. Almost exclusively, Caucasian and a few distinctive Hawaiian families were the subjects of society reports. This was perhaps the ideal life situation from a purely Caucasian point of view, for it allowed status, comfort, security, and a boundless future for most of this group, except perhaps for the increasing number of uniformed military to whom the islands were only a way station in a chain of overseas rotations.

An attitude of Americanism prevailed in Hawaii through World War II. The Caucasians represented the traditions of the nation whose revolution and pronouncements of 1776 had inspired the world; in Hawaii as on the mainland the drive of the immigrants was to share fully in those ideas and to become full-fledged, integrated members of the society and political system that produced them. They were told to become Americans, to lose their identity as Chinese, Japanese, and so on. In other words, despite many changes the dominant culture was Caucasian and to a certain extent it remains so today. Caucasians had the best jobs; they were in full command of politics and the economy; they received more rapid promotions and drew higher pay—all of which resulted in occupational division along ethnic lines and contributed significantly to ethnic tensions.

It appears that Caucasian dominance and paternalism, based in part on cultural ignorance and insensitivity, gave birth among the patronized and suppressed to ethnic enmities that, although submerged, have not wholly disappeared despite the erosion of Caucasian control. It has to be said, however, that this anti-Caucasian feeling also contains some element of the envy that is universally directed toward any dominant group.

The great change began with World War II. The rule of the civilian Caucasian oligarchy was replaced by military government and martial law which, although predominantly Caucasian, was tied to the mainland and the national security and not to the relative parochialism of a small island territory. The changes brought by war set off chain reactions which hastened the spread of a more genuine democracy and weakened Caucasian influence. The centralized economy based on *kama'āina* firms was destroyed by war and the aftermath; by defense spending; by postwar tourism; by the rise of a generation of war-experienced, proven young Americans of Japanese ancestry and their entrance into politics, business, and the professions; and by rapid advances in transportation and communications.

Once World War II ended, Caucasians were attracted to residency in the islands because they had first been there in military service or as tourists. Veterans took advantage of the GI Bill of Rights at the University of Hawaii, shifted their trades and professions learned in the service to the civilian sector, and gradually and then more and more rapidly took advantage of opportunities in the development of tourism. As fast, frequent, and most of all, affordable plane service between California and Hawaii increased, travel brought more and more mainlanders, almost all Caucasians, many of whom returned to settle. So, at the same time that Orientals of the second and third generation left their traditional (even though short-lived) stations of life on Hawaiian plantations and in low-paying service jobs to move into the rapidly expanding occupational, educational, and political opportunities, Caucasians without *kama'āina* ties or long-standing background in the islands also vied for niches in the expanding residential and occupational spheres. Previously, only a few non-Caucasians had entered the most prominent or desirable professional positions, medicine, law, and banking. Corporations' top echelons were still almost exclusively Caucasian, with a few Hawaiians and even fewer Chinese among them. The appointed governor of the Territory was always Caucasian, or a *haole*fied, distinguished Hawaiian, the traditional ally.

The Contemporary Caucasian Situation

The entire island situation, however, shifted rapidly following statehood in 1959. A Caucasian politician, later the influential and widely revered governor of Hawaii, John A. Burns, not only recognized the talent and aspirations of non-Caucasians, but correctly assessed their political drive, if not their impatient quest for leadership positions and open opportunities. As territorial representative to the federal government, he was the force instrumental in bringing about Hawaii's new place in the nation. His empathy and interest probably stemmed from his upbringing in Kalihi, a lower-middle-class section of Honolulu near Fort Shafter, and from his acquaintance with the *nisei* during his career as a Honolulu police detective. His contributions to Hawaii's politics assumed gigantic proportions and are still evident in the fiber of the present-day local political structure.

Statehood initiated the final process, diluting the predominance of the *kama'āina* Caucasian and, at the same time, opening the islands to new and large waves of migrating Caucasians *(malihini)* from other states.

Swelling numbers of "new" Caucasians, individuals with a variety of skills and occupations, were attracted to Hawaii as residents; their numbers are still the most rapidly increasing of all groups. Their attraction to Hawaii may have come about through a personal yearning to visit the islands and the subsequent or sudden availability of professional opportunities. Many physicians, lawyers, engineers, accountants, bankers, managers of businesses and scores of other occupationally specialized individuals came to Hawaii in this manner and are now perhaps the largest contingent of Caucasians in terms of the arbitrary divisions we are suggesting. As mentioned earlier, a considerable number of Caucasians in these many fields know Hawaii through the time they spent in the service, or because of service-connected travel and brief stays in the islands; many of them married island women and stayed. Since statehood a large number of companies with headquarters on the mainland and branches in other states have opened facilities in Hawaii which needed partial staffing by established company executives and staff. Until quite recently the tendency was to move someone from the mainland into such positions. Increasingly, however, local individuals who began by working for national companies in Hawaii are assuming such positions, and the somewhat colonial approach to staffing by mainland companies, which was the cause of a great deal of Caucasian influx, is shifting.

The retirees who have come to Hawaii form by far the smallest and, as yet, least significant group in terms of Caucasian impact. Many retirees in Hawaii have been residents here for a long time, due to military service connections, or have chosen the islands for retirement, as so many choose Florida, simply because of the high standard of living. Some Caucasians come after retirement because one or several children have settled here. They either find their own housing or, in more typical present-day Caucasian style, join one of the growing number of retirement homes or colonies. Few of this small group of Caucasians are likely to settle here without some previous acquaintance with the islands and some knowledge of its culture and lifestyle, not to speak of costs. The long-range impact on Hawaii of these Caucasians remains to be seen; at present, their numbers are growing and, in terms of their accumulated knowledge, experience, and different perspectives from those of many residents, it could be considerable. In this group the sex ratio favors women because of their greater longevity.

Among the newcomers to Hawaii have been many Caucasians who came for educational reasons, whether as students, faculty, or administrators. This group, at first glance, may seem odd because it encompasses a quite divergent set of characteristics. The common trend is an educational background based heavily on university training, continuing education, and professional contacts, with the university campus as an important center and focal identification point. Although the University of Hawaii is sometimes accused of being too aloof from the community, a large number of Caucasians in professional positions came to Hawaii as students (often with a service background as a first step to residence) or as young professionals just graduated on the mainland. The university, therefore, has become one major processing institution where Caucasians first learn about the islands while they are receiving academic training and are establishing ties to the community. For a long time the university drew a majority of its faculty members from the mainland; only in the last decade has this situation changed somewhat, but by no means completely. The professional schools, in particular medicine and law, now give clear and acknowledged preference to local residents for admission, but other graduate programs still attract many mainland Caucasians who seek the specialities offered by the university because of its location and focus on Asia and the Pacific. While there are no reliable statistics on the role of the university as an initial focus for Caucasian immigration to the islands, either for faculty, staff, or students who eventually find jobs in Hawaii, the number of Caucasians who settled in Hawaii via this route must be considerable.

A 1976 report indicated that 32.7 percent of the Caucasian population consisted of members of the armed forces and their dependents. Their numbers are significant because without them the percentage of resident Caucasians was 21.5 percent, making the Caucasians the second, rather than the largest, population group in the islands (Schmitt, 1977). Of family heads in the civilian sector, 67.1 percent were in professional, technical, business, managerial, or office jobs. The figures here, briefly, give some idea of the scope of Caucasian in-migration to Hawaii since statehood and a measure of Caucasian placement in the more advantaged occupations.

The experiences of *malihini* ("newcomers") who recently moved to Hawaii from the US mainland reflect some parallel experiences of other immigrant groups in Hawaii, as well as some significant differences. Many of the recent mainland arrivals first visited Hawaii as tourists or transients. Their idealized expectation of an island paradise influences their adjustment from "recent newcomer" status to "typical haole". Many of these newcomers find themselves at first isolated from local residents and relying on other transients for contact and establishment of social networks. Waikiki is one environment where they can find others of comparable background in a similar situation. In some ways the entire experience, from the decision to move to settlement in Hawaii, is part of a life-crisis experience involving integration into the new social fabric and the establishment of a new identity (Whittaker, 1978).

While all this may not be too different from the experience of migrants in general, the majority group of Caucasians from the mainland United States do not usually consider themselves as migrants. They expect others to have to adapt, not themselves. That these expectations are further mitigated by economic factors is evident. Mainland haoles who move to Hawaii with a job waiting for them, or with a financial base which permits them to pay for the high cost of housing, have a clear advantage over the many haoles and other migrants who come with modest means or no other support than that provided by relatives.

Another group of Caucasians, the most difficult to categorize, is important for its impact on island living and lifestyles. Since the mid-1960s an increasing number of young Caucasians sought and found, in the scenic beauty and relative remoteness of some island localities, the idyllic setting for a new lifestyle. They were quickly joined by more and more seekers, some religious in orientation, who were willing to work with their hands in some cases and who became increasingly desperate for jobs and for a peaceful place in which to find meaning in this competitive society. Mixed with surfing, with some university or other educational activities, with bumming, with preaching, with following, and with gardening, this Caucasian influence has assumed major proportions. Aided by low airfare, liberal welfare and health maintenance programs, and the pioneering successes of those who preceded them, these young people came first from the western states, then more and more from any state to which Hawaii is alluring. During 1978, according to the State Department of Planning and Economic Development, half of the in-migrants from the mainland, the great majority of whom were Caucasian, were under 24.4 years of age, so that the increase of Caucasians reflected in overall demographic terms is probably largest in this category.

Legal, welfare, health, and psychiatric systems feel the burden from this group, especially because once arrived in Hawaii and in need of intervention or support, the return to another state is fraught with difficulties. Unlike other states—with vast expanses of land on which to settle away from communities that are reluctant or hostile toward these people—community contact in Hawaii is immediate and intense. The ingenuity of these Caucasian seekers in finding ecological niches in the community, given the high cost of housing, food, and of any service, is impressive, though seldom acknowledged. Whether one cites the establishment of pedicab service in Waikiki, seemingly one of the commercial ventures of young Caucasians, or the many attractive stores and open-air stands displaying and selling special foods, crafts, books and magazines, or any of the multitude of enterprises that have directly or indirectly sprung from the influence of these young Caucasians, there is no doubt that their impact has been considerable and deep. As in California where the young generation has long set a tone that influenced crucially a life-style associated with their state, a new lifestyle has blossomed in the islands to an extent where, although some think of this influence in terms of California, others see it more in terms of a happy blending of Californian and Hawaiian styles with a bit of Oriental influence. An ecology consciousness, now widespread in Hawaii, must clearly be traced to the impact of these young Caucasians.

Following the termination of warfare in Vietnam and a realignment of American economic and political relationships, both nationally and internationally, migration to Hawaii continues. Federal welfare and other service supports also continue, though more and more shakily, to aid the influx of Caucasians. But the economic expansion and opportunities seem to have dwindled or at least reached a plateau. The current place of Caucasians in the total Hawaiian social pattern has drastically changed if viewed from its historical origin. It is far from stagnant, however, as is true for all ethnic groups in Hawaii. Somewhat analogous to the international position of the United States, vis-à-vis other countries, Caucasians remain an important influence, but one which increasingly appreciates the historical problems and current efforts of other ethnic groups to further their economic and social positions. In short, a social homogenesis has occurred in an ethnic sense. Increasingly, economic and political opportunities are more evenly distributed among ethnic groups in Hawaii, if not inversely lopsided from a historical perspective, at least in the case of political leadership.

Haole Stereotypes and Myths

The Caucasian resident, as viewed by his local neighbors, is often automatically stereotyped as successful, independent, and self-confident. His aggressiveness, as perceived in business and interpersonal relations, results in such labels as "loud, insensitive, bossy, outspoken, prestige and power oriented, boastful and conceited." It may be true that Caucasian values emphasize independence, self-assertion, and individual achievement from a very early age, in contrast to the pervasive *aloha* spirit where emphasis is on smooth interpersonal relationships through control of feelings which, if expressed, might cause disruption, and where every effort to avoid confrontation that would offend is given the highest priority. But haole-style communication, in comparison to that of many others, is marked by an emphasis on openness and frankness (speaking one's mind directly, complaining when one feels like it) and on neighborliness and interpersonal relations without too deep an involvement. Haole style is low on, or devoid of, ritual in comparison with other ethnic styles. This is expressed in characteristics of housing, garden arrangements, social events, and leisure time activities—all of which are associated with the term *suburban*. To delineate the components of haole lifestyle through contrast, haoles are more likely to go to lunch and pay individually; locals are more prone to try to quietly pick up the tab for each other. Haoles tend to state outright and sometimes loudly their accomplishments or their opinions, but locals refrain from such open expression or revelation of their thoughts; they often associate haole style with immodesty and loudness. Haole style may also imply a middle-class style of consumption, or perhaps just a preference for certain foods or drinks. Any example here is difficult because there are no clear lines; the distinction is so subtle that it may be one of only perceived differences rather than one of real differences in preference. In another vein, what was haolefied fifteen or twenty years ago is now a widely accepted island pattern, yet a certain type of haole style continues: in speech, dress, patterns of social relations, expression of personality, leisure time activities, and a number of other ways. While Caucasians may refer to themselves as haoles, the term has a series of subtler meanings which shift from unflattering or somewhat jealous to quite neutral dimensions depending on the context and the individuals referred to, as well as the primary identification of the user. "She is haole" may be a purely factual statement in some cases. In others it may be quite critical or disparaging, and, should there be any initial doubt, the adjectives "damn" or "dumb" will leave none.

Given the "neutral" nature of Caucasian culture mentioned earlier, it is amazing how much cultural style one may be able to distill that in turn relates to psychological characteristics. Caucasians are generally described as driven toward constant activity and achievement and as talkative and noisy, if compared to standards of other groups. Youth, activism, optimism, futurism, progress, success, humor, conformity, health and cleanliness, democracy, and romance are values commonly attributed to Caucasian culture and used as points of comparison with other ethnic groups. These may be turned into caricatures and stereotypes by others.

For example, a study by Arkoff, Meredith, and Iwabara (1964) compared Caucasians with other ethnic groups in Hawaii. Members of the other ethnic groups made systematic evaluations of Caucasians, specifically comparing Caucasian students with students of Polynesian Oriental ancestry. (The latter included mixtures of Polynesians with Chinese, Japanese, Filipino, and part-Hawaiian students.) The conclusion was that Caucasian men, as viewed by the other groups, score high on needs for dominance, aggression, autonomy, achievement, exhibition, and heterosexuality, and low on needs for deference, abasement, nurturance, affiliation, order, and endurance. In this study, Caucasian women scored relatively high on the need for exhibition and heterosexuality and low on needs for dominance, deference, and order. The study rated both Caucasian men and women higher on the activity scale than their Asian counterparts. Another comparison by Garside (1965) indicated that Caucasians are not only more extroverted than Polynesians, but also more defensive.

A University of Hawaii student (Kaleialoha, 1966) dealt with the characteristics of mainland Caucasian women in-migrants to Hawaii. Her thesis developed this profile: aggressive, independent, assertive, and ambitious, with a dislike for conventional and conservative values and rigid behavior. A Caucasian in-married (that is, married to a local Hawaiian man), on the other hand, was motivated by the need for emotional stability which appears to stem from an emotionally deprived upbringing.

Meredith and Meredith (1966) discussed acculturation and personality among Japanese American college students in Hawaii. Their analysis compared Caucasians and Japanese and found Caucasian men less reserved, humble, shy, and conscientious, and more outgoing, expedient, assertive, venturesome, and imaginative. Caucasian women appeared less affected by feelings than Japanese women, less obedient, suspicious, and apprehensive, and more emotionally stable, independent, trusting, and self-assured.

Any description of a group of people conforms to some norms or uses a contrastive approach. As seen by many of the other ethnic groups, different as they are among themselves, Caucasians are considered insincere, less warm, less committed, even less intense in their interpersonal relationships with their families, their friends, and their fellow workers. A typical exchange may not seem odd to the Caucasian involved in it who hears from his Oriental colleague that his parents are coming to visit and to stay in his house for a month or longer. Yet the Caucasian's expression of sympathy—referring to the demands of older persons, the generation gap, the possible crowding which results, and a number of other factors—seems quite odd to the colleague of Oriental background for whom this visit is a natural and desirable event, and who could never consider it an imposition.

This more impersonal or differentially oriented approach to relationships may have a considerable effect on interethnic understanding, to the point where acceptance of a Caucasian is considerably influenced by that individual's ability to recognize and adopt a relationship style more characteristic of other island ethnic groups. Sociologists have seized on these facts and described them in fanciful words such as *universalistic* (referring to the generalized rules of interrelations) as opposed to the *particularistic* (those factors which structure relationships in terms of individual considerations in each case). Caucasians follow more of a universalistic approach than do others in the islands who seek a personal factor, even at work. Common meals, exchange of gifts, the simple exchange of concern, all these may be construed differently by the typical mainland-raised Caucasian than by those familiar with the local style.

For Caucasians in mixed gatherings—ethnic, social class, occupational—the fine nuances of expressing relationships as practiced by non-Caucasians may not be recognized for a long time. Alcohol can become an effective catalyst, but so can the greater interpersonal sensitivity of non-Caucasians. Sense of humor is related here, though difficult to abstract ethnically. Caucasian men are given more easily to the obviously sexual or scatological types of humor found in public affairs as well as in bars than are other men who appreciate more the subtler humor involving puns and the foibles of humans and of relationships. Here is a whole area of as yet unexplored cultural styles in Hawaii where the Caucasian pattern undoubtedly could be given separate identification.

What amazes more traditional non-Caucasians is the ease with which Caucasians can state their opinion, their judgment, their evaluation of a situation or of a person. There is little that is guarded in Caucasian expression of opinions if compared with that of non-Caucasians. This is as much a feminine as a masculine characteristic and often earns the epithet "loud-mouthed haole." Openness, coupled with the more strident quality of voice attributed to them, makes Caucasians stand out in groups. And finally, there is the flow of words which often exceeds that of anyone with a different background. Where verbal skills and expression are also highly valued in Polynesian groups, and therefore a virtue, they are quite differently structured and expressed. A person from another, especially Oriental, ethnic group who shows such verbosity may be considered *haole*fied by the older, traditional Orientals.

Mental Health Problems of the Caucasian Group
GENERAL PROBLEMS

If we now review the personality characteristics and values that are identified with the Caucasian group, we may be able to isolate some general trends pointing toward conditions that are symptomatic of difficulties in achieving certain desires and goals. It is important to keep in mind, however, that the Caucasians of Hawaii reflect diverse regional and ethnic backgrounds and are perhaps more heterogeneous than any other group. Second, the lack of common regional ties and loyalties among the Caucasians, together with the lack of support found in the extended family tradition of some of the other ethnic groups, leaves the Caucasian in Hawaii more vulnerable in the overall social network. Third, when a Caucasian arrives in Hawaii, it is often his first experience in a multicultural situation, a fact which may precipitate, or intensify, any existing potential for internal or interpersonal personality conflict. Fourth, many Caucasians feel pressure to live up to the stereotypic views other ethnic groups have of them: successful, independent, confident, and prosperous, even if the stereotype does not fit.

If we recognize the limitations involved in generalizations, yet acknowledge that independence, self-assertion, and achievement are highly valued characteristics in the Caucasian group at large, and thus are promoted in families with growing children, we may begin to recognize the common signs in the many members of the Caucasian group who do not achieve these ideals. For example, depression is perhaps the most common symptom found in Caucasians today, not only in Hawaii, but on the mainland as well. In Hawaii, it can often be related to a discrepancy between one's *ideal* of individual achievement, and the reality of one's *actual* achievement. Depression in the Caucasian group is often associated with alcoholism, a disorder found to be significantly overrepresented in the many studies comparing the Caucasian with other ethnic groups. The counterpart of this in the preadult population is drug abuse. Both of these conditions have been associated traditionally with the frustration growing out of a need to be dependent and cared for in a group that values independence and self-assertion. In addition, these cultural values of independence and self-assertion also may be related to the high occurrence of marital problems, that is, conflicts between husband and wife which result in a higher divorce rate among Caucasians than in other ethnic groups, and to that of family conflicts which often involve nonconforming children and adolescents.

COMMON PROBLEMS OF SUBGROUPS

Large numbers of *malihini* Caucasians, the largest group of Caucasians in-migrating from the mainland United States, are brought to Hawaii for management positions at various levels of the business and corporate community. Many of these managers and their relatively young families are rootless and see their stay in Hawaii simply as one more step on the way up the corporate ladder. As is true throughout the country, the heads of such families are frequently subject to intense pressure to return profits that are satisfactory to the distant home office, and often they also are afflicted with personal financial problems in their struggle to maintain appearances and standards of living thought to be essential to their present position and future careers in an area of the country in which the cost of living is very high. To the general conditions mentioned above is added the problem of suddenly being a minority member in a multiethnic setting. Much of the personal stress becomes focused on realistic issues, such as concern over the current crime situation which is largely attributed to non-Caucasians, but problems most often surface as "rock fever" or "island fever." It should be noted that there are two varieties of island fever. One is spatial or geographic and the other psychological. The first is captured in the mainland visitor's question to local inhabitants: Isn't it difficult to live in the confined space of an island? The mainlander is usually brought up abruptly by the counter question: How much space do you move around in geographically during your normal day on the mainland? But the deeper meaning of island fever is the feeling of being closed in by surrounding ethnic groups more than by water. A mild defense and remedy is choosing to live in the predominantly mainland-haole neighborhoods. "Seeing water wherever I go," or "not being able to drive for miles and miles,'' however, are often just the superficial complaints of patients whose island fever has reached a state of anxiety. Psychiatrists who have seen these patients report that the defensiveness caused by being "surrounded" (or "excluded") by *kama'āina* may break out as hostility toward those groups or as feelings of loneliness and isolation.

A special segment of this population is the retirees. These older persons are subject to all of the biological and psychological problems of the aging everywhere. Isolation and decline in self-esteem, traceable to society's low premium on the elderly, especially in the Caucasian group as opposed to the Oriental; the progressive loss of friends and relatives, as well as the loss of one's own capacities with advancing age; all may play a part in forming psychological disabilities in this group which may be further complicated by the development of organic brain disease related to the aging process. The high cost of living, with its increasingly intense pressure on the retired person of fixed income, and the separation from friends, family, and familiar surroundings can come as a shock to those who choose to retire in the islands, lured by visions of a benign climate and simplicity of life. These factors intensify rather than alter the varieties of mental disturbance observed among retired persons in Hawaii. Among the problems most frequently seen are agitated states, depression, and preoccupation with suicide, together with disorders resulting from organic brain disease.

At the other end of the age scale are people who have come to Hawaii to seek alternative lifestyles. They come to find the meaning of life, to live a relaxed life, to get on (or off) drugs, or any combination of these. Their problems are expressed as states of confusion, emptiness, or "identity crises," and range all the way from disillusionment with "the search" and accompanying depression to serious mental illness and complete loss of the sense of one's identity. The turnover among this group is great; indeed, they may be considered a transient population. Some, having "dropped out," seek help in order to learn how to "drop back in" because they have lost touch with the simple means of communication in a larger society. They may wish to find a job, settle down, and adjust to the real or "straight" world even though disillusioned with it. They, like many Caucasians, both men and women, have found the '70s a contrast to the '60s when job opportunities were greater. Indeed, Hawaii is the state with the highest proportion of husbands and wives who work. Many Caucasians now have problems, however, in locating appropriate jobs, especially professional positions. University expansion has leveled off. The tourist and travel industries, perhaps the source of greatest employment, turns more and more to established local residents of different ethnic groups as its employees. Caucasians, once the dominant group as employers and employees, now express feelings of insecurity and inadequacy, real or fancied, as Hawaii strives to even out the racial balance in occupations.

The problems suffered by Caucasians in the military are characterized by alcoholism, episodes of depression, anxieties about authority and dependency which cannot be satisfied, and antisocial behavior. This may seem paradoxical because authority and structure are the very factors which often are sought by those who are attracted to a military life as a career. It is hypothesized that one would find higher scores for symptom discomfort and lower scores for stability among Caucasian military families than among civilian Caucasian families as measured by standardized scales. The difference presumably would be accounted for largely by the women because they appear to be more adversely affected than men by the isolation of the military from the civilian communities.

For some of the women and children of service families the frequent absence of husbands requires constant shifts and readjustments within the family which may lead to special vulnerabilities. Especially among some Navy families, husbands may be absent for several months on regular rotations; in such a family the wife and children must shift roles and interaction patterns every time the husband leaves or returns. The man often feels excluded by the family's need to close ranks in his absence, and has difficulty reintegrating himself on his periodic returns. He in turn may overreact with efforts to exert discipline out of context, which is resented by wife and children. Such special demands placed on the mothers in military families and precipitated by male absence, together with the relatively closed pattern of military living, often preclude independent and educational pursuits on the part of these women in the community.

Children of military families usually attend public schools and often it is the teacher who first identifies learning, behavioral, and/or emotional problems which need professional intervention. These children not only carry some of the burdens of families that frequently are uprooted, and which are not participating in the life of the more open community, but they also frequently display difficulty in establishing rewarding peer relationships among the children of the local population.

The lives of single service personnel, especially enlisted persons, involve deprivations and frustrations which differ somewhat from those of families. Young single Caucasian men, with or without provocation, sometimes become involved in fights with non-Caucasians and in other antisocial behavior. While much is said publicly about these involvements, that is, "training in aggressive behavior during the day is hard to turn off in the evening," little is really known about the loneliness of single military personnel who find Hawaii expensive, who feel far from home, and who, in many cases, have left home early in their lives for the glamor and attraction of faraway places such as Hawaii—all factors that are characteristic of the single military in any service and of any ethnic background.

Finally, let us consider the *kama'āina* Caucasians. Here problems often reflect identity conflicts brought on by a dramatic shift in status between the generations or by a mixture of old and new realities. The independence, risk taking, and self-righteousness of the early members of the oligarchy reflected the frontier personality of any group in a similar situation. Their intermarriage with Hawaiians and years of insulation while perpetuating conservative "plantation psychology" values, except for the Oriental ones which gradually infiltrated and became very powerful, have produced an interesting mixture of old and new. The social conscience of recent generations of *kama'āina* has emerged from the old paternalistic "colonial" rule. Yet psychiatrists who see this group as patients commonly describe the need for maintaining control over emotions as a contributing factor in the resulting depressions which are so frequent in these overly controlled personality types. Strict need to maintain an image as a model for others, particularly those seen as socially inferior may, if it becomes a family trait and expectation, lead to similar styles in younger generations who adopt the family role, or to exactly the opposite in those who rebel against its strictness, for example, the passive playboy who cannot compete or achieve on his own and disappoints the family and "cousins."

Many of these descendants have experienced conflict in their efforts to identify with the traditional *kama'āina* patterns of behavior

while at the same time adjusting to a modern and drastically different Hawaii no longer under their sole dominion. They have inherited
and sought to perpetuate symbolic roles and forms of social interaction which become less and less viable in an increasingly complex and
competitive island social system. As this conflict intensifies, social
grouping among the *kama'āina* descendants tends to be less stable
and psychopathology, reflecting an inability to establish a sense of
personal identity, tends to occur increasingly. Younger members of
this *kama'āina* subgroup seeking psychotherapy have been noted to
experience depression and alienation, inability to compete, and addiction to alcohol. In other words, those members of this group who
have psychiatric problems often relate these problems to the change
from a previous generation which felt a moral and intellectual superiority which was reinforced by being surrounded and outnumbered by
people of different ethnic backgrounds and which required isolation
for protection of those values. The special work ethic of the *kama-
'āina* by which self and others were judged (juxtaposed to the stereotype of the Hawaiian as interested only in food and basic pleasures)
has come home to roost with the difficulty the present generation of
kama'āina have in living up to the strict values of their parents and
grandparents.

THERAPEUTIC APPROACHES

In general, it is important in attempting to help Caucasians with
problems to keep in mind Caucasian personality traits and ideals of
self-direction, independence and achievement, the importance of
success in work and social life, and a problem-solving approach to
conflict. When Caucasians develop symptoms of emotional distress
the chances are they may seek professional help more quickly than
will members of other ethnic groups. They may appear more open
and verbal and may readily introduce such matters as sex, aggression,
divorce, and alcohol. They will more readily divulge and discuss intimate family details, both present and past, in contrast to other
groups which consider these to be privileged communication and
which take longer to confide in an outsider. Although a therapeutic
relationship and rapport are always important to develop, they may
develop more rapidly and openly with the "businesslike" Caucasian
than with a member of a group in which a subtle and prolonged peri-

od of "talking around" a topic must occur initially, like peeling an onion: layer after layer of paper-thin defenses are discarded. A specific problem-solving approach directed toward the Caucasian patient after an adequate period of history taking identifies and groups together the significant data in his life and leads to a plan for treatment. Crisp, straightforward identification of the problem—that is, 1) what is wrong, 2) how it happened or got that way, and 3) what will be done about it—is often the best approach to this kind of person. A "time limited" period of treatment, that is, a number of appointments which are preset and thus are goal-oriented, is often preferred.

Conclusion

In spite of their large number, which constitutes a certain power base and predominance in the society, the Caucasians who in-migrate to Hawaii experience the same acculturation problems faced by the many non-Caucasian groups at their initial coming to America. Increasingly, the haoles who settle in Hawaii are culturally more sophisticated and open than their predecessors of years past. They have traveled, often have visited Hawaii before settling here, and have participated in the national and worldwide trend of sensitization to pluralistic existence in a community. It is not likely that they would, or could if so determined, force cultural styles upon a society of groups rich with traditions and customs still practiced by so many of their people. The often rootless haole, through genuine attempts at interaction and social assimilation, has more than once found his place and home.

References

Arkoff, Abe; Meredith, Gerald; and Iwabara, Shinkuro. Male-dominant and equalitarian attitudes in Japanese, Japanese-American and Caucasian-American students. *Journal of Social Psychology,* 1964, 64:225–229.
Beaglehole, Ernest. *Some modern Hawaiians.* Honolulu: University of Hawaii Research Publication no. 19, 1937.
Daws, Gavan. *Shoal of time: A history of the Hawaiian Islands.* Honolulu: University Press of Hawaii, 1974.
Fuchs, Lawrence H. *Hawaii pono: A social history.* New York: Harcourt, Brace and World, 1961.
Garside, Jayne G. A cross-cultural comparison of personality. Ph.D. thesis, Brigham Young University, Laie, Hawaii, 1965.

Hormann, Bernhard L. Hawaii's mixing people. In Noel P. Gist and Anthony G. Dworking, *The blending of races*. New York: Wiley and Sons, 1972, 213–236.

Judd, Lawrence M. *Lawrence M. Judd and Hawaii: An autobiography*. Rutland, Vermont: Charles E. Tuttle, 1971.

Kaleialoha, Carol J. Adjustment in intermarriage between local part-Hawaiian men and mainland Caucasian women. M.A. thesis, University of Hawaii, 1966.

Meredith, Gerald M., and Meredith, Connie G. W. Acculturation and personality among Japanese-American college students in Hawaii. *Journal of Social Psychology*, 1966, 68:175–182.

Simpich, Fredrick. *Anatomy of Hawaii*. New York: Avon Books, 1973.

Schmitt, Robert, and Kawaguchi, Paul. *Population characteristics of Hawaii, 1976*. Hawaii Department of Health, Research and Statistics Office. Issue no. 9, October 1977.

Whittaker, Elvi W. The ideological and experiential world of the mainland expatriate in Hawaii. Ph.D. thesis, University of California, Berkeley, 1973.

Wright, George. *Hawaii Hochi*. Honolulu: May 10, 1932.

Wright, Theon. *The disenchanted isles: The story of the second revolution in Hawaii*. New York: Dial Press, 1972.

CHAPTER 4

The Chinese

Walter F. Char
Wen-Shing Tseng
Kwong-Yen Lum
Jing Hsu

Roughly 4 percent of the population, the Chinese of Hawaii are one of the smallest ethnic groups in the islands. Yet, due to certain cultural traits and fortuitous circumstances, they wield influence far out of proportion to their numbers in nearly every field of endeavor: business, education, government, law, politics, medicine, and art.

History of Chinese Immigration and Early Settlement in Hawaii

There are some recently arrived Chinese from Hong Kong and Taiwan, but the majority of Hawaii's Chinese are second, third, and fourth generation descendants of Chinese from the South China province of Kwantung who came in the late nineteenth century to work as laborers on the sugar plantations. These field hands, imported under plantation labor contracts, numbered approximately fifty thousand and arrived at various times between 1852 and 1898. Prior to the arrival in 1852 of 180 men and 20 houseboys on the *Thetis,* a few skilled Chinese workers had come as early as 1823 to help set up the sugar mills, but the influx of unskilled field labor which followed was far greater.

During their early days on the plantations most of the Chinese had little or no intention of staying in Hawaii; their plan was to return to China with their savings as soon as possible. About half (approximately twenty-five thousand) did return to China.

Long strenuous hours in the hot sun, meager pay, and frequent conflicts with non-Chinese bosses were the lot of the early immigrants. Because most of the men were bachelors, they lived in camp barracks. Few of them knew Hawaiian or English; thus they were strangers in a strange land who had little contact with the outside world. Although there were some incidents of bosses severely punishing workers for minor infractions, the Chinese received fair treatment from their plantation bosses, who needed their labor, and from the native Hawaiians, who were by nature a hospitable people.

There were very few Chinese women in Hawaii. Therefore some of the men married Hawaiian women and started families. Others sent for brides from their home villages or brought back wives from China on subsequent visits to their homeland. A great many Chinese men, however, never were able to establish families in Hawaii, an important factor in the return of so many to China and in the later establishment of a home in Hawaii for elderly Chinese men.

As their labor contracts expired, many of the Chinese left the plantations for the larger community and became involved in small retailing, in crafts such as carpentry, and in taro farming and rice planting. They also formed clan societies, established temples, cemeteries, language schools, and Chinese newspapers to retain their cultural identity. For many, Hawaii was no longer a temporary stopping place, but a permanent home. They grew from 71 Chinese among 1962 foreigners and 84,165 native Hawaiians (according to an 1851 census) to 20 percent of the population by 1893. Subsequently the importation of Chinese was abruptly stopped in 1898 to avoid the establishment of an excessively large Chinese population.

Economically and socially the Chinese moved ahead rapidly in Hawaii. Their cultural emphasis on personal industry, adaptability, education, and achievement was in large part responsible. Many second and third generation Chinese in Hawaii owe their success to the sacrifices their parents (many of whom were semi-illiterate) made to give them an education in undergraduate and graduate schools on the mainland. In two generations, from 1890, six of every ten Chinese entered the preferred occupations: professional, proprietary, clerical, or skilled (Fuchs, 1961). According to the census of 1971, 27 percent went to college and 10.4 percent to graduate schools.

Well before the start of World War II in the Pacific in 1941, many Chinese had reached middle management levels. Aided by the social and economic upheavals of the war, they became the first nonwhite ethnic group to penetrate the so-called "better" residential areas of Honolulu which hitherto had been occupied exclusively by Caucasians.

The Chinese and the Chinese Hawaiians were also successful in politics. Some adopted Hawaiian names because, being so small a part of the total population, they had to rely on support from other groups, particularly the Hawaiians, to win election. Many of the first Chinese physicians in Hawaii practiced in the lower socioeconomic neighborhoods and developed strong relationships with Hawaiians and other nonwhite patients. This was an important factor which contributed to the developing power base of the Chinese.

The 1941–1945 war in the Pacific had a major impact on Chinese culture in Hawaii, greatly accelerating the assimilation of the various ethnic groups, including the Chinese. Such concepts as "patriotism" and "Americanism" forced many common Chinese practices to the side. For example, Chinese language schools were closed during the war. Also, because the war restricted the import of Chinese foodstuffs, the local Chinese turned increasingly to a Western diet.

By moving into the vacuum created by a partial withdrawal of Caucasian interests from Hawaii during the war years, the Chinese made great upward strides for themselves into key areas of business and politics. By war's end many Chinese had risen to top management positions in established businesses or had created successful enterprises of their own. This gain was further advanced after 1945 as the domination by Caucasians of the economic, political, and social life in Hawaii was diluted by events which occurred during and after World War II.

Not long after the war, the Speaker of the Territorial House of Representatives was Hiram L. Fong. After Hawaii became a state in 1959, Fong went on to become Hawaii's senior member of the US Senate. There are, of course, many other examples of outstanding achievement by the Chinese, but Fong, as dramatically as any, personifies the rapid rise of the Chinese, in less than a century, from contract labor to positions of wealth and influence, thus making significant contributions to the professional, business, and political life of Hawaii.

The "Hakka–Punti" dichotomy is no longer a problem in Hawaii. Originally, in the southern Chinese province of Kwantung, the people made distinctions among themselves; one group was the Punti or "local" group and the other, the Hakka, was the "guest" group. The latter were descendants of a group of people who migrated from central China to Kwantung many centuries ago. Carrying their class prejudices with them from China, the Punti people used to consider themselves to be of a higher class than the Hakka people. In earlier days of Hawaii, a Punti mother would be upset if her daughter married a Hakka boy. Now the Hakka versus Punti issue is seldom even mentioned except out of curiosity or as a point of family origin, rather than as an issue of prejudice.

Many Chinese have intermarried and thus their children have more than one ethnic heritage. Many Chinese also have gone to the US mainland for an education or to work and thus have been exposed to the culture there as well. Some Chinese, particularly in the past, uncomfortable as Chinese, consciously rejected their Chinese heritage, but others clung vigorously to it. Most, however, without deliberate effort became thoroughly Americanized, yet at the same time retained, to varying degrees, elements of their culture.

Hawaii's Chinese today run the gamut from scholar to unschooled worker. With the change in the immigration law that permits more nonwhites to emigrate to the United States there has been a noticeable increase in recently arrived Chinese from Hong Kong and Taiwan, so there are now in Hawaii many Chinese whose island roots go back more than one hundred years and many who have just stepped off the plane.

Thus, within the Chinese, as within other ethnic groups, there are many differences that make cultural generalization difficult. It is important to keep in mind that each individual must be viewed as such, despite membership in a distinctive group. Even so, there are basic and strong influences from their traditional culture on all Chinese, even on those who have tried to reject their background.

Traditional Chinese Culture

To understand the culture of the contemporary Chinese in Hawaii in comparison to that of other ethnic groups, it is necessary to know something of the traditional culture of China.

One demographic fact of China is that a large proportion of the population are farmers. Agriculture tends to keep the family in rural areas and thus encourages family cohesiveness. In the China from which Hawaii's immigrants came, society was organized along family lines and embraced the extended family. Some villages were made up entirely of a single extended family and were named, for example, Wong's village or Chun's village. Though this traditional extended

family system has been weakened in today's China by moderniza-
tion, urbanization, industrialization, and communism, the tendency
to emphasize the family is still strong.

Associated with the family system is an extreme concern for interpersonal relationships, which dates back to Confucius (Tseng,
1973*a*). Terms setting out precise relationships within the family are
common in everyday speech. For example, speaking to or of an uncle, Chinese use *pak-fu* for the father's older brothers, *shu-fu* for his
younger brothers, and *kau-fu* for the brothers of the mother. In addition, each individual is designated numerically according to the rank
of his age within the generation, as in the first *pak-fu,* second *pak-fu,*
and so on. The purpose of this system is to preserve a sense of precise
order within the family, with the paternal side of the family accorded
higher rank than the maternal side. Incidentally, the Hawaiian slang
word for Chinese is *pake,* which is derived from the Chinese word
pak, ''uncle.''

This ancient system of parent-child, husband-wife, and sibling relationships, which dates from the time of Confucius and persists with
little change today, is patrilocal and patriarchal. The family is rooted
in the village of the paternal side and the paternal side rules, with the
father-son relationship as the backbone of the family system. Yet, as
frequently occurs in many cultures, the mother is usually closer to the
children and far more influential than the father in the emotional life
inside the home, while the father dominates in external affairs (Hsu
and Tseng, 1974). The mother-son relationship is a close one during
childhood and remains so into the son's adult years. The mother may
tend to overprotect her son and keep him from being involved and
learning from others, including peers, and thus, from the Western
point of view, may be inhibiting his psychosexual development.
Among most Hawaii-born Chinese, however, this continued relationship is considerably relaxed.

The life of the traditional Chinese woman deserves special attention. Although, philosophically, the relationship between man and
woman is considered a harmonious and complementary one, as represented by the Tao's symbolism of yin and yang, from a social point
of view the woman's status is always secondary to man. The life of the
Chinese woman, however, is a process; her roles may change from
lowly and underprivileged daughter to revered and honored dowager
in the course of her life.

Traditionally, the chief role of the Chinese woman was that of an obedient daughter and wife. In the past, marriages were arranged between the mother of the groom and a prospective bride's family. The choice of a good wife depended not just upon her suitability to a husband-to-be, but just as strongly upon her ability to serve, respect, and obey the whim and wish of her mother-in-law. Once a match was made, the daughter-in-law remained subservient and unimportant until she produced children. Her position was bettered considerably if she provided a boy or boys as heirs for the husband's family. As the years passed and her children, with her guidance, developed into obedient and responsive individuals, her position increased and improved. In the years of midlife and beyond, she was rewarded with the respect and maternal dominance she once gave to her mother-in-law.

As was mentioned, the traditional Chinese society is a patriarchal one in which sons are more highly valued than daughters. In practice, however, the Chinese woman often does not assume a subordinate role in the family. The Char woman in the Chinese section of James Michener's *Hawaii* was characterized as an extremely strong and able individual, and it was through her efforts that her family achieved so much. This type of woman is not uncommon in Chinese families. In Hawaii not only the Chinese sons but also the daughters have received fine educations, become successful, and are leaders in various community organizations.

Many basic aspects of traditional Chinese culture are reflected in works of fiction, in art, and in the daily living situation (Hsu, 1953). In the Chinese novel emphasis is placed on what the characters do rather than on what they think and feel. In art the important thing is the individual's place in nature. In daily life the emphasis is on one's appropriate place and behavior among one's fellows. Perhaps to a greater extent than in other cultures Chinese society is governed by formal rules; the Chinese tend to make their thoughts and actions conform to social reality rather than attempting to force reality to conform to their wishes. Chinese society, in other words, does not encourage strong individualism; it is situation-centered rather than individual-centered. This does not mean, however, that the Chinese are blind conformists. Being adaptable and practical by nature, the Chinese, within the context of reality, can do much to change things to fit their needs and goals.

Chinese philosophy emphasizes harmony. It holds that the yin and yang principle, which dictates perfect harmony between yin (the female element) and yang (the male element), is essential for health and that disharmony causes illness. Early Chinese medicine perceived that the life function is based on the cooperative action of the visceral organs—heart, lungs, kidney, liver, and spleen—and that illness results from disharmony among these organs. Certain foods thought to have this yin or yang quality are used to correct bodily disharmony (Tseng, 1973*b*).

Although the influence of emotions on physical illness was recognized by Chinese medicine in ancient times, nevertheless, the treatment of emotional problems was through the use of herbs—the core of Chinese medicine. The Chinese people, however, also have depended for psychological treatment on folk therapy such as shamanism, fortune-telling, physiognomy, and divination in the temple (Hsu, 1976). Few among Hawaii-born Chinese really believe in the traditional Chinese medicine; in fact, it is noteworthy that a large percentage of the modern, scientifically trained physicians of Hawaii are of Chinese descent. Even so, in times of crisis when patients do not seem to respond to Western medicine, they may be induced by an older member of the family to resort to ancient Chinese medicine. It is perhaps a reflection of Chinese practicality that a Chinese of Hawaii—not missing any bets—may try both Western medicine and the ancient Chinese approach simultaneously.

Stereotypes of the Chinese

As with almost any ethnic group, there is no lack of stereotypic myths about the Chinese. There are those who consider the Chinese a mysterious and inscrutable people who do things backwards. This misunderstanding is the result of faulty communication and a common psychological need to describe another race as mysterious. Such negative thinking is encouraged by the sterotyped portrayal of Chinese characters in movies and on television. Some may believe the Chinese think in reverse because they write from right to left instead of from left to right. The Chinese method of writing is simply a matter of custom and does not mirror a reverse linear approach to thought and reasoning. This matter of things being reversed in Chinese is also interestingly reflected in crude sexual jokes about the Chinese female genitalia being reversed.

Another common stereotype is that of the Chinese as a nation of launderers and restaurant operators, one which stems from the fact that the early Chinese immigrants to the United States were from the uneducated peasant class, who did in fact open laundries and restaurants. These occupations were often the only pursuits, other than common labor, for which many of the immigrants were qualified. Also, in some instances, these new arrivals were stopped by racist barriers from engaging in other vocations. The descendants of these Chinese immigrants now rarely become launderers; instead they capitalize on the universal popularity of Chinese food and open larger and more successful restaurants, often with the manpower and financial support of Taiwan and Hong Kong interests. Many of the smaller Chinese restaurants and retail shops in Hawaii now are being formed or taken over by recent Chinese immigrants who work long hours on marginal capital to try to make a success in their new home, thus repeating experiences of the earlier immigrants.

The Chinese are sometimes viewed negatively by others as being shrewd, and too frugal and hardworking. This stereotypic prejudice is similar to that which some may have of the Jews. In fact, the Chinese have sometimes been called the "Jews of the Orient."

The reputed Chinese tendency to be frugal is not totally valid since the Chinese do not hesitate to spend money on what they consider to be important. They spend money on the education of their children, the support of the aged, the purchase of property, and the support of a family or clan cause. As noted, the older Chinese tend to identify with family far more than with the larger community, which inclines them to channel their money into family causes rather than into public charities. Yet, with younger generations of Chinese in Hawaii, many of them not only contribute generously to public charities but also have become leaders of fund drives for such charities.

From a sociohistorical point of view, the Chinese, originally predominantly farmers, placed a high premium on land ownership. An important goal was to acquire land through hard work and thrift, land on which to live and work which could be passed on to descendants. Probably, it is this goal that has led to a greater percentage of Chinese owning their own homes than is true of almost any other ethnic group in Hawaii. In addition, much of the Chinese fortune in Hawaii has been gained from parlaying wise real estate investment into more and more real estate or other types of business investments.

A frequent misconception about the traditional Chinese is that they say "yes" when they mean "no" and vice versa. The Chinese consider it impolite to deny or refuse a request directly, and, if it is necessary to say "no," they seek to convey the message subtly and indirectly. For anyone versed in Chinese culture there is no problem understanding the message, but for those who are unfamiliar with the culture the result is often distortion and misunderstanding. With westernization, however, many young Chinese have become as vocal and outspoken as their Caucasian counterparts.

There also exists the misconception of the Chinese as cold, stoic, and unemotional. They may avoid freely expressing their inner feelings, thoughts, and problems, especially to strangers, and particularly if the feelings are negative. Like all others, they do have deep thoughts, feelings, and personal problems, but they prefer to explore such matters privately. This tendency is present even in many Hawaii-born Chinese, who may be almost completely westernized. Yet, here again, many of the younger Chinese can be open and free with their thoughts and feelings.

Contemporary Situation

Having sketched the salient aspects of the traditional culture of China, we will now sharpen the focus upon the contemporary Chinese of Hawaii. The extended family system of the older local Chinese has been replaced by the inclination of the younger generation toward the nuclear and stem family. The emphasis on family is not as strong as formerly, but it is still greater than among Westerners.

Another break from former patterns is an increasing incidence of marriage outside the ethnic group. In 1977, combined data for Chinese men and women showed that 64.7 percent of marriages were to non-Chinese; 26.1 percent of these outmarriages involved Japanese, 20.7 percent Caucasian, and 9.8 percent part-Hawaiian (Hawaii Department of Health, 1977).

The continually decreasing emphasis on family is reflected in the increasing rate of divorce, although the divorce rate for the Chinese is still lower than that of other ethnic groups. Statistics for 1950 show that the divorce rate for Chinese families was 12.6 percent (far lower than the 25.1 percent for Hawaiians and 26 percent for Caucasians in the same year); however, for 1956–1960 the divorce rate for Chinese increased to 19 percent (still lower than the 29 percent for Caucasians during the same period). In 1970, 3.27 percent of individuals of all ethnic groups age seventeen or older listed themselves in the divorced status while 2.17 percent of all Chinese were in this status.

A 1968–1969 sociological interview study (Young, 1972*a*) revealed that the Chinese of Hawaii saw their primary concern in life as obtaining good jobs and providing a comfortable standard of living for their families. The interviews cited little emphasis on attaining group recognition, on contributing to the larger society, or on having many friends. The traditional Chinese values of education, hard work, financial security, and family responsibility apparently still maintained a strong hold on even the third and fourth generation Chinese in Hawaii. Here again exceptions can be noted, however. For example, some of the leaders of the Third World movement (Asian activist movement) here and in the mainland United States are Hawaii-born Chinese youths.

The traditional culture also remains strong in the area of child rearing. Most Chinese parents in Hawaii still are concerned that their children perform well in school and become thoughtful, considerate, responsible, and obedient children; however, especially among the younger parents, they also are greatly influenced by current Western concepts on child rearing, which emphasize respect for the individuality of the child. Therefore, in practice, there is a blending in different degrees of Chinese and Western child-rearing concepts.

As with the other ethnic groups, the Chinese usually tend to associate with their own kind in intimate social activities (Young, 1972*b*). In business and professional activities, however, they mix well with other racial groups.

A notable cultural difference between the Chinese of Hawaii and those of China (or even those Chinese residing elsewhere in the world, including San Francisco) is that few Hawaii Chinese are able to read and write Chinese. If they can speak the language at all, they do so poorly. This lack of linguistic ability is especially true of the younger generations. There are still several small Chinese language schools operating in Honolulu, however, which attempt to teach Chinese to the children who come to them in classes offered on Saturdays or on weekdays after regular school hours. Probably because of the time problem, the enrollment in these classes is small and the only children who attend are those whose parents place a high priority on learning Chinese. Classes in Mandarin are offered as a foreign language elective in colleges and in some intermediate and high schools.

An unusual, and perhaps distinctive, feature of the Hawaii Chinese is that it is not uncommon for different members of the same family to be affiliated with different religions (Hsu, 1951). Many Hawaii Chinese are Christian; and in the same family, for example, the daughter may be Roman Catholic, the son a Methodist, while the mother retains the custom of worshipping at the Chinese temple. This scattering of religious affiliations is compatible with the pragmatic nature of Chinese culture. It is a common and acceptable practice in Hawaii to see Chinese Christian children, without conflict, assist their Buddhist parents in carrying out their religious rituals, such as participating in ancestor worship on Chinese memorial day.

Again, it must be emphasized that the foregoing description of Hawaii's modern Chinese is based on broad generalization. As is noted frequently throughout this volume with respect to various ethnic groups, there are many varieties of Chinese and each must be approached as an individual with the understanding that a common cultural background does not necessarily predicate common characteristics. It can be said, however, that the more recently a Chinese has arrived in Hawaii, the more strongly he is likely to be influenced by the traditional Chinese culture.

With less stringent immigration laws for Orientals, there has been a recent influx of a number of Chinese to Honolulu. Figures from the Immigrant Service Division show that, between 1970 and 1976, 3156 immigrants from China and Taiwan entered the United States and reported Hawaii as their state of intended residence. Although the numbers fluctuated in that seven-year period, from 423 in 1970 to 631 at the latest reporting in 1976, the trend is toward a continual rise of newcomers. This has made a noticeable impact in the community. There are now three movie theaters in Honolulu that show Chinese films exclusively. The majority of the Chinese food stores in Chinatown and most of the Chinese restaurants are now run by these new arrivals, who provide a continuous pool of skilled cooks, waitresses, and kitchen help. The Cantonese language is spoken much more freely in Hawaii these days, because most of these immigrants are Cantonese from Hong Kong. Their presence has imparted a more pronounced Chinese atmosphere in Honolulu, especially in Chinatown. They, like the forebears of the *kama'āina* Chinese, face the adjustment and language difficulties of assimilation into Western society.

A point which warrants mention is that Chinese in Hawaii have developed a unique subculture of their own, so that although still distinctly Chinese in many ways, at least to the professional observer, Hawaii's Chinese are markedly different from more newly arrived immigrants from Hong Kong or Taiwan, or even Chinese Americans from the mainland United States. In some ways the Hawaii Chinese have been softened in a positive way by the unique blending of cultures in Hawaii. They are more comfortable and less defensive about being Chinese and much less wary about other races, including Caucasians, than their counterparts from either the East or West. The insecurities and fears noted in *The Woman Warrior,* written by a second generation Chinese of her life in Stockton, California (Kingston, 1976), would be found to a far lesser degree in a Chinese growing up in Hawaii.

Comments and Suggestions Concerning Mental Health

In psychiatry, studies have shown that the percentage of Chinese seeking psychiatric treatment is relatively low compared with that of other ethnic groups in the islands. A 1967 study of admission rates to the Hawaii State Hospital revealed that Chinese accounted for 3 percent of all admissions (Gudeman, 1967), although at that time the Chinese represented 6 percent of the population. According to the Hawaii Department of Health (1972), the figures remain substantially the same for Chinese patients under care in state-operated outpatient mental health facilities in 1970–1971, representing only 3.1 percent of the total patient load.

Explosive uncontrolled behavior that accompanies mental disturbance in other cultures is not common among the Chinese. The Chinese tend to somatize their emotional difficulties. This tendency to present somatic complaints is more prevalent among Chinese of lower socioeconomic groups, as it is in most ethnic groups.

Sexual conflicts may be manifested in a fear of impotency rather than in sexual activities such as homosexuality, rape, and sexual promiscuity. Problems of aggression tend to show up in antisocial behavior, such as gambling, rather than in more overtly aggressive acts, such as homicide, assault, and armed robbery. Mental problems of the traditional Chinese typically reveal themselves more as signs of inhibitions than as acts of aggression (Muensterberger, 1951). This probably still holds true even among the modern Chinese in Hawaii.

According to police and court records from 1925 to 1940, the number of Chinese charged and convicted of sex crimes and manslaughter was disproportionately smaller than those of other races (Hsu, 1951). The general impression is that as a group the Chinese are still a law-abiding people and commit proportionately fewer crimes, especially violent crimes, than do others in Hawaii.

Homosexuality, a topic which is being evaluated anew in many mental health circles, is an area in which careful evaluation is required in reference to the Chinese. In their traditional society, intimate, prolonged relationships between members of the same sex are permissible during childhood, adolescence, and even beyond. The role of gender is clearly defined by Chinese society so that the problem of gender role confusion seldom occurs. Although many young Chinese may maintain close relationships with members of the same sex, and delay heterosexual relationships, the practice is normal socioculturally. Therefore, it is wise not to suspect the presence of homosexual difficulties in the Chinese in the absence of more definite clinical evidence.

The traditional Chinese man may not experience guilt feelings about sex, but he nevertheless may suffer from sexual disorders. Sexual intercourse is seen not only as a means of achieving conception but also as strengthening the man's vitality by allowing him to absorb the woman's essence. The woman is seen as deriving physical benefit by the stirring of her latent feminine nature. A neurotic Chinese man thus may view the woman as a threat to his energy, able to induce weakness or illness by absorbing his sperm and energy (castration anxiety) and causing him to have neurasthenic symptoms (Rin, 1965). Interestingly, in psychotherapy it is often found that Chinese women can talk more freely about their problems, including sexual ones, than can Chinese men.

Traditional Chinese culture tends to foster repression and suppression of unacceptable thoughts and feelings. Forms of mental disturbance that result from this include such disorders as morbid anxiety about health (hypochondria), nervous prostration (neurasthenia), and psychosomatic disorders.

Alcoholism, a prevalent problem in some ethnic and cultural groups, seems to be rare among the Chinese (Lin, 1953; Wang, 1968). The typical traditional Chinese drinks alcohol only with meals, usually on ceremonial occasions; and drinking is confined largely to the men. The purpose of the drinking is to promote socialization and is used as a symbol of masculinity. In such a social setting men sometimes are encouraged in a competitive fashion to overindulge to the point of acute intoxication. As a general rule, however, drunkenness is strongly condemned. There is little solitary drinking among Chinese. Aside from the use of alcohol on social occasions, drinking is considered to be a sign of weakness and deterioration. Recent studies (Wolff, 1972) show that the Chinese react to alcoholic intake with more uncomfortable vasomotor reactions, such as flushing or nausea, than do other racial groups. This tendency toward considerable physical discomfort partially explains why Chinese generally do not acquire a taste or interest in liquor and it may also contribute to the low alcoholism rate for their group.

In contrast to the available figures on mental health treatment in public facilities, there is no systematic way to establish the extent to which Chinese are under private treatment for mental problems. The general impression of private practitioners is that the Chinese, as compared to Caucasian patients, still tend to avoid consulting psychiatrists unless their problems are severe. This may also be changing, however; a private practitioner of Chinese descent estimates that 15 to 20 percent of his patients are Chinese, and that they come to him for types of problems comparable to those of his Caucasian patients. Some of the problems he treats are intergenerational ones, those between more traditional second generation Chinese parents and their third generation offspring who are much more westernized.

The Chinese traditionally are taught to respect authority (elders, parents) and to be obedient and compliant, and authority takes it for granted that respect, obedience, and compliance will be shown them by their subordinates (children) (Tseng and Hsu, 1972). Under such a system youth may suffer. For example, a young man may wish to marry someone of whom his parents disapprove. The therapy indicated may be the encouragement of the youth to make the decision according to his own wishes. But such advice should not be given in a manner that will cause the youth to feel guilty about rebelling against authority. At the same time, this action should be done in such a way so as to avert or minimize hurt and humiliation to the parents and to avoid a collapse in family relationships.

Among Chinese, mutual dependence is encouraged; social independence is not emphasized and is seldom achieved until adulthood and marriage. Consequently, by Western standards, a Chinese patient may be considered as being too dependent and immature. Yet, within the culture, this state is normal and a therapist must take this into consideration while treating and evaluating the patient.

The emphasis on the family rather than on the individual in the Chinese culture may indeed be a potential source of conflict and problems among the Chinese in Hawaii, particularly for the younger Hawaii-born Chinese who have been exposed to a greater extent to the cultures of other groups which value independence, individuality, personal privacy, and self-expression. How this problem is handled by the individual, however, is influenced greatly by personality and family relationships.

The rearing of children in the traditional Chinese culture is characterized by an almost overgratification of the child's needs and wants, and this probably helps to explain why somatization of psychological problems is so prevalent among the Chinese. Were an adult neurotic to complain of feeling depressed or anxious, he most likely would not receive the desired concern and care from others because the culture considers depression and anxiety a part of daily life. But the patient who complains of physical illness usually receives the immediate gratification he wants; attention, care, and the concern of others.

Therefore, in dealing with a "Chinese" patient, one who identifies with the more traditional culture, the physician must evaluate the somatic complaint to determine whether it is merely an overture for an emotional complaint, a culturally determined method of seeking attention through somatization, an emotional problem expressed by means of organ-oriented language, a primary psychophysiological disorder, or a symptom of an organic disorder (Tseng, 1975). In the "westernized" Chinese, the evaluation of a somatic complaint is perhaps similar to that of a Westerner since he might express his emotional difficulties in ways other than somatization.

The traditional Chinese cultural ban against open and direct expression of aggressive and negative feelings was mentioned earlier. This cultural disapproval is emphasized in child rearing to varying degrees, even among the Chinese born in Hawaii. In the event of a fight between two brothers, for example, the elder is blamed for not giving in to the younger and the younger is scolded for failure to respect the elder. No matter what the cause of the fight, both brothers are likely to be punished for aggressive behavior.

Therefore, it may be a mistake for a psychotherapist to initially encourage his traditional Chinese patients to express aggressive negative feelings openly and directly, although this may be an eventual goal. A premature effort disregards the fact that they are culturally trained to handle negative feelings subtly and delicately, and such a problem must be dealt with slowly and sensitively.

Although the traditional Chinese look upon sex as natural and without sinful connotation, they nevertheless feel it shameful to display sexual desires openly. Parents do not exhibit their sexual feelings in front of their children, and a sexually neutral atmosphere is maintained within a crowded Chinese family home. Thus, because the traditional Chinese are not accustomed to discussing or expressing sexual desires or fantasies freely in public, it may be a mistake for the therapist to encourage these patients to do so prematurely. Any judgments of masculinity, femininity, and sexuality should be made with the cultural context in mind. The extent to which a Chinese husband and wife are openly affectionate with each other should be evaluated on a relative basis and not on Western standards.

Patterns of depression and suicide among traditional Chinese are culturally distinctive. Because of the strong family system and the emphasis on gratification during childhood, together with delayed independence and separation from family, Chinese in general may suffer less from problems of isolation and loneliness. Depression as a reaction to loss is present, but because of their strong support system the Chinese are less prone to it.

The situation is quite different, however, for certain groups of Chinese in Hawaii. For those newly arrived, as for any immigrant in an unfamiliar place, the loss of original family social ties and the absence of or reluctance to utilize a new support system makes them vulnerable to depressive situations. This is particularly true for women born in the home country who intermarry with Americans, and who have very little knowledge of the lifestyle and customs of the new land to which they have come. Another vulnerable group is the students who come to this country and face the challenge of being excellent in an unfamiliar academic setting, as well as all the other problems of acculturation—language difficulty, social orientation, loneliness—faced by any newcomer (Bourne, 1975).

A third group especially prone to depression is the middle-aged women who are accustomed to the traditional lifestyle of their culture which promised them a seat of reverence in their later years.

Many of the women who have suffered and tolerated their existences as obedient wives, dutiful daughters-in-law, and doting mothers now find themselves robbed of their awaited maternal reverence because of the change in culture.

Today, marriages are not as strictly arranged by the families; children often move away from the area in which their families or mothers live; and consequently, daughters-in-law, if so inclined, are not close enough to serve or respect their mothers-in-law. In the case of a difficult and unhappy marriage with little or no opportunity for divorce, this loss of a birthright or right to devotion in one's later life is especially acute and creates virtually a lost generation of Chinese women.

Although the divorce rate is increasing, divorce is still theoretically regarded as a disgrace and hence an almost unthinkable method for solving marital discord among the traditional Chinese. They usually will try to keep a marriage intact, regardless of marital difficulties, because the family is far more important than the individual. Therefore, a clinician should be cautious and not advise too quickly a divorce as a solution to a marital problem when working with a traditional Chinese couple.

Although it is usually no problem to get a traditional Chinese family to assemble, this does not mean that it is easy to conduct family therapy with them. The parents usually feel uncomfortable discussing private feelings in front of their children, and the children are unaccustomed to expressing their feelings toward parental authority —particularly if those feelings are negative. Therefore, it may take longer for a Chinese family to feel sufficiently comfortable to discuss problems openly in a family therapy session. Even then, the wise therapist will be well advised to keep in mind the difficulty that members of a Chinese family may have in being frank with one another. The therapist should realize that premature suggestions for a family session may be antitherapeutic.

Particular mention should be made here of the increasing numbers of Chinese newcomers from Hong Kong (Cantonese-speaking) and Taiwan (Mandarin/Fukenese-speaking) who culturally are prone to the same emotional and psychological vulnerabilities, but who for various reasons fail to receive the assistance and care they require. The absence of Cantonese-speaking specialists, and the minimal number who speak Mandarin and are available to aid this group, point to the need for a more specialized mental health system which can easily adapt itself to the cultural and situational factors present in a constantly evolving ethnic community.

Taiwanese immigrants are generally more financially prosperous on their arrival in Hawaii than are those from Hong Kong, and may be able to utilize private services where some language resources are available through which to communicate their needs. Those from Hong Kong are much more dependent on the public mental health services where Cantonese language specialization is not yet available.

Both groups, however, share as immigrants the same problem of the negative stigma attached to mental illness in their traditional culture. There is an additional problem: immigrants are asked whether they ever have been hospitalized as mental patients. Thus, utilizing any mental health services may be seen by them as possibly jeopardizing their immigrant status. The reluctance to talk about a personal mental problem, or one in the family, is probably heightened in this group.

With westernization, the Hawaii-born Chinese attitude and behavior regarding sex and aggression, the kind of emotional problems they have, and the behavioral and clinical manifestations of them are becoming more like those of Westerners. This is especially true of the third and fourth generation; thus, the management and treatment of their difficulties may not require methods or approaches any different than those used for other groups of people. Nevertheless, the Chinese culture is strong and in varying degrees it still exerts an influence on all the Chinese in Hawaii.

It is significant to note that recently there has been a heightened interest in the Chinese culture in Hawaii. A Hawaiian Chinese Historical Society has been formed to encourage and support historical research on the Chinese in Hawaii and to preserve the Chinese heritage for future generations. Through a personal communication with Irma Tam Soong of the Center, we learned that at present in Honolulu there are more than seventy Chinese organizations listed as active by the United Chinese Society of Hawaii.

Like other groups, the Chinese of Hawaii are seeking their roots. With the recent opening up of China to visitors, those able to are making trips back to their homeland to become more familiar with their beginnings. Instead of being ashamed of being Chinese and wanting to become completely Americanized, as was the trend in the past, most Chinese of Hawaii are now proud of their Chinese heritage and of its presence in Hawaii. This phenomenon has been aided by the increased worldwide interest in, and value placed on, China and things Chinese since the lifting of the Bamboo Curtain.

References

Anonymous. A Chinese family in Hawaii. *Social Process in Hawaii,* 1937, 3:50–55.

Bourne, Peter G. The Chinese student—Acculturation and mental illness. *Psychiatry,* 1975, 38:269–277.

Char, Tin Yuke. *The sandalwood mountains: Readings and stories of the early Chinese in Hawaii.* Honolulu: University Press of Hawaii, 1975.

_____. *The bamboo path: Life and writings of a Chinese in Hawaii.* Honolulu: Hawaii Chinese History Center, 1977.

Chow, Richard. The Chinese-Hawaiian mixture. *Social Process in Hawaii,* 1935, 1:11–13.

Fuchs, Lawrence H. Success, Pake style. In *Hawaii pono: A social history.* New York: Harcourt, Brace and World, 1961.

Glick, Clarence E. Residential dispersion of urban Chinese. *Social Process in Hawaii,* 1936, 2:28–34.

_____. Changing ideas of success and of roads to success as seen by immigrant and local Chinese and Japanese businessmen in Honolulu. *Social Process in Hawaii,* 1951, 15:56–70.

Gudeman, Howard E. First admissions to the Hawaii State Hospital: A cohort analysis. *Hawaii Medical Journal,* 1967, 27(1):37–45.

Hawaii Department of Health, Mental Health Register, Research and Records Division. *Psychiatric outpatients program, state of Hawaii fiscal year 1970–71.* October, 1972.

Hawaii Department of Health. Statistical Report. 1977.

Hsu, Francis L. K. The Chinese of Hawaii: Their role in American culture. *The New York Academy of Sciences, Transactions,* 1951, 13:243–250.

_____. *Americans and Chinese: Two ways of life.* New York: Henry Schuman, 1953.

Hsu, Jing. Counseling in the Chinese temple: A psychological study of divination by *Chien* drawing. In William Lebra (ed.), *Culture-bound syndromes, ethnopsychiatry, and alternate therapies.* Honolulu: University Press of Hawaii, 1976.

Hsu, Jing, and Tseng, Wen-Shing. Family relations in classic Chinese opera. *International Journal of Social Psychiatry,* 1974, 20:159–172.

Kingston, Maxine H. *The woman warrior: Memories of a girlhood among ghosts.* New York: Alfred A. Knopf, 1976.

Koran, Lorrin M. Psychiatry in mainland China: History and recent status. *American Journal of Psychiatry,* 1972, 128:970–978.

Li, Min Hin. *The relation of Chinese shrine worship in Hawaii to modern medicine.* Honolulu: Territorial Hawaiian Medical Association, Transaction of Annual Meeting, 1926, 42–46.

Lin, Tsung-Yi. A study of the incidence of mental disorders in Chinese and other cultures. *Psychiatry,* 1953, 16:313–336.

Michener, James. *Hawaii.* New York: Random House, 1959.

Muensterberger, Warner. Orality and dependence: Characteristics of Southern Chinese. In Geza Roheim, *Psychoanalysis and the social sciences,* 1951, 3:37–39.

Rin, Hsien. A study of the etiology of Koro in respect to the Chinese concept of illness. *International Journal of Social Psychiatry,* 1965, 11:7–13.

Singer, Karam. Drinking patterns and alcoholism in the Chinese. *British Journal of Addiction,* 1972, 67:3–14.

Sue, Stanley, and Sue, Derald W. Chinese-American personality and mental health. *Amerasia Journal,* 1971, 1:36–49.

Tom, Winifred. The impact of war on Chinese culture. *Social Process in Hawaii,* 1943, 8:45–48.

Tseng, Wen-Shing. The concept of personality in Confucian thought. *Psychiatry,* 1973*a*, 36:191–202.

———. The development of psychiatric concepts in traditional Chinese medicine. *Archives of General Psychiatry,* 1973*b*, 29:569–575.

———. The nature of somatic complaints among psychiatric patients: The Chinese case. *Comprehensive Psychiatry,* 1975, 16:237–245.

Tseng, Wen-Shing, and Hsu, Jing. The Chinese attitude toward parental authority as expressed in Chinese children's stories. *Archives of General Psychiatry,* 1972, 26:28–34.

Wang, Richard P. A study of alcoholism in Chinatown. *International Journal of Social Psychiatry,* 1968, 14:260–267.

Wolff, P. H. Ethnic differences in alcohol sensitivity. *Science,* 1972, 175:449–450.

Yap, Pow Meng. Hypereridism and attempted suicide in Chinese. *Journal of Mental Science,* 1958, 104:34–41.

Young, Nancy F. Changes in values and strategies among Chinese in Hawaii. *Sociology and Social Research,* 1972*a*, 56:228–241.

———. Socialization patterns among the Chinese in Hawaii. *Amerasia Journal,* 1972*b*, 1:31–51.

CHAPTER 5

The Japanese

Terence Rogers
Satoru Izutsu

As with all immigrant groups, the degrees of separateness and assimilation of Hawaii's Japanese can be traced to such factors as their original culture, the impact of their new environment, their resilience and adaptability to the new environment, and the concurrent changes in that environment itself. In this chapter, we will review the history of the Japanese in Hawaii, describe the factors impinging on their assimilation, and discuss those factors which are relevant by virtue of the Japanese cultural heritage.

Historical Summary

In the early nineteenth century the sugarcane industry had a relentless demand for manpower and, with the suppression of the slave trade, the planters sought other forms of cheap labor. In many parts of the world, this led to the importation of contract workers from China or India under conditions comparable to the horrific prototype of kidnapped Africans. In Hawaii the declining native population displayed disinterest in life as plantation workers, which led to the importation of Chinese laborers between 1823 and 1898. The Chinese were the first to leave the plantations to set up their own enterprises in Hawaii, or to return to China.

In 1868 the first 148 Japanese immigrants arrived in Hawaii, followed by the recruitment of the next large cadre of workers in 1885 (Schmitt, 1977). There were three major waves up to 1924; the last group included many women and children. The recruitment negotiations were carried out with the seeming concern of the government of Japan, which insisted on humanitarian safeguards about the treatment and rights of the contract workers. Yet the actual conditions of plantation life came as a shock to workers, most of whom were poor farmers from the southern prefectures of Japan—Hiroshima, Kumamoto, Fukuoka, and Okinawa—who were not by any means expecting the proverbial roads paved with gold.

One can speculate about the reasons for the brutal conditions. Undoubtedly, there was a cultural carry-over from the management of slaves in the literal sense, and an ever-present fear of a violent revolt of the workers. The irony is that the early Japanese immigrants were already inured to hard work, plain food, and simple dwellings. The provision of some respect for their humanity and an opportunity to organize their own supervisory hierarchy would have eliminated many humiliations and resentments, of which some embers still smolder today in those who remember plantation existence, or whose parents and elders relayed stories of misery during those early years in Hawaii.

The hardships on the plantations could be lessened by family life. Many men sent for their wives and single men negotiated for brides from Japan whom they had never seen except in photographs. There are women living in Hawaii today who recall leaving their village homes as adolescent "picture brides" for a new life in a strange land with an unknown partner.

Although conditions improved, the overwhelming trend was for the Japanese workers to leave the plantations at the earliest opportunity. Upon arrival in Hawaii, there were two common plans: one was to return, rich and triumphant, to the home village in Japan, and the other was to make a home in the new land and to achieve comfort and security. Of the approximately 180 thousand immigrants, about 40 thousand returned to Japan and a similar number moved on to California and other parts of the US mainland. Some remained on the plantations and achieved security in that hierarchy.

Clearly, not all of the forty thousand who returned to Japan did so rich and triumphant. Similarly, it is difficult to determine the levels of choice among those who stayed in Hawaii. Some could have returned to Japan, but preferred to stay; others may have been inhibited about returning less than rich, and others must have been trapped in Hawaii by their poverty. One can only speculate about the mental health impact of such "failure" upon the latter and their children.

The majority who remained in Hawaii settled in Japanese villages called "camps" in which were found all of the small businesses, Japanese schools, temples, and other familiar cultural forms. Most of these camps have been abandoned or have disappeared into urban sprawl, but a stranger may still be given directions based on the location of "the old Japanese camp."

Prosperity came slowly to Japanese families in the 1920s and 1930s. The Japanese tradition of hard work, thrift, and the value set upon education is virtually indistinguishable from what is known as the "Protestant work ethic." The Japanese forged ahead as meticulous and reliable artisans, owners of small businesses, and in the helping professions as school teachers, nurses, social workers, and, to a lesser extent, doctors and lawyers. Perhaps because of Buddhist principles, the traditional Japanese could derive great fulfillment from a service occupation without the Western concern that it may be servile. Or it could have been that the helping profession was educationally affordable, a step into the American middle class, nonthreatening to the Caucasian minority, and the simple result of an absence of role models other than their uneducated parents. Any cut above eighth grade became an accomplishment in the late '20s and '30s. Nonetheless, the distinction between work and leisure was not clear, and long hours in the family business are recalled today as family time rather than drudgery.

Families made great sacrifices in educating their children, especially the boys and younger siblings who displayed intellectual talents. There were families where the eldest son or daughter contributed their wages to the family income so that educational expenses could be met. In many instances, older brothers and sisters dropped out from school and delayed marriage so that one child in the family could attend college. Today, it is an unwritten understanding that the successful lawyer, doctor, or teacher who was helped by older siblings will in turn help their children pursue educational goals.

During this period the *tanomoshi* was a popular method of mutual assistance in financing tuition, transportation, books, and other expenses which required lump sum payments. A group of ten to twelve persons would begin by agreeing on the amount to be contributed monthly by each member. The life of the group usually depended on the number of members; that is, ten months for ten members. At the monthly meeting members offered a sum of money (bid) for the month's total amount. The highest bidder would take home the lump sum and the bid was divided as interest among the remaining members. In a variation of this system the group agreed on a set amount of the monthly bid. Then, each month, the members would pick lots. The "lucky" person for the month was compelled to take the "pot." In all *tanomoshi* groups each member could bid once during the life of the group. Therefore, the last person to bid collected the most interest.

A requirement for belonging to a *tanomoshi* group was that one needed a "second" who would pay the monthly amount should the member not have the required money. Many long-term friendships were destroyed because at a crucial moment, the endorser or the primary member reneged and, therefore, could not come up with the monthly payment, or the second could not be found in time of need.

In the context of education, a custom prevalent especially during the '20s which produced the unusual *kibei* ("return to America") group should be cited here. A husband and wife would often be too busy working on the plantation or elsewhere to care properly for their children. The children were sent to Japan to be raised by their grandparents in the home villages, and to return to America as thoroughly Japanese adolescents. Other children were sent or taken when they were older, with the principal motive of securing for them a proper Japanese education which was honestly believed to be superior to that available in the West. Many recall the terror of their abandonment to strange relatives in Japan, their homesickness for the blue skies and tradewinds of their real homes in Hawaii, and their lack of language facility. Some were stranded in Japan by World War II and returned later as young adults: American citizens with poor English and forgotten roots in Hawaii. From the mental health standpoint, there was the critical event of parental rejection. These *kibei* persons, now in their middle age, have especially ambivalent feelings about the support of aging parents—a matter ordinarily beyond discussion in a Japanese family.

It is interesting to note that most Japanese families in Hawaii have no role model in the care of the aged since parents were not seen relating to grandparents. The *nisei* (second generation in Hawaii) has no precedent other than to establish patterns which may be followed by *sansei* (third generation) and *yonsei* (fourth generation). Family obligations related to the care of the aged seem to be causing strain due to crowded living conditions, need for a livable income by having both the son and daughter-in-law employed, and the gradual disintegration of family cohesiveness.

World War II had the most profound effect on the Japanese of Hawaii. Their pride in things Japanese, an ethnic exclusiveness, and a personal reserve had left them open to criticism from other groups in Hawaii. This flared into open hostility and suspicion after the Pearl Harbor attack. Nevertheless, cool heads on both sides prevailed with work by committees from the Japanese community which interfaced with the military government (Hawaii was under martial law until the end of World War II). The consequence was that Hawaii's Japanese did not suffer the disruption of the "relocation" camps experienced by Japanese of the west coast of the US mainland. (The exceptions were an estimated one thousand men, women, and children who were sent from Hawaii to the mainland for internment.) In addition to common sense and humanity, there was also the realistic consideration that the Japanese in Hawaii comprised 30 percent of the population, and the economy and war effort would have ground to a halt without them.

Soon after Pearl Harbor the organization of the 100th Battalion and the 442nd Regimental Combat Team brought a huge volunteer response from young Japanese. The bravery and tenacity of these units are legendary, and they laid to rest questions about the loyalty of Americans of Japanese Ancestry (AJAs). In addition to the intrinsic qualities of these young soldiers, the whole Japanese sentiment of serving one's country above all, with reckless bravery and loyalty unto death, was *completely* transposable to the adopted country—both by the soldiers and their proud parents. At the beginning, there was probably also an ironic element of being closely observed by the rest of the army and the country. For these and other reasons, these units had the highest number of decorations (and casualties) in the entire army.

The overwhelming authority of martial law had already eroded the authority of the elders *(issei)* when the returning soldiers (who were *nisei)* arrived with their heads and hearts set upon a new order in Hawaii.

A still permeating difference between Hawaii AJAs and those of the US mainland is the World War II experience. Virtually all of the West Coast *nisei* were sent to camps with their parents under the most humiliating circumstances, which have left great bitterness. Ironically, the young *nisei* left the camps only as they reached draft age and entered the military. In the broadest sense, World War II was a time of acceptance for Hawaii AJAs rather than of rejection.

Although the majority of Hawaii's Japanese were spared internment, the Martial Law Administration of the territory ordered the closing of Japanese language schools and the dismantling of most of the Japanese cultural network that bound the people to their homeland. There was an overall "de-Japanizing" thrust, with corresponding slogans on "Americanization" and "Speak American" with the sincere cooperation of the Japanese themselves, to the extent that there was a complete blackout of the Japanese language and cultural activities during World War II. In an effort to be American, children and young adults, during these years, adopted Christian names given to them by teachers, ministers, friends, and siblings, and they often selected their own. To this day, these names are not legally registered. Some of the common names were: Betty, Thelma, Jane, Grace, Dorothy, Winifred, Beatrice, Harriet, Judy, Nancy, Edith, Alan, David, Robert, Richard, Ronald, and Ted. A small but highly illustrative example is that Japanese children born after that time nearly always have an official Western first name with a traditional Japanese name relegated to second place. Some were even named after American war heroes.

The egalitarian ideas of the returning AJA soldiers affected the Japanese family's hierarchial structure as much as they did the long-standing Caucasian oligarchy that dominated government and trade in the islands. It will be appreciated that this pattern among the younger Japanese was superimposed and added to the worldwide trend toward rejection of established lines of authority—family and otherwise—after World War II. A strong traditional culture enabled the Japanese to survive and flourish against odds in Hawaii, but the traditional culture itself had to adapt to meet the needs of headlong social and economic changes.

Prior to World War II Hawaii was a relaxed garrison outpost for the military, the playground of a few wealthy tourists, and the base for large-scale agriculture in sugar, pineapple, and cattle. The interests controlling agriculture were tightly bound by economic class and family loyalties, and by an honest conviction that they were united in preserving a uniquely good way of life for the islands. Their control, based classically in land ownership, extended into every facet of society to a degree that seems almost inconceivable in retrospect. They controlled shipping, finance, wholesale distribution, major retail outlets, the newspapers, the political apparatus, and the judiciary. The relentlessness with which dissidence was pursued and neutralized was not restricted to conventional targets, such as labor organizers or radical school teachers. Small-business owners, even "mom and pop" grocery stores, that displayed any untoward enterprise found themselves with delayed shipments, restriction of credit, and a drifting away of embarrassed customers. In one rural high school, plantation management prohibited the teaching of shorthand and typing to young girls since it meant losing manpower to the city. This was a way by which some of the immigrants' children were held in place to follow the footsteps of their parents.

In this environment the Japanese were second-class citizens, whether they were still direct employees of the plantation or theoretically "independent" within the controlled economy. This environment itself, however, changed rapidly after World War II and the Japanese social, political, and economic advances were no longer conducted in an otherwise static situation. The very scale of the Japanese advances was a major factor in the overall societal changes, but the incursion of out-of-state business enterprises undaunted by the oligarchy's control, the fact that the oligarchy itself was probably experiencing a failure of nerve and energy, and the rise of other liberal elements to challenge the status quo were equally important factors.

On the home front, the war brought defense workers to Hawaii from the West Coast. Until then it was unimaginable that *nisei* would be working side-by-side with *haole* (Caucasian) laborers, who lived in low-rent housing along the waterfront and spoke with a Southern drawl which sounded uneducated. Some of the imported laborers from the West Coast were "Okies" who left Oklahoma in abandonment of the dust bowls of the '30s to find the land of plenty in California. Furthermore, the social behavior of soldiers and sailors was outrageous compared to the almost puritan ethics which the immigrants drilled into their children. (Sexual inhibitions were seen as conducive to desirable behavior.) The "superiority" of haoles as a racial group began to diminish. The social advance of the Japanese sprang also from the determination of the returned soldiers that things would be different, from the educational opportunities pro-

vided by the GI Bill of Rights, and from a whole national climate of
more equal opportunities. Further, the returning GIs had related to
Caucasians in a different context, in the deep South where they
trained and in war-torn Europe from which some of the *nisei* brought
back brides.

A political leadership emerged from this group of returned *nisei*
soldiers, and an alliance was formed with Caucasian liberal elements
in the Democratic party, and especially with the increasingly strong
labor unions that were simultaneously challenging the oligarchy.
This tale has been told many times (Coffman, 1973). The result was
an almost complete reversal of the political power structure in local
politics and, within a short time of achieving statehood in 1959, in
the US Congress and the judiciary. In retrospect, the restraint exhibited by a largely Japanese legislative leadership after a series of land-
slide election wins, which all but buried the Republican representatives of the traditional power structure, is impressive. Also, on an
ironic note, some of the original radical leadership who have been so
long in office are now perceived by young Japanese voters as ponder-
ous symbols of the present establishment. Although the most spec-
tacular success stories for Hawaii's Japanese occurred after World War
II, there had been a few older individuals who had previously made it
from the plantations into the higher reaches of the arts and professions without the benefit of the later assistance.

While attention has been appropriately focused on those *nisei*
leaders who became state and national figures, many others moved
quietly into the professions. Today AJAs are adequately represented
(on a population *pro rata* basis) in medicine, law, architecture, and
the social services. Their representation in the ranks of public school
teachers and the broad range of administrative and clerical jobs in
state and county governments is even stronger, to the point that some
newcomers perceive an ethnic bias in recruitment. The basis for this
AJA "over-representation" is, however, that civil service opportunities were the first white collar jobs to be opened up to genuine competition (as has been the case elsewhere in the United States and with
other ethnic minorities). Accordingly, there is an AJA preponderance
(now at the middle management levels) in consequence of an earlier
lack of choice. Also, the structured hierarchy of such occupations is
attractive in the Japanese cultural tradition, especially when coupled
with a perceived upward social mobility. The mobility element was

more apparent in the 1950s by comparison with pre–World War II conditions than by comparison with the relative rewards of skilled blue collar occupations today. Finally, it must be recognized that to-day's predominantly Japanese supervisors in some areas would be less than human if they were not attracted to job applicants who display personal characteristics traditionally recognized as appropriate in the young by the Japanese culture and, to a large extent, by all white collar middle management standards, even without ethnic bias in the crudest sense.

In striking contrast to the success of Hawaii's Japanese in politics and the professions, there has *not* been a parallel success in large corporate endeavors (to match those of the much smaller Chinese minority, for example). There are notable exceptions, of course, but it seems that a sense of competition, jealousy, and distrust prevail among non-blood-related Japanese which will not permit close business collaboration. The exception is the Okinawans who have formed business ties and have assisted each other in successful ventures. This cohesive behavior can be attributed to the prejudice expressed by the mainland Japanese immigrants who did not consider the Okinawans as Japanese. This feeling extended to looking askance at marriages between those of mainland Japanese parentage *(naichi)* and those of Okinawan parentage.

The cultural base for Hawaii's Japanese was rural and conservative, even by the standards of 1900. They left a rural culture in the southern prefectures which was relatively unchanged despite the intellectual and political ferment in the mainstream of Japanese life during the period from the Meiji Restoration in 1868 to the adoption of an approximately "Western" constitution in 1889. Consequently, modern Hawaii can provide glimpses of rural Japan of the Meiji and pre-Meiji eras. Some visitors to Hawaii from modern Japan are surprised (and frequently touched) to find that the very Americanized Hawaii Japanese unknowingly perpetuate minor practices, verbal expressions, and attitudes that seem incredibly old-fashioned. In some instances, the Japanese from Japan see the Hawaii Japanese as being economically well off, but culturally poor.

Although peasant origin and isolation from the subsequent happenings in the Japanese culture are important, attention should be drawn to some exceptions. The disruption of the pre-Meiji feudal system meant that the then unemployed samurai had to be reassimilated into society. It is likely that the samurai who drifted downward socially would have been attracted to the new chance offered by emigration, and so this kind of cultural leavening remains an intriguing possibility. In addition, many Japanese families sent their children back to Japan to be educated, again providing a cultural infusion and diminishing the impact of total isolation. Furthermore, the immigrants themselves maintained ties with their families in Japan even to the extent of multiple visits in the period between the two world wars. Finally, the doctors, priests, language teachers, and other educated persons serving the Japanese community were mainly brought for that purpose from the homeland.

In general, however, the Japanese cultural base in Hawaii was conservative and authoritarian, which has served to increase the tensions between generations in modern Hawaii.

Stereotypes of the Japanese and Hawaii's Japanese

For a newcomer to this state, and especially for anyone who plans to work and live as part of the community, identification of general and positive stereotypes of the Japanese as seen by others might be useful. For example, the Japanese like to be seen as possessing qualities of personal cleanliness, orderly behavior, and stoicism under physical pain and poverty; they also like to be known for their appreciation of hard, meticulous, and completed work with an overlay of thrift.

In addition, the Japanese are oriented to the group rather than to the individual. They feel a deep sense of obligation to family, village, and country. Moreover, the loyalty and obedience of a child toward parents and siblings are the basic virtues which are prototypes for other loyalties. Outward expressions of respect and consideration for the aged and love for children are a common observation in the Japanese. The good name of the family (or other unit) takes precedence over all personal considerations. Personal achievement is valued for the honor it brings to the family and, reciprocally, humiliation of the family is the ultimate shame.

Finally, there seems to be a keen awareness and acceptance in the Japanese of a well-defined hierarchy whether it be in the family, institution, or society in general; there is comfort in knowing one's place in the hierarchy.

Negative stereotypes of the Japanese by the non-Japanese might include descriptions such as: clannishness and ethnic exclusivity, stubbornness, reluctance to state an opinion on issues or to acknowledge personal error, lack of originality, and a disinclination to articulate or show emotion. Negative impressions of the Japanese by the Japanese might include those listed above, although concurrence would usually be of the "yes, but—" variety. As with the rest of the world, the Japanese tend to dwell upon their cultural virtues rather than list their failings. Further, the generally acknowledged "failings" are seen as virtues. For example, one might hear "We Japanese have the failing of being too straightforward, kind, trusting, and honest. That is how other groups take advantage of us."

An examination of these stereotypes, especially the positive ones, can leave an impression that the Japanese culture is not very different from those Western cultures with traditions of strong family authority, soldierly virtues, stoicism, hard work, thrift—in fact, the whole Judeo-Christian work ethic set in Sparta without the Helots. This superficial similarity is enhanced in Hawaii because the AJAs seem so intensely American middle-class. Families clip immaculate lawns around suburban tract homes, attend Little League and PTA functions, watch national television programs, and keep up with the Joneses (or the Morikawas).

The operational similarity of traditional Japanese values to the dominant WASP culture of the United States has been a major factor in the assimilation of the AJAs. Further, an important characteristic of Japanese culture in Japan has always been its adaptability, to absorb and assimilate those parts of other cultures perceived as useful —whether Chinese, European, or American. All this can be misleading for those citizens of Hawaii (of all ethnicities) who seek a deeper understanding of AJAs beyond the prevailing cordial neighborliness. The need for examination becomes especially important when Japanese and non-Japanese persons are engaged in enterprises involving close interpersonal communication, including complex enterprises as well as, for example, a doctor-patient relationship.

The basic Japanese culture is more different than appears superficially, and is much more pervasive in the family lives of Hawaii's AJAs than the middle-class success story would suggest. AJAs experience unique emotional stresses because of the tensions between traditional family expectations and the American lifestyle of personal achievement and acquisition; illness, loss, or other misfortunes exacerbate these problems because of what can be called a "cultural regression" (in an individual) as a paradigm for the regression to an earlier stage in personality development under stress.

Ruling Concepts of Japanese Community
OBLIGATION

A sense of obligation *(on)* is the substance of the traditional Japanese hierarchy. Although that hierarchy is manifestly vertical (Nakane, 1967), the *on* is reciprocal, and the vertical relationships are interdependent.

The deference accorded the head of the traditional Japanese family is based on a sense of obligation on the part of the junior members, but the leadership role involves *responsibility,* as contrasted with the simple assumption of authority (as in the stereotyped Prussian family), and yet it is the authority that is so superficially obvious. In reality, the leader of a Japanese family or other organization is reluctant to make unilateral decisions. The usual course is first to test confidence in an extensive consensus. The individual or small group conferences for this purpose are psychologically valuable expressions of the reciprocity of *on*. Furthermore, the achievement of a consensus is greatly assisted by the inclination of individuals to align themselves with the group or, at least, a disinclination to express disagreement. The motivation is the seeking of agreement as a positive good in itself, almost independently of private feelings and certainly not from fear of the leader. The consequence, however, is that the leader's pronouncement may then sound authoritarian to the outsider or to an Americanized younger member of the family. This is not to say that there are no Japanese domestic or institutional tyrants, any more than it is to suggest that informal base-touching with a support group is unknown among leaders of Western-type hierarchies.

On also forms a network of interdependence among peers or near-peers and probably has origins in the exchange of labor among small farmers through the rhythms of the agricultural year, as well as in the vertical feudal context.

It is emphasized that *on* is taken extremely seriously, to an extent that can easily be underestimated by Westerners. It extends beyond the reciprocal good-natured helpfulness of neighbors (even of Western pioneer days) and compares more with the total commitment to each other of some high-morale, small military units, or to the uncompromising "duty, honor, country" of the professional soldier. This makes sense to Westerners when observed in the self-sacrifice of AJA combat units in World War II, but can be underrated as a social force when the current issue seems trivial and the original assumption of *on* is long forgotten.

Not surprisingly, the rigidity of the code regarding *on* makes for undertones of resentment, especially in Hawaii, as family obligations impinge upon personal desires and the external achievement orientation of later generations. The ideal of family or group solidarity at all costs also establishes resentments of the obligations that demand that harmony. The obligations of children to their parents (and vice versa) probably present the most common psychological stresses among AJAs. The adoption by the *nisei, sansei,* and *yonsei* of the American concepts of personal achievement and advancement bring them into conflict with parental authority even though, paradoxically, the parents may be immensely proud of the achievements in question. If it is assumed that a revolt against parental authority is a common human condition, that revolt which we see in modern Hawaii Japanese results from the dilution or breakdown of the traditional means of resolving it. Further, assimilation (especially of the parents) has not progressed to the point at which the usual Western patterns for resolving conflict with parents are useful. In consequence, the Hawaii AJA tends to have particular difficulties with authority figures in general. This could stem from the constant reminder from parents that one must never lose, must be at the top, the best, and above all, must not be second to a peer of another racial extraction. Therefore, following orders and directions may be placing oneself below the person who is seen as not having the right to be in an authoritarian position. Other cultural factors mask this, especially since resentment is seldom displayed overtly and the *forms* of respect for parents, teachers, and community leaders are followed.

Since about 1968 overt rejection of traditional expectations has been especially noticeable in some of the AJA student population at the University of Hawaii. This has taken forms that would be unremarkable elsewhere in the United States, but even in the 1960s one did not see many Japanese students living communally or in pairs in the same city as their parents; one did not see Japanese girls riding bicycles—and never in short shorts or halter tops—nor were AJA students prominent in protest movements or activism generally. Today's younger AJAs are leaders of the environmental protection activities, for example, and what one might loosely summarize as a "counterculture lifestyle" is sufficiently commonplace to attract no attention. This can be regarded as a further stage of assimilation, although, because nothing is simple, some of the rejection of acquisitive WASP culture takes the form of reaffirming the ancestral culture. At this point there is little information about the family tensions induced or the psychological price paid by the young people for their separation.

It is clear that *on* was an effective network substance which held together a traditional feudal society and provided a priceless stability for Hawaii's Japanese in the new land. The evoked resentments, which were always present even in the traditional system, seem like powerful factors in the assimilation of Hawaii's Japanese, and they must still be taken into account in interpersonal transactions.

Once established, *on* is reversible only by treachery or similar outrage. Therefore, in the traditional society most persons were alert to inadvertently evoking *on* by being the unthinking recipient of a casual kind act from a stranger. Reciprocally, good manners demanded a kind of inverse considerateness in not placing strangers under obligation through the sort of busybody kindness taken for granted in an American small town. This guardedness was applied to strangers because responsibilities toward family were taken for granted, and socially adept persons carefully guarded their warmth and kindness toward others, ranging from inner family to total outsiders. Even in modern Japan, the inverse considerateness can be seen in the restrained behavior of bystanders at minor traffic accidents where there is no effusive helpfulness. In real emergencies, however, bus drivers, firemen, and others perform acts of selfless heroism.

Perhaps because of the influence of the Polynesian tradition of cooperativeness, this guardedness is not so noticeable publicly in Hawaii, but must be taken into account in personal transactions. An anxiety about incurring *on* comes up especially when the potential benefactor is an older Japanese person. Influential assistance for the employment of a younger relative, for example, is often sought from persons of other ethnicities because of this sensitivity.

On a lighter note, an aspect of the endless cycle of *on* that causes wry amusement among the Japanese themselves is the exchange of gifts at every conceivable occasion. The codification in the Japanese language of the different types of gifts is illustrative of the complexity of these rituals within the culture: *kōden* is given for funerals, *senbetsu* is money given when someone leaves for a trip, and *omiyage* (probably the most general term) is a gift, like a memento or souvenir, brought back by someone who has returned from a trip. This aspect of *on* is closely allied to *kōsai,* one's social give and take. Many families maintain files of who gave what to whom, so that on similar occasions celebrated by the giver, the identical amount or more can be reciprocated. In some instances, this file is inherited by the eldest son or another family member when the parents are no longer capable of functioning as the head of the household.

A manifestation of *on* that had perhaps the largest impact on the political history of Hawaii was the *on* felt by the *issei* and *nisei* for John A. Burns, a granite-faced Caucasian police detective, who took the responsibility to work with the Hawaii Japanese leadership for security and restoration of calm in the hysteria immediately after Pearl Harbor. He showed his unconditional respect for and trust in the Japanese community and thereby established the *on* which became a cornerstone of his electoral strength during his subsequent political career. This career did not begin in earnest until his 1956 election as the Territorial Delegate to the US Congress and his election as Governor for the first time in 1962. The Hawaii Japanese community perceived an obligation to John A. Burns, and it is characteristic of that culture that it was met matter-of-factly and undiminished in the subsequent years (Coffman, 1973).

THE IMPORTANCE OF FAMILY

A useful way of looking at the structure of the traditional Japanese family is to consider the prevalence of the word *uchi* in so many terms relating to the family. *Uchi* is actually the pronunciation for two different characters, one meaning "inside" and the other meaning "house." A person refers to his or her own home as *uchi,* and relatives are called *miuchi* which suggests persons "intimate" with the speaker. A man's (own) wife is *kanai,* which translates "the person inside the house." This identification of the house (as a structure) with the family has some correlation with the English usage "the House of Tudor," although there are other words in the Japanese language which suggest the idea of clan, lineage, or kinship. Certainly, the family was originally composed of the persons living in the house, and the English word "household" comes to mind. These persons comprised two, three, or four generations plus maiden aunts, widows, and so forth; in fact, all of the people who were born in the house or came to live in the house (sons and daughters-in-law, for example) are included.

This concept of "inside" and "outside" marked more than genealogical distinctions; it also related to Japanese emotional life. Doi (1973) uses the terms *omote* and *ura* to suggest dual concepts of traditional Japanese personality. The *omote*, which literally means the "front" or "surface," is the public and more formal side of Japanese manner which would be used in addressing guests or respected outsiders. *Ura*, which refers to the rear or the private side of the Japanese, is used and shown only to those most familiar to them. These distinctions are present in one's manner as well as in the choice of vocabulary and grammatical structure used. This view of Japanese personality is thought to be complementary rather than divisive and should be noted by Westerners in their interactions with Japanese, especially of *issei* and *nisei* age groups.

Notions of people "inside" and "outside" have a further set of implications. In the positive sense, the normal individual was guaranteed unconditional support from an inside group against the outside, and more negatively (for a Western bias), the wishes and welfare of the group took precedence over anything that could be regarded as private and personal plans for self-realization. Traditionally, there was little conflict between group welfare and individual welfare because the latter took a subservient role. It is rare when an outsider is included in the privacy of the nuclear family. Outsiders may be invited to family functions, but they quickly sense that they are just visitors. Relationships with an AJA group can be viewed in five concentric circles. The core is the family; the next circle is the extended family, and may include those whose parents came on the same ship, from the same prefecture or village in Japan, or who grew up together in the plantation camps; the third is classmates and schoolmates; the fourth is close business associates; and the fifth is acquaintances.

From this brief description of the traditional family structure, it is clear that the adoption of American patterns of advancement would set up tensions, some of them almost intolerable.

The adoption of Western ambitions for self-realization and personal freedom is almost incomprehensible to persons with traditional Japanese assumptions about family loyalty. Nevertheless, the stability of Hawaii's AJA families is testimony that the necessary accommodations *have* been made. In general, the basic code of obligation and respect for the elders, for example, has been maintained inside the family, while a persons's life outside the family may follow conventional American lines. Even in the latter context, however, the AJAs are, as noted, team players; they are not pushy, not opinionated, and they act in a manner generally consistent with the traditional pattern.

Housing is expensive in Hawaii, and the high cost of living is accepted as the reason for Hawaii having the largest proportion of wage-earning married women in the United States. These factors fortuitously maintain the pattern of several generations living under one roof. Grandparents are thereby housed with dignity and economy and are essential for the care of children whose mothers are employed. Although the working mother seems a consequence of the high-consumption habits of American affluence, we might consider that the middle-class "norm" of a vigorous young matron devoted entirely to home duties is really, on a world scale, the exception. Young women have *always* worked outside the house and left the care of children to grandmothers. In such households, the conflicts between mother-in-law and daughter-in-law are timeless and, accordingly, there seem to be workable patterns of accommodation.

In traditional (and modern) Japan an older son brought his wife to live in his parents' home, where his mother was indisputably in charge. In Hawaii the usually more prosperous son (or the not so prosperous son who needs the help of his parents' savings for the down payment on a house) will bring his aging parents to live in a house which he and his wife own, setting up a crucial shift in the balance of power. Also, as finances permit, more and more AJA couples prefer to assist aging parents to maintain their own separate, and sometimes, original home, more in the direction of other segments of American society. Independent living arrangements are also demanded by the aging parents who insist (on the surface, at least) that they do not want to be a bother to their children. One of the consequences is that eventually the frailty of old age leaves the parents unable to cope with their own establishment and sets up the classic American ambivalence about care of the aged at home versus the "old folks' home." For Japanese adult children this dilemma is especially wrenching, and for aged Japanese parents the merest suggestion that they are a problem is interpreted as a personal rejection and a dereliction of filial duty.

It is noted in this context that even in modern Japan a man who marries an only child goes to his wife's home as if he were the oldest son of that family, adopts his wife's family name and becomes the heir, with all attendant rights and responsibilities. This *yōshi* pattern is *not* followed in Hawaii today. This leaves the parents of a female only-child in Hawaii in an unusual position, by Japanese standards, in their old age.

Although the trend among AJAs is toward the Western-type nuclear family (as contrasted with the multigeneration household), the family life may be much more Japanese than appears on the surface to the outsider. For example, the basic relationship in a Western-type family is between husband and wife, whereas in Japanese society, the parent-child relationship is the *real* one. This makes for the possibility of more "distance" between Japanese spouses than is consistent with the Western ideal and correspondingly enhances (or exacerbates) the parent-child interaction. AJAs subscribe to the Western myth of "fall in love, get married, and live happily ever after" and somehow superimpose a surprisingly traditional relationship with their children. There are no solid data, but individual cases have been cited where the mother routinely sleeps with the youngest child and the father with one of the other male children. It is emphasized that this may not be a conjugal rejection, but the maintenance of a traditional custom. The significance, of course, is not in who sleeps with whom, but the interdigitation of Western and Japanese family styles. This practice may occur less frequently in the *sansei* and *yonsei* groups.

Japanese families tend to be close and supportive, but ordinarily not verbal. The origins of this are complicated, but one fact is that the closeness of the family is so taken for granted that the ritualistic endearments and politeness in families of other cultures would be regarded as unnecessary. In the Western cultures the polite expressions, such as "please," "thank you," and "would you," are as routinely used among family members as with other people. This would be inconceivable to a close-knit Japanese family because the polite forms (in which the language abounds) are for strangers. In fact, the use of a polite form in the family would be cold and rejecting. As in so many other matters, Hawaii's *nisei* and *sansei* strike various compromises, but generally a good-natured grunt (in the family) is the equivalent of several minutes of Latin thanks. This is an important point for non-Japanese persons working with an older AJA supervisor to remember. Caucasians and others are accustomed to receiving verbal strokes for work well done, but if a Japanese supervisor feels close to his subordinate he will not diminish that closeness by the kind of routine acknowledgement he would make to an outsider. In Hawaii the admixture of Japanese and Western culture makes interpretation of a Japanese supervisor's reaction difficult. The absence of conventional expressions of gratitude can be taken as an index of "belonging," but total silence could mean similar pleasure or mean that the supervisor is too embarrassed to complain overtly about the job performance. Everything we have stated here with respect to supervisor-subordinate roles would apply in both directions to student-teacher, doctor-patient, and social worker-client relationships. Non-Japanese persons married to Japanese or AJAs need to take many comparable factors into account or else feel a lack of verbal affirmation.

Assimilation of the *sansei* and *yonsei* AJAs has progressed to the point where a lack of verbal responsiveness in the family may cause some problems comparable to those described in the previous paragraph. This is intensified by a communication difficulty common to other immigrant groups in many countries. The *issei* spoke rural Japanese and learned pidgin English. The *nisei* usually speak almost childish Japanese, which they learned from their parents, and the pidgin English demanded by peer pressure from schoolmates. A hurdle for *nisei* seeking a higher education was to acquire articulate standard English in the teeth of peer disapproval for talking haole. Those *sansei* and *yonsei* persons who achieve a higher education speak standard American English, although many are "bilingual" in pidgin. Now the problem is that they usually cannot speak Japanese (except for baby talk learned from interaction with their grandparents). Therefore, their only communication with their parents is in pidgin English because pidgin English and "pidgin Japanese" are the parents' languages. This is not to pass a value judgment on pidgin, but there is something sad about *nisei* and *sansei* who have full access to neither Japanese nor English. They are cut off from both languages, each of great richness and beauty. Similarly, students describe the difficulties of communicating complex emotions to their parents and their shame at consciously inserting pidgin expressions as a vain reassurance that they are in tune.

In addition, the developmental years of the *nisei* were superimposed with the Western (American) education which they attempted to adopt in extreme ways, such as changing their names, not eating rice, not using chopsticks, and not speaking Japanese. Yet, in later years when the *sansei* came about, the *nisei* would project those very values and customs, such as the Saturday morning classes (*shushin,* "moral and ethical values") in the Japanese schools that extolled the virtues of honesty, thrift, hard work, and filial piety and which every *nisei* remembers and, as a younger person, tried to ignore and reject. This generation gap, then, is not only of language, but the handing down of value systems which are not well expressed by the *nisei* nor totally understood by the *sansei* and *yonsei.*

STATUS OF WOMEN

Sex roles were strongly delineated in the traditional Japanese culture, but the actual authority of women, especially in the farming communities, was (and is) much greater than the forms suggest. In modern AJA families women have made the same kind of advances in status as they have in the rest of the United States, but probably to a lesser degree; in any event, these advances have coincided with an erosion of the traditional authority of the male.

In most Japanese families women still elaborately defer to their husbands in front of their children and the community, but in reality they control the family finances, child rearing, and other major decision making.

Upward mobility for AJA girls in Hawaii was typically through teaching or nursing, while working as secretaries, retail clerks, and waitresses remained the norm—essentially as in the rest of the United States. Despite marked recent advances by AJA women into executive positions, the professions, and elected office, the other sex-typed roles remain the usual, just as elsewhere, with perhaps a somewhat slower rate of advance in Hawaii.

Traditional family expectations and emphasis on career opportunities for sons are the main inhibitors of women entering the learned professions. AJA women applicants to medical school have described ridicule from their families as an extremely painful deterrent. Not unexpectedly then, AJA women medical students are noted as highly assertive by AJA standards, which in turn has tended to discourage sexist attitudes from their classmates. Curiously, the most notable sexist attitude among medical students at the University of Hawaii is the resistance of AJA men to the authority of women faculty. This may be a cultural carry-over of a discomfort with a perturbation of the traditional pattern of authority, or it may be simply that a woman professor of pediatrics evokes uncomfortable echoes of grade school.

Emotional and Psychological Problems

Potential emotional and psychological problems in the Japanese are in some sense related to the type of family system and the individual's relationship within or separate from the family. In a modern era of espousing the rights of the individual and the quest for personal identity and fulfillment, the possibility for conflicts between individual needs and the obligation and compliance to a group ethos, especially in terms of the family, indeed looms large for some Japanese. Permission and the blessing of one's parents is still desirable in the selection of a husband or wife. Siblings often frown upon the choice of a partner whom they term not good enough for a member of their family.

There is the general reluctance by the individual to state an opinion at variance with group consensus, or often a reluctance to state an opinion at all. There is a *very* strong inhibition against making oneself conspicuous. This extends even to asking questions in class, far less to a determined assertion of a policy recommendation. As noted, the family environment encourages conformity; at times, this may have been reinforced by the large number of public school teachers who are from similar families. Not surprisingly, once an individual feels strongly enough about an issue to break through the inhibition, the resulting assertion or complaint may seem, to the non-Japanese, unreasonably passionate.

The traditional pattern of family loyalty is carried over, to a lesser extent, into groups centered on work, military associations, and school. Just as the unquestioning family loyalty has been somewhat diluted by the assimilation of subsequent generations of AJAs, so has the comfort with total group identification. Modern Japanese tourists (in Hawaii), for example, are noted for their strong group discipline, whereas AJAs seem to have largely broken away from that pattern.

Not only is the individual versus the group a potential problem; the discontinuity between the lifestyles and values of different generations has also become a source of discontent between members of families. The criteria of success and happiness is not always the same for the *sansei* son as it was for his *nisei* father. In families where three generations are present, the inability of the grandchildren to speak or understand Japanese still spoken by a grandparent also widens the gaps of communication.

Two other family systems pose difficulty. Under certain circumstances family members share a particularly close emotional tie. Traditionally, the Japanese widow does not remarry, but will devote the rest of her life to raising her children, or an unmarried sister and brother will live together. The overattachment and special dependence in these relationships are a potential problem, especially in the event of an unexpected separation or loss of one of the parties of the relationship. It would be a mistake to assume that such a relationship can always be interpreted as the intimate and emotional connection typical of Japanese family relationships. There may be, in fact, the suggestion of a possible pathology.

In contrast to the dependence and overattachment in some family relationships is the rivalry or antagonism that can exist between siblings. Often, the problems result in an elder-younger situation, one common in Oriental families in which the older brother, as first heir, is revered and favored, while the younger son may feel left out of his parents' and grandparents' pride and affection for the first son of the family. There is also the case in which siblings are of opposite sexes. In a traditional family, discipline and treatment were definitely sex linked; the restrictions on a daughter's behavior were much more stringent than on a son, and the family expectations for success were placed upon the son rather than upon a daughter. Today, in a family with a progressive daughter, the tensions and resentment can be considerable if she questions her subjugated position, or if she demands her rightful share of the family's interest and support for her ambitions.

The emphasis on the family's good name, and the high priority placed on protecting the family from shame, has many positive consequences summarized as honorable behavior. Ruth Benedict (1967) triggered years of debate by her distinction between a shame culture (Japanese) and a guilt culture (Western). The position taken on this by Doi (1973) is perhaps the most useful in the present context since he raises the matter above a simplistic guilt versus shame issue. Whatever may be the form of the guilt undoubtedly experienced by a traditional Japanese person, shame is an extremely powerful emotion of great significance to an understanding of family dynamics.

Prior to about 1950 shame incurred by a Japanese person would affect the entire Japanese community in Hawaii. A newspaper account
of a Japanese youngster in trouble with the police would cause supper
to be late in many homes while fathers thundered about the shame.

Many diseases, such as tuberculosis, cancer, and leprosy were regarded as shameful and treated as dark secrets within the family;
mental retardation and psychiatric illness fell into that same category. In the days when a matchmaker still negotiated the arrangement of marriages, it was customary to ask if there was anyone in
either family who had any peculiar illnesses or characteristics. Even
today, families still question their children about the background of
their friends, especially in dating situations. The medical community
still cites the presence of the stigma on mental illness in the Japanese
community. There is still a reluctance in the individual to seek psychiatric help and a reluctance of the family to seek hospitalization for
a member who needs it. The number of psychotic Japanese patients
brought to the various clinical facilties is less than predictable on a
population basis, but their symptoms are correspondingly more advanced and more severe, and their subsequent hospitalization is
longer. Accordingly, it can be assumed that Japanese families maintain, at home and untreated, many persons with highly disruptive
symptoms, partly because of the shame involved in exposure of the
problems by seeking help.

There are several groups of Japanese who might be labeled as vulnerable to the occurrences of mental illness. Women in their late
middle age, after a lifetime of caring for their children, are suddenly
set emotionally adrift as their children marry and leave home. In
many cases, the only tie between husband and wife has been their
children, and other interests were separately cultivated. The sense of
loss because of their children's absence and the prospect of years with
a resented stranger are often the cause of emotional problems.

A second group of women may be classified as vulnerable to mental illness. In spite of the stigma against divorce in the Japanese community, some women choose to end an unhappy marriage rather
than suffer for the sake of their children. The result is often social ostracism, subtle or overt, from family and friends, thus any problems
must be handled without the usual support system. These women
even come to look upon themselves as failures or as an underprivileged group.

If an individual does not carry out his social obligations, or com-

mits some unthinkable wrongdoing, his family or friends may completely cut off all association and contact with him. Such an individual may have reneged on his promise as a second in a *tanomoshi*
group, disgraced the family by his ugly behavior and unsavory com-
panions, or just not lived up to the family's plans for his future.
Isolated and scorned by the community because of his family's rejection of him, such a person is often a prime candidate for psychiatric
help, but is not the sort of individual likely to present himself at a
facility for any assistance.

A very important factor to note is how the Japanese make constant
reference to feelings *(kimochi)*—"I don't have good *kimochi* about
this matter," "You don't understand my *kimochi!*"—in their daily
lives. In the groups noted as vulnerable to emotional disturbance and
in the Japanese generally, interpersonal conflicts are often the result
of a misinterpretation or a lack of regard for someone's feelings.
Westerners often misinterpreted the unwrinkled brow or the dry eye
of an Oriental as a sign of a lack of feeling or of an unperturbed, im-
penetrable nature. Japanese feelings are handled in two seemingly
opposing forms. They are well controlled, sometimes even suppressed in a public or deferential occasion; yet, in the proper setting
or situation, tempers are allowed to fly and tears flow quite freely.
How the Japanese handle emotions and feelings is part of the *omote-
ura* dichotomy mentioned earlier in the chapter.

The constant concern for proper behavior and the stigma against
mental illness are probably two explanations for the general tendency
of the Japanese (as compared with Caucasians) to somatize all illness
and to deny the possibility of an emotional component. Being "ill"
is a legitimate, socially acceptable manner of getting care; consequently, patients' complaints are usually physical. Without drawing
a firm line about which diseases are psychogenic and which are not,
clearly the management of gastric ulcers, hypertension, or colitis becomes difficult with patients who insist that the stresses of their lives
are nonexistent or unrelated. Even when the emotional symptoms are
unmistakable, the self-referring patient is likely to insist on the mental health worker's not making contact with the family under any circumstances. The difficulties this imposes upon the acquisition of a
history, far less treatment, hardly need description.

Several other areas which might be observed or considered in dealing with a Japanese patient and which are often misunderstood by an
unaware therapist warrant mention. Just as the Japanese have been

incorrectly labeled unemotional, so also have they been called inarticulate and nonverbal. Constant verbal communication is seen as unnecessary by many Japanese. It is often more important to communicate through attitude, action, and feeling than through words. A talkative person is often considered a "show-off" or insincere, thus the Japanese are not taught to speak out at every opportunity. Unfortunately, this quiet behavior may be misread as antisocial, passive, and even passive-aggressive. This kind of behavior in its extreme form may indeed occur in a Japanese as a kind of "acting out" behavior which is radically different from violent, explosive, or disruptive behavior observed in a Western patient. The difference between a normally quiet Japanese individual and a pathologically withdrawn person, however, is easily discernible. A normal individual, regardless of whether the setting is a social or therapeutic one, if asked to speak or participate will do so. The individual whose behavior is pathological, however, or who is indeed acting out, will react hostilely if pressed or will become more withdrawn or physically agitated when addressed or approached.

Another area of misunderstanding is the Westerner's view of the "desexualized" Japanese woman. It is not uncommon to encounter an older Japanese female patient who has not had sexual relations with her husband for some time because of a long-term physical separation, or to learn of a widow who, years after her husband's death, still has no sexual partners; culturally accepted long abstinence should not be mistaken as a sign of sexual dysfunction or maladjustment.

Problems with alcohol are minimal in the Japanese community. Alcoholism occurs occasionally, however, in the women who live an "out of group" lifestyle (a small part of the population) and consequently may drink as part of their outcast, unsanctioned behavior. The Japanese generally are not copious social drinkers; they, like most Orientals, prefer to share food with their friends. Here in the islands, when the social occasion is a cocktail party given by a haole friend, the Orientals will sometimes in jest (sometimes in earnest) make arrangements to eat before or after because there will usually be more to drink than to eat at the party.

Suicide, thought by the Westerners to be a common occurrence in the Japanese, is not frequent among the Japanese in Hawaii. In the past a person might have taken his own life to show sorrow or to make amends for a crime or disgrace he may have caused. His death would bring forgiveness to his name, because there is no concept of punishment after death; every man is considered a follower of Buddha and thus a good spirit when he dies. Attempted suicide as a cry for help is frowned upon as an act of cowardice. Suicide is not a sanctioned form of solving one's problems, but anyone so inclined usually does so quickly and effectively, with no desire to scandalize or burden friends or family.

Conclusion

The Japanese in Hawaii are an example of the American dream. In three to four generations, descendants of poor immigrants have entered the American middle class, economically, socially, and in many ways, emotionally. Instead of assimilating into the rest of the population, however, the Japanese in Hawaii have maintained their own identity and a critical mass. This block is often identified as having influenced the determination of persons to be elected to the highest political offices in the state, thus perpetuating the solidity of the group.

The Japanese Americans in Hawaii have been chided as "bananas," yellow-skinned and white inside. The latter refers to the aspiration of being like the haole middle class toward whom, ironically, the Japanese aim their prejudice and reservations. Mental health workers should guard against thinking that they are working with a white middle-class person when confronted with a Japanese client. It is suggested that the professional worker take into consideration, in most instances, some of the intricacies described in this chapter, with the reminder that the Japanese in Hawaii are unique because of their history and interpretation of values through the generations. In essence the Japanese Americans in Hawaii today, while middle-class in appearance, remain Japanese in heritage.

References

Beall, Lynnette. The psychopathology of suicide in Japan. *International Journal of Social Psychiatry*, 1968, 14:213–225.

Benedict, Ruth F. *The crysanthemum and the sword; patterns of Japanese culture.* Cleveland: World Publishing Co., 1967.

Berrien, F. Kenneth; Arkoff, Abe; and Iwahara, Shinkuro. Generational differences in values: American, Japanese American and Japanese. *Journal of Social Psychology*, 1967, 71:169–175.

Blane, Howard T., and Yamamoto, Kazuo. Sexual role identity among Japanese and Japanese-American high school students. *Journal of Cross-Cultural Psychology*, 1970, 1(4):345–354.

Caudill, William A., and Doi, Takeo. Interrelations of psychiatry, culture and emotion in Japan. In Iago Galdston, *Medicine and anthropology*. New York: International University Press, 1963.

Coffman, Tom. *Catch a wave: Hawaii's new politics*. (2nd ed.). Honolulu: University Press of Hawaii, 1973.

Cohen, Judith B. Sociocultural change and behavior patterns in disease etiology: An epidemiologic study of coronary disease among Japanese Americans. Ph.D. thesis, University of California, Berkeley, 1974.

DeVos, George. The relation of guilt towards parents to achievement and arranged marriage among the Japanese. *Psychiatry*, 1960, 23:287–301.

Doi, L. Takeo. *[The anatomy of dependence]* (John Bester, trans.) (1st ed.). Tokyo, New York and San Francisco: Kodansha, 1973. (Dist. by Harper and Row).

_____. Omote and ura: Concepts derived from the Japanese two-fold structure of consciousness. *Journal of Nervous and Mental Disease*, 1973, 157(4):258–261.

Kalish, Richard A. Suicide: An ethnic comparison in Hawaii. *Bulletin of Suicidology*, December 1968, pp. 37–43.

Kondo, Akihisa. Morita therapy: A Japanese therapy for neurosis. *American Journal of Psychoanalysis*, 1953, 13:31–37.

Lebra, Takie Sugiyama. Acculturation dilemma: The function of Japanese moral values for Americanization. Reprint. *Council on Anthropology and Education Newsletter*, 1972, 3(1):6–13.

_____. Reciprocity and the asymmetric principle: An analytical reappraisal of the Japanese concept of "on". *Psychologia*, 1969, 12:129–138.

Lee, Dorothy D. Ethnic structures in Hawaii: A report based on the Hawaii health surveillance program survey. *Population Report*, no. 6. Honolulu: Hawaii Department of Health, Research and Statistics Office, 1976.

Lin, Tung Kuang; Kim, John H. C.; Dung, William M. H.; Miyawaki, E. H.; and Bennett, James G. Myocardial infarction in Kaiser Hospital, Honolulu (1959–1967)—A long-term analysis. *Hawaii Medical Journal*, July-August, 1972, 31(4):257–261.

Lum, Doman. Japanese suicides in Honolulu, 1958–1969. *Hawaii Medical Journal*, 1972, 31(1):19–23.

Moellering, Robert C. Jr., and Bassett, David R. Myocardial infarction in Hawaiian and Japanese males on Oahu—A review of 505 cases occurring between 1955 and 1964. *Journal of Chronic Diseases*, 1967, 20:89–101.

Nakane, Chie. *Tate shakai no ningen kankai* [Human relations in a vertical society]. Tokyo: Kodansha, 1967.

Ogawa, Dennis M. *Kodomo no tame ni—For the sake of the children: The Japanese American experience in Hawaii*. Honolulu: University Press of Hawaii, 1978.

Ohara, Kenshiro. Characteristics of suicides in Japan—especially of parent-child double suicide. *American Journal of Psychiatry*, 1963, 120(1):382–385.

Schmitt, Robert C. *Historical Statistics of Hawaii*. Honolulu: University Press of Hawaii, 1977.

Stokes, Joseph R.; Bassett, David R.; Rosenblatt, Gerald; Greenberg, Donald; and Moellering, Robert C. Jr. Coronary disease and hypertension in Hawaii. *Hawaii Medical Journal*, 1966, 25(3):235–240.

CHAPTER 6

The Portuguese

Eugene W. Carvalho

The Portuguese in Hawaii today represent approximately 6 percent of the state's population. To understand the situation of this ethnic group it is necessary to go back to the year 1878, to see what was then happening in Hawaii and also what was happening nearly halfway around the world in Portugal.

The Portuguese have always lived close to the sea and sailing has been a way of life for them. In the fifteenth century, Portuguese explorers settled the group of islands in the Atlantic Ocean now known as Madeira and the Azores. In addition, the Portuguese established colonies in other areas of the world. The Portuguese empire reached its peak in the sixteenth century. Following this time, because of internal political problems, Portugal failed to participate in the industrial revolution. In 1822, the absolute monarchy which had dominated Portugal's politics since the twelfth century was replaced with a modern constitution. This was followed, however, by a period of political instability, civil war, and a return to a constitutional monarchy. A government survey in Portugal in 1851 showed that Portugal had fallen behind western Europe in development, with few good roads, no railway system, and no telegraph lines. Moreover, during the 1850s the vineyards of Madeira were laid waste by a blight, which crippled the wine industry on that island for several decades. A consequence of this was high unemployment and hunger. As conditions worsened, Madeirans looked for a better way of life and began emigrating to Brazil, Hawaii, and the United States (Felix and Senecal, 1978).

In the 1870s in Hawaii, the island economy had specific needs which had to be met. The growing sugar industry needed workers for its plantations. Because the local population could not fill the demand, the industry began importing workers from China. Several thousand began emigrating to Hawaii during the 1860s and 1870s. As a result of the distinct cultural differences between the Chinese and the other residents of Hawaii, however, there was considerable pressure to end the large-scale importation of workers from China. In 1876, Jacinto Perreira, a Portuguese citizen and owner of a store in Honolulu, suggested that the Hawaiian government consider the importation of Portuguese to solve the labor and population problems of the islands. The Hawaiian government subsequently contacted Dr. William Hillebrand, who was at that time residing in Madeira. Acting as an agent for the Hawaiian government, Dr. Hillebrand arranged the first importation of Portuguese emigrants to Hawaii.

Immigration

In a letter to the Hawaiian government describing the Portuguese people prior to the first immigration, Dr. Hillebrand wrote,

> In my opinion your islands could not possibly get a more desirable class of Immigrants than the population of Madeira and the Azores Islands. Sober, honest, industrious, and peaceable, they combine all the qualities of a good settler and with all this, they are inured to your climate. Their education and ideas of comfort and social requirements are just low enough to make them contented with the lot of an isolated settler and its attendant privations, while on the other hand their mental capabilities and habit of work will insure them a much higher status in the next generation, as the means of improvement grow up around them (Kuykendall, 1967).

By 1878, before the ship *Priscilla* arrived in Hawaii, there were already approximately four hundred Portuguese living here. Most had arrived as sailors on various shipping vessels and had become cattle ranchers and dairymen. Hawaii's expectations of the new immigrants were clearly reflected in *Thrum's Hawaiian Almanac and Annual* for 1879 and subsequent years: "The government have also been successful in procuring an immigration of men, women and children from Madeira, who were immediately taken up. These people promising to be a valuable laboring class, measures were immediately taken to procure an ample supply, and defeat, if possible, the pernicious effect of continued male Chinese immigration."

This importation, however, did not immediately solve the needs of the local industry, and Thrum's almanac for 1881 states: "There have been free arrivals of Chinese, Portuguese, and South Sea Islanders since our last writing, but the demand is not met. There is a prospect of more near at hand, including a number of Norwegians, which it is hoped will relieve planters of their difficulties. The Chinese are found to prefer engaging with their own people in the cultivation of rice, rather than to engage on sugar plantations while the South Sea Islanders have not proved all that was hoped for in them, being unused to the climate and work." The almanac for 1882 states: "The Norwegians, as a whole, have failed to satisfy the expectation of the promoters of this costly scheme, as have the South Sea Islanders, while the Portuguese seem to present claims for favorable consideration and will prove likely to become permanent settlers, evincing already the inclination to become small farmers."

A difficulty with the Portuguese immigration, however, was the fact that they brought their entire families with them. Thus, the cost of importing these immigrants was the highest of any group that was brought to Hawaii. As a result, immigration was briefly halted in 1882, but was subsequently resumed after protest from the local sugar industry.

The labor contracts arranged with the Portuguese immigrants were generous. The terms proposed to the immigrants in the contracts of 1877 were as follows: passage money was prepaid; employment was guaranteed by the Board of Immigration at the rate of $10 monthly for men, $6–$8 for women, with food, lodging, and medical attendance provided; a day's ration was to consist of one pound of beef or one-half pound of fish, one and one-half pounds of rice, one-half pound of taro or other vegetable, and one-third ounce of tea; in addition, the time of service contracted for was thirty-six months, of twenty-six working days each, ten hours being counted to the day. With this contract, the first Portuguese immigrants arrived at Honolulu on 29 September 1878. The group numbered 120 persons, consisting of 60 men, 22 women, and 38 children. Subsequent shipments, however, became progressively more unprofitable from the planters' point of view. The Portuguese persisted in bringing their families, men and women, young and old, until the Board of Immigration was forced to make a new arrangement. The arrivals of the next three years amounted to 7700, and the laborers commanded better and better wages. In 1884, the Board was required to offer $16 a month plus lodging and fuel. The total cost of the Portuguese immigration cannot be stated, but a tabulation covering the five shiploads, 2750 persons, which arrived in the years 1884 to 1886 showed a total of $246,197.78 of which amount the planters paid approximately $102,000 and the government $144,000 (Kuykendall, 1967).

Early Life in Hawaii

Early life on the plantations in Hawaii for the Portuguese is well described in a personal recollection by Nettie dos Reis, whose experience was typical.

> My father was assigned as a field laborer on a sugar cane plantation . . . on Maui. He quickly learned that the recruiting agents in Madeira had misrepresented both working and living conditions on the plantation. He knew nothing about farming, and had a difficult time completing his three-year contract. After three months of laboring in the cane fields, his hands and feet ached constantly. Luckily, the plantation manager, Mr. Henry P. Baldwin, learned that father was a shoemaker, and transferred him from the fields to the plantation stables to be head stableman and harness maker. . . . Father continued as head stableman and harness maker for the plantation until his three-year contract ended. The period had been a difficult one; plantation life was hard with long days of rough work and low pay and few opportunities for economic and social advancements. Furthermore, the only two children born to this family on the plantation also died there. . . . Father moved from Hamakuapoko and opened his own leather shop, and earned an improved living making shoes, saddles, bridles, harnesses and other articles for whoever needed them. Mother supplemented the family's income: being a professional dressmaker, she converted a spareroom into a dressmaking shop. (Felix, 1978)

Generally, in the plantations the Portuguese lived in camps provided by the plantation companies. A young Portuguese immigrant interviewed by Hideko Sasaki in 1935 described the conditions in the camp:

> We went to live in the long house in Camp 4. There was six families in this long house. One Portuguese family stayed next to us and we come good friends. We never pay attention to the other families. This family next to us came with us, so we good friends. My father cut a door in the wall and the children can go between the two 'apartment' easily. The

kitchen was outside and the floor was dirt. When it rain, we were like ducks in the mud. My father used to pity my mother, but everybody was the same. Everything was new and so my mother never grumble. We sleep on stick beds, just like bench. My father and mother and my sister sleep in one room, us three boys sleep in the other room. No furniture, only one table and the beds.

The family structure in early Hawaii among the Portuguese was the same as it had been in Portugal. Dorothy Jose (1937), gives a flavor of early Portuguese family life:

My father was the boss in our home, but he handed my mother his pay check every month and she took care of it. . . . We each had duties which had to be performed on pain of punishment. All our earnings were put into the family fund, and our mother gave us what she thought was necessary and no more. We were taught to respect each other in our family and especially our parents and guests. . . . Swearing was absolutely forbidden; there was no backtalk allowed; we had to take punishment without a murmur and we feared the strap which my mother used for punishing us. . . . At the table we always said grace before and after meals and no talking was allowed. The table was a sacred place in our home. . . . We had some superstitions—I remember when a chicken crowed like a rooster, it had to be killed immediately unless some catastrophe should take place. Dogs howling at night always meant a death in the family or neighborhood. Many of the families believed and still believe in what they term *fetseras,* a word for fairies who are supposedly actual people possessed of the power to change into various animals at night.

Early Portuguese in Hawaii also formed several benevolent societies and most Portuguese men belonged to one of them. The first was the San Antonio Society formed in Honolulu on 1 January 1877, prior to the arrival of the *Priscilla.* The society began as a cooperative economic and social benevolent organization to assist members in times of need. So great, however, was the demand for assistance that the societies subsequently limited benefits to provide funds against sickness and, in case of death, to provide the widows with support to educate and raise their children (Jubilee of the San Antonio Society, 1926).

Early family life of the Portuguese in Hawaii was thus dominated by traditional mores based on southern European, Roman Catholic values. The great majority of Portuguese retain their Catholic religion today, although there have always been small numbers belonging to other religions. In the family, the father was obeyed and respected and his authority in the home was reinforced by the Church. Courtship and marriage also followed traditional Catholic patterns. Although changes are now occurring, the double standard in sex and the traditional overprotectiveness toward girls still exists. The Catholic emphasis on the importance of the family unit also survives, and extended kinship is common.

Early Portuguese also had a system of folk medicine which is still known today, especially among the older Portuguese people. Healers known as *curadeiras* are still sought by some for the relief of *bucho virado*, or "turned stomach." These healers are generally older women who have learned the methods from other practitioners. They massage the abdomen with oil and apply cabbage or taro leaves and bandages. They also use vacuum cups for local pains, the vacuum being obtained by burning cotton in the inverted cup (Cabral, 1948).

Portuguese culture has made considerable contributions to pidgin, the lingua franca in Hawaii. The first Portuguese word recorded in Hawaii was heard by a Spanish explorer in 1791. He entered in his journal the word *piquinini,* translated as "small thing." Other Portuguese loanwords to pidgin, especially names of ethnic foods, are commonly used in Hawaii (Carr, 1972). In addition, the "Portuguese lilt" or intonation of sentences from Madeira and the Azores may have contributed to Hawaii's pidgin dialect. The position of Portuguese living on the plantation as middle man between English-speaking *haole* and the Oriental workers may have contributed to such linguistic blending. Although English was used for communication, the syntax or phraseology used was often adopted from the Portuguese grammatical style. *

Assimilation

When the initial immigration process came to an end, the Portuguese began the task of assimilation. The degree to which assimilation has taken place is a controversial subject. What is generally agreed is that the Portuguese made every effort to completely assimilate into Hawaii's society. They sought citizenship as soon as they were eligible. Laws favoring Caucasians for citizenship assisted in this

---

*Herbert Carlos, President, Hawaii Council on Portuguese Heritage, personal communication, 1979.

respect. Assimilation for the Portuguese, however, was not only a political but also a social process. The Portuguese were often subjected to stereotypes and derogatory ethnic jokes. The haole might laugh at the propensity of the Portuguese for talk and repeat the cliche "Telephone, telegraph, teleportuguese."

Fuchs observed, "In Hawaii the inner Haole elite determined policy, the Scotch managed, and the Portuguese supervised" (Fuchs, 1961). As time went on, however, the Portuguese on the plantation never advanced past the *luna* ("foreman") or supervisory status, and by 1915 no Portuguese had yet been appointed as head overseer. This discrimination fueled an exodus of Portuguese from the plantations into the towns, where most became skilled workers or went into business independently. No matter how hard the Portuguese tried to identify with the haoles, they were not accepted as such. By 1940 they were still not accepted as Caucasians and in fact began to slip behind the Orientals in income and occupational prestige. This increased the pressures on the Portuguese to fully assimilate into the Caucasian group (Fuchs, 1961).

The Portuguese reaction was twofold. A large number of Portuguese women solved the problem of ethnic identity by marrying haole men; between 1912 and 1934, at least 20 percent of the Portuguese women did so. Substantial numbers of Portuguese girls married part-Hawaiians too, thus removing themselves further from Caucasian identity and perpetuating the problem of nonacceptance of the Portuguese as haoles. The Portuguese attempt to assimilate, in view of the surrounding discrimination, was not unrecognized. An observer in 1940 summarized the problem at that time:

> Since they first came to the Islands, the Portuguese have improved their economic status tremendously. . . . Also, the Portuguese are property owners and home owners and take great pride in the cleanliness of their homes. . . . Today, the Portuguese are a highly literate group. . . . They want to be allowed to belong to American clubs and societies, and to progress in business to the level indicated by individual ability, rather than by a "haole" established level beyond which a Portuguese is not permitted to rise. . . . The "haole" group is no longer justified in its prejudicial practices toward the Portuguese. Assuming that such practices ever were justifiable, their continuance in recent years has apparently been due to two factors on the part of the "haole" group: cultural lag, and the desire to keep the Portuguese competition out of the higher labor

brackets. It appears very likely that the "haole" group has used the former low status of the Portuguese as a tool and a justification to keep them out of active economic rivalry. (Estep, 1941)

Government reaction to this discrimination was prompted by the Portuguese themselves, who demanded recognition as Caucasians in official census data. In 1940 the Portuguese were officially recognized by census enumeration as Caucasian. The prejudicial "other Caucasians" classification was eliminated. As a result, in official documents the Portuguese became an indistinguishable part of the Caucasian group. This meant that, to some extent at least, official discrimination against the Portuguese was reduced. From 1940 on, Portuguese groups and the remaining beneficial societies were disbanded. By 1954 external evidence that the Portuguese still constituted a separate immigrant group was negligible.

Beyond Assimilation

A sociologist observer who attended a Portuguese folk-dance festival in 1954 noted that speeches given emphasized the importance of preserving Portuguese culture and the significance of being Portuguese. This marked a new trend among the Portuguese toward the revival of their ethnic culture and toward the organization of persons of Portuguese ancestry into a separate ethnic group, apart from the dominant Caucasians. While acknowledging past discrimination toward the Portuguese, it was pointed out that new feelings of ethnic pride were beginning to appear. In her words:

> According to those sponsors (of the folk dance groups), they began to feel that the Portuguese had something worthwhile to show to other peoples. As they repeated their experiences of public display of their folk dancing, they realized the public's appreciation of the Portuguese culture instead of encountering contempt. Such experience helped them to re-evaluate their folk culture. Also, as they displayed their folk dances . . . they became more willing to compare themselves with the Orientals on an equal basis. . . . Their comparison of themselves with the Orientals no longer makes them feel involved with a lower social or economic class. (Kimura, 1955)

The year 1978 represented a symbolic turning point for the Portuguese in Hawaii. In that year, the centennial celebration of the arrival of the first immigrant ship to Hawaii was celebrated. The Portuguese cultural revival which had begun in the mid-1950s reached its full fruition and the year was marked with great pride over numerous cultural events. Hence, one hundred years after the arrival of the first ship of immigrants to Hawaii, after slow and painful attempted assimilation from plantation life into the Hawaiian lifestyle, after subsequent assimilation by fiat in 1940, and after abandonment of the European culture they had brought with them, the Portuguese realized that their culture was worth retaining. They had reached a state where it was no longer an embarrassment to be Portuguese.

The removal of assimilation pressures has enabled the Portuguese to more fully participate in the expanding Hawaiian economy and lifestyle. Presently, Portuguese in Hawaii are represented in all areas of business. Many are employed in management in larger corporations, or are owners of small businesses. A large number of Portuguese are skilled craftsmen and mechanics. In addition, there have been numerous prominent Portuguese politicians and lawyers. The relative lack of Portuguese in medicine is a curious fact. There have been only a few Portuguese physicians in Hawaii, and the presence of a medical school at the University of Hawaii has not yet alleviated this underrepresentation. With two-thousand practicing physicians in the state, a fair representation would be about 5 percent, or one hundred Portuguese physicians, but there are only two currently in practice. The reasons for this underrepresentation are not clear.

Mental Health

There are very few studies available that describe the Portuguese as a separate group in Hawaii because separate statistics have not been available for this group since 1940. In a study during the 1960s of 210 patients at the Hawaii State Hospital, a number of characteristics were noted among patients who identified themselves as Portuguese that distinguished them from other ethnic groups. They were found to be older, predominantly Roman Catholic, more often married and living with a spouse. They had the highest average length of stay in the hospital, their educational level was the lowest, but their social class was second to the highest. The Katz Adjustment Scale ratings described them as more helpless and suspicious than they had been as nonpatients (Katz, 1963). Relatives described them as less belligerent and verbally expansive. This, however, differed from the clinicians' observations in which they were rated high in hostility or belligerence. The reasons for this discrepancy between relatives' observations and clinicians' observations is not apparent. It may be due to different cultural concepts about emotional experiences, or different interpretations of the affect associated with these emotions.

A study during the period 1972 to 1976 at Queen's Hospital on psychosomatic disorders showed some differences between Portuguese and other groups in this class of disorders. Portuguese accounted for approximately 4 percent of all admissions to Queen's Hospital. This group of patients represented 7 percent of myocardial infarctions, 9 percent of cases of angina pectoris, and 10 percent of the cases diagnosed as obesity. Whether this implies a higher incidence of these disorders in the Portuguese population or conversely indicates that Portuguese patients do not come to the hospital as often for other types of illnesses as they do for these types of problems remains unclear (Tseng, 1977).

My personal observations and clinical impressions of the Portuguese suggest that there is no significant difference in the frequency or severity of major psychiatric disorders such as schizophrenia, affective disorders, organic mental disorders including retardation, and drug abuse disorders between the Portuguese and other ethnic groups. Quantification of these impressions remains to be done, but the success of this approach will be contingent upon the willingness of the Portuguese patients to identify themselves as such, and upon the hospitals and state health department to attempt to keep more accurate demographic data on the Portuguese in Hawaii. Unfortunately, many of the people taking personal data for admission are often unaware of the possibility that a patient may be Portuguese. Failing to ask the right questions, they may enter erroneous data, resulting in great difficulties for the researcher. Proper questioning by therapists will often lead to unexpected responses and, occasionally, new insights into therapy with the patient. In addition, the therapist should be mindful of the fact that not all Portuguese patients will want to be identified as such and will prefer to be regarded as Caucasian. The Portuguese in Hawaii today sometimes have mixed feelings about their heritage, and the issue of ethnic background may be a sensitive one for some patients.

Summary

In discussing the Portuguese in Hawaii, I have avoided cultural stereotypes, as I feel these are not applicable today. Rather, I have attempted to delineate, through the history of this group in Hawaii, the forces that played a prominent role in shaping the Portuguese community until the present. The most striking fact about this group today is that it stands out least as a separate group. There are few distinguishing characteristics to which one can point and say, "That is typical." In the older generations there were found the attitudes and beliefs discussed earlier in the chapter. The younger generation has lost most of the cultural patterns brought here from Europe. There are now modified values and problems which emerged in the development of this group in Hawaii. That the history of the Portuguese is dynamic and still evolving is apparent from the cultural revival that has occurred and accelerated in recent years.

References

Cabral, Elma T. The romance of Rosa Das Vacas. *Paradise of the Pacific*, 1948, 60: 67–100.

Carr, Elizabeth Ball. *Da kine talk: From pidgin to standard English in Hawaii.* Honolulu: University Press of Hawaii, 1972.

Estep, Gerald A. Social placement of the Portuguese in Hawaii as indicated by factors in assimilation. M.A. thesis, University of Southern California, 1941. Summarized in Felix and Senecal, *The Portuguese in Hawaii.*

Felix, John H., and Senecal, Peter F. *The Portuguese in Hawaii: Centennial edition.* Honolulu: published by authors, 1978.

Fuchs, Lawrence H. *Hawaii pono: A social history.* New York: Harcourt, Brace and World, 1961.

Jose, Dorothy. A Portuguese family in Hawaii. *Social Process in Hawaii,* 1937, 3: 70–75.

Jubilee of San Antonio Society 1877-1927. Honolulu: San Antonio Society, 1926.

Katz, Martin M., and Lyenly, Samuel B. Methods of measuring adjustment and social behavior in the community. *Psychological Reports,* 1963, 13:503–535.

Kimura, Yukiko. A sociological note on the preservation of the Portuguese folk dance. *Social Process in Hawaii,* 1955, 19:45–50.

Kuykendall, Ralph S. *The Hawaiian kingdom: The Kalakaua dynasty* (Vol. 3). Honolulu: University Press of Hawaii, 1967.

Sasaki, Hideko. The life history of a Portuguese immigrant. *Social Process in Hawaii,* 1935, 1:26–31.

Thrum, Thomas G. *Thrum's Hawaiian almanac and annual* (1879, 1881, 1882, 1883). Honolulu: Honolulu Press Publishing Company.

Tseng, Wen-Shing, and Streltzer, Jon. Psychosomatic disorders in the multi-ethnic society of Hawaii. In *Proceedings of the 4th Congress of International Colleges of Psychosomatic Medicine.* Kyoto, Japan: 1977.

CHAPTER 7

The Okinawans

William P. Lebra

Introduction

At the present time persons of Okinawan ancestry make up approximately 5 percent of the civilian population in Hawaii. They were the last major group to migrate to Hawaii from Japan. When the first of their numbers arrived in early 1900, the Japanese already comprised 40 percent of the population. As with their fellow countrymen, they mostly came from small, overcrowded, and impoverished farms and possessed a modicum of formal education, but they differed markedly from other Japanese nationals in terms of language, behavior, dress, and diet, which served to set them apart and at the bottom of the local Japanese hierarchy. Their experience in Hawaii, until quite recently, has been that of a "minority within a minority" (Ikeda, Ball, and Yamamura, 1962). There were, of course, other regional divisions and schisms among the Japanese, but the major cleavage in Hawaii Japanese society was between the Naichijin ("Homeland people") and the Okinawa-kenjin ("Okinawa Prefecture people") or Uchinanchu.

Although the two groups may have appeared nearly indistinguishable to outsiders, to the Japanese the Okinawans were shorter in stature, wider eyed, somewhat darker skinned, and more hirsute. Moreover, prior to their encounter in Hawaii, the Okinawan and Japanese had had relatively little firsthand contact with one another; consequently, even minor cultural differences loomed large. For example, Okinawan women were customarily tattooed on the backs of their fingers, hands, and arms, whereas tattooing practices were associated with criminal and outcast elements by the Japanese. Okinawan speech was wholly unintelligible to Japanese ears, as distinct as French from Italian. The cut, pattern, and styling of the kimono were different in each group; even the manner of tying the sash was different. According to one account, because of differences in the fashioning of their sandals, Okinawans tended to walk with toes pointed outward, while that of the Naichijin pointed inward. Like the southern Chinese and Filipinos, the Okinawans were pig raisers, and lard was an indispensable item in cooking. Not only was their food considered greasy by Japanese standards, but the image of the Okinawans collecting garbage for pig feed came to be readily conjured up by the pejorative epithet *Okinawa-ken ken buta kau kau,* "Okinawans *kau kau* (Hawaiian pidgin for "eat") pigs." On the plantations Okinawans were termed "Japan Pake" (Hawaiian for "Chinese"), suggesting that those in close association with the two groups were well aware of their differences. Commonly, the Okinawans and the mainland Japanese occupied separate settlements apart from one another; thus, on Kohala Plantation the Japanese lived in Shimokawa, the Okinawans in Shimabukuro; on Hoea Plantation Japanese resided in the main settlement, the Okinawans at Camp 9; and so forth.

Traditional Culture of the Okinawans

The distinctiveness of Okinawans from other Japanese can be partly understood in terms of geography. Lying 600 km southwest of Kyushu, the southernmost of the four main islands of Japan, Okinawa was never a part of the mainstream of Japanese culture; nor does it represent, by any anthropological standards, a merely isolated or provincial development of Japanese culture. Rather, there is ample evidence of direct cultural sharing with China, Korea, and aboriginal Taiwan, as well as with Japan.

For five hundred years Okinawa was a nominal tributary of China, sending students to study in Peking and incorporating many aspects of Chinese culture. And for two hundred sixty years Okinawa was tributary to the Satsuma Daimiate in southern Japan. The dual cultural and political relationships with these large neighbors were evidently well recognized, for a Japanese observer early in the seventeenth century noted that there was then a saying among the old people, "Think of China as mother and Japan as father."

Okinawa long enjoyed a political existence apart from Japan, which permitted the development of distinct values and modes of civil life. Pacificism appears to have been a deeply embedded trait. Nineteenth-century Western visitors repeatedly commented on the kind and gentle character of the people. Their dislike of violence found expression in oft repeated sayings: "When anger rises, hold hands down," and "When hands rise, hold anger down." Some would even contend that the Okinawan version of karate lacks an aggressive stance. Most decidedly the incidence of homicide and suicide were significantly below the national average for Japan prior to World War II. And it should be particularly noted that the Japanese romanticization of suicide to the point of investing the act with honor was decidedly alien to traditional Okinawan thinking. Not surprisingly, therefore, more than a few of the migrants to Hawaii were motivated, at least in part, by a desire to evade military service.

Okinawa was incorporated into the Japanese state as one of the home prefectures, not a colonial territory, but when the first migrants departed for Hawaii in 1899, only twenty years had elapsed since the departure of their king. It was the land reform of 1899–1903, which ended the communal system of tenure and community tax payment, that brought about the first major alterations of rural life. Thereafter the Japanese government steadily sought to integrate Okinawans more fully into the national society.

The Okinawan and Japanese languages, though related, are not mutually intelligible, yet the rather demeaning term *hōgen* ("dialect" or "brogue") is applied by Japanese, scholars and laymen alike, in referring to the Okinawan language. In the establishment of a Japanese public school system and in the spread of universal education, Okinawa was behind the nation as a whole. Japanese was the second language for much of rural Okinawa until well after World War II. Although later migrants to Hawaii included some well-educated persons—physicians, teachers, priests, and editors—a majority of those migrating from the rural areas were simply not articulate in Japanese. As of 1900, when migration commenced, 32 percent of the primary-school-age boys and 65 percent of the girls were not attending school (Ryukyu Government, 1966). While these figures had dropped to 6 percent and 17 percent respectively by 1905, even then the total period of schooling was often limited to only three or four years; moreover, attendance was not strictly enforced.

Girls generally attended for even briefer time spans and received a more inferior education than the boys. Prior to World War II (by which time the period of compulsory education had reached six years) limited opportunities for education beyond primary school were available in the larger towns and cities. While there were no restrictions on advanced education for country children, the odds favored the urban children and/or those of more affluent families. According to one account, Okinawan draftees frequently had a difficult time in military service because of a language handicap (Kinjo, 1974).

The intention here is to note that the average migrant from Okinawa to Hawaii learned Japanese language and Japanese culture in Hawaii. It was related by one of the migrants in the first group from Okinawa that only three or four could communicate in Japanese (Yamazato, 1960) and that the services of interpreters were required while shopping in Yokohama enroute to Hawaii. By way of contrast, the migrant from Hiroshima Prefecture or Yamaguchi Prefecture had to learn only sufficient pidgin (Hawaiian English) to survive in his employment, whereas the Okinawan carried the extra burden of having to learn pidgin for his employment and Japanese for life among his compatriots. Undoubtedly, this linguistic handicap contributed significantly to compounding the "minority within a minority" problem.

The traditional Okinawan village was an inbred, tightly knit community until well into this century. Each formed a production unit for agricultural foodstuffs, a tax unit, a religious collectivity, an endogamous unit for marriage, and for many tasks a collective work force. Restrictions on marriage and mobility (by decree or sentiment), as well as the spatial separation of villages, ensured social isolation and homogeneity; in fact, this was so marked in some villages that as late as the 1950s minor differences in dialect were detectable between neighboring communities.

There was a deep attachment of Okinawans for their native place, and this was reflected in the commonly used terms *shima chōrē* or *kuni chōrē* ("village sibling," "village brotherhood," or "siblinghood") applied in reference to all others in the community, kinsmen and neighbors, men and women alike. Although Okinawan society was marked by rank hierarchies, within the *shima chōrē* relationships were idealized as essentially egalitarian.

The village itself was viewed as a collectivity of families; thus, the basic unit of reference within the community was the family-household, not the individual. Commonly, a person was identified by house name (family names or surnames are relatively new) and kin status within that house. The "pivotal position" (Glacken, 1955) was occupied by the first son, the only legitimate lifetime occupant of the house, all others married in or out. Because brothers were not supposed to live under the same roof after marriage, younger sons moved out and established branch houses, but ritual ties with their house of origin were retained during their lifetimes and by successive generations of direct descendants in their first-son line. Sisters and daughters also married out, joining their husbands' households. An eldest son carried the responsibility for the ancestral altar, care of the parents in old age, and perpetuation of the house, principally through providing a male successor.

Among the villagers considerable freedom was accorded young adults of both sexes in mate selection; this was institutionalized in the form of *moo-ashibii* (literally "playing in the hills," an evening get-together of unmarried young people). When a couple found each other to their liking, they became *yung nu miitu* ("nighttime couple"), which gave the young man sleeping rights at the girl's house in return for assisting her father in farm work. If the couple became devoted, or more importantly, if a child was born, marriage resulted; if not, they were both free to form new attachments without stigma. This system was, of course, limited by the rule of endogamy to unmarried villagers.

Okinawan society was characterized by a collectivity focus—the basic unit of reference was the family, not the individual; individualism was de-emphasized and aggressive pursuit of self-interest deplored. Children were socialized for mutual interdependence, and ideally people were expected to live up to their responsibilities and to honor obligations. Those who were more highly endowed (by intelligence, strength, or position) might be expected to assume leadership and responsibility, which did not confer the privilege of exploiting others for personal advantage, but rather made it incumbent upon them to offer nurturance to those weaker and/or less able.

To the outside observer, especially from Western culture, the Okinawan propensity for group activity and group identification may seem gregarious to the point of compulsiveness. Group action in task accomplishment, however, seems to have been the preferred mode and cooperation a highly esteemed value.

When cooperation is an esteemed value, compromise is a necessary corollary. To form and sustain effective cooperative work relationships, to foster and maintain harmony within the collectivity, and to minimize potential conflict in the group, interpersonal differences are best muted and individual proclivities set aside or repressed. In return the collectivity provides an identity for the ego and the security of its support.

The observance of propriety, cooperation, compromise, deemphasis of the individual in preference for group togetherness, and self-sacrifice for the collectivity were some of the principal features constituting the Okinawan ethos at the beginning of this century. In addition, the dislike of violence and aggression, the aversion to things military, and the low incidence of suicide and homicide were characteristic of the Okinawan group. Drunkenness was also without violence or overt aggression, and sexuality was equated with naturalism. Moderation and reasonableness, adjuncts of cooperation and compromise, were prized in interpersonal relationships. In essence, there was an absence of absolutes—human nature was viewed as inherently comprised of good and bad, and it was society's function to curb the latter. Even in crime, victim as well as aggressor was viewed as sharing some measure of fault.

In religious life there was believed to be a reciprocity between man and the spirit world; in return for ritual supplications by the priestesses on the behalf of the collectivity, the ancestral spirits and *kami* spirits were expected to assure the good harvest, health, and well-being of all. Failure to provide or sustain ritual could result in withdrawal of their support leading to misfortune and unhappiness. Yet, in essence, the orientation was this-worldly. When things went wrong, especially if unexplainable by usual rational means, then supernatural explanation was assuredly sought, primarily by resorting to the shaman, but essentially the basic concern was man and the ordering of human relationships, anthropocentric and pragmatic (Lebra, 1966).

The Okinawan migrants transplanted to Hawaii undoubtedly carried some traits and values at variance with those of the adopted society, but they assiduously applied their capacity for hard work, frugality, and endurance to the tasks at hand. Some of the more repressive features of the old society which limited individual initiative and ability were cast aside, but other aspects, such as their talent for organizing social and work groups for the common good were set up, refashioned, and made useful instruments in effecting their adjustment, achievement, and success in Hawaii.

Okinawan Migration to Hawaii

The first group of migrants from Okinawa, twenty-six men who arrived in Honolulu on 16 January 1900, was sent to Ewa Plantation. Later in June of that same year the Organic Act took effect, implementing the laws and the Constitution of the United States and theoretically freeing the migrants to change their employers and means of employment. At the time these men arrived there were more than sixty thousand Japanese in Hawaii, comprising almost 40 percent of the total population. Quite likely, the Okinawan arrival scarcely stirred a ripple on the local scene, but it may be assumed that their status was low in the pecking order of the by then well-established Japanese community.

The men in these first two groups (a second group of thirty-five arrived in 1903) ranged in age from twenty-one to thirty-eight years (Ishikawa, 1976, 1977). Most were from farm villages. Apparently, most were married and had left their wives and children behind. One thirty-one-year-old migrant, whose case may be somewhat atypical, left a pregnant wife at the time of his departure, and it was not until 1918 that he was reunited with her and the grown son.

By 1911, more than ten thousand migrants had arrived. At first, all of the migrants were men, but in 1905 fifty-two women were included and thereafter they came nearly every year until World War II. Although some of the earliest arrivals, as in the case cited above, waited years before being joined by a wife or *yobiyose* ("person summoned"), in most instances it seems that the average man waited a shorter period of time than did the earlier arriving Japanese or the later arriving Filipinos.

A common pattern was for a man to labor a number of years, accumulating savings, and then with the help of the *mūyē* or *tanomoshi* (rotating credit group) send for his wife and children. Bachelors followed a similar path, saving, joining a *tanomoshi,* and then having his family or friends back home arrange for a suitable bride. Not uncommonly, after the preliminary negotiations had been completed, the bride-to-be took up residence with the man's parents and siblings, thereby becoming familiar with her in-laws and their lifestyle before leaving Okinawa to join her spouse. (Often the woman's name was entered into the family registry and they were officially married before she arrived in Hawaii, though Hawaii authorities for a long time enforced a dockside ceremony.) Very often, the bride was selected from the same village or local district *(son)*. Apparently, there was no lack of takers, and in some instances young women from proper, but impoverished, gentry families used this avenue for escaping an unwelcome arranged marriage in Okinawa.

The year 1907 was important for all Japanese in Hawaii, for it marked the implementation of the Gentlemen's Agreement which, in essence, precluded Japanese emigrating from Hawaii to the mainland United States or to adjacent Canada and Mexico. The higher wages and more attractive working conditions on the mainland had siphoned off large numbers of Japanese from the plantations. But, seemingly, the mainland had not held quite as much attraction for Okinawans as for other Japanese. For one thing, the climates and flora of Hawaii and Okinawa have more in common with each other than with Japan; Hawaii thereby provided more of a look of home for the Okinawans. Moreover, cane sugar, which is not grown in Japan proper, was long a familiar crop to Okinawan farmers, and their particular skills and knowledge in this respect stood them well not only on the plantations, but also later when they left and took up farming of cane by contract. While not a few of the Okinawans cherished the dream of accumulating wealth in Hawaii and returning home to live in comfort and security within their native villages, to be weighed realistically against this were the pervasive poverty back home, a heavy tax burden, compulsory military service, and a relative lack of opportunity for their children. Most, therefore, sent for their wives or brides and elected to remain in Hawaii.

The Immigration Act of 1924 closed the door on further free entry of Japanese laborers into all of the United States. (Teachers, priests, ministers, students, and the wives and children of permanent residents were not excluded from entering.) During the remainder of the twenties and throughout the period up to World War II, on the average about a hundred per year came to Hawaii. From the time of the China Incident (1936) their numbers began to rise, some of them apparently earlier returnees who now opted for permanent settlement in Hawaii. Approximately twenty-one thousand Okinawans had migrated to Hawaii between 1900 and 1938 (Ishikawa, 1974).

Following World War II, Okinawa and the Ryukyuan Islands to

the south, principally the Miyako and Yaeyama groups, were detached from Japan. These islands were placed under the direct control of a US military administration which lasted until reversion in 1972. Enormous military bases, nurtured by the Korean and Vietnam Wars, were constructed and maintained. Thus, for more than thirty years after World War II thousands of American soldiers, as well as civilian employees of the military and their respective families, have been stationed on Okinawa. In addition, a number of American businesses and their employees moved there to service the bases and their personnel. A disproportionately large number of men and women from Hawaii saw service or found employment there, in part because of Japanese language skills and also simply because of proximity and opportunity. Not a few of the men have taken Okinawan wives. While the majority of these Okinawan women married Americans of Naichi Japanese and Okinawan ancestry, there were also marriages into other ethnic groups found in Hawaii—Chinese, Korean, Filipino, Hawaiian, and Caucasian. Commonly they have been referred to as "war brides," now an outdated term and scarcely appropriate.

These new migrants to Hawaii in the post–World War II period offer some striking contrasts with the prewar immigrants. They represent, of course, an entirely new generation with different perspectives. As the period of compulsory schooling was increased to nine years (through junior high school) in postwar Okinawa and because high schools were made available in some rural areas (with about 50 percent attending), on the average they are a more educated group. Because the school system, even under the Americans, remained Japanese, they are probably much more assimilated in the direction of Japanese culture than were the majority of those who migrated between 1900 and 1924.

The present number of Okinawans in Hawaii is a figure in need of clarification; unfortunately, the salient features of that population are somewhat obscure and likely to remain so. From the viewpoint of the federal government and the state (territorial) government, the Okinawans have been perceived as Japanese nationals, little different from those migrating from other prefectures. Thus, from the official American perspective there have been no valid reasons to establish separate categories for the Japanese prefectures, save for the time period of 1945 to 1972 when Okinawa was detached from Japan and under the direct administration of the US Army military government. From the Japanese side, the records are more detailed and useful to our purposes; yet, these too become progressively less reliable after World War II as successive American-born generations shed their Japanese identity and merge with the larger population.

Given the various estimates of the Okinawan population in Hawaii, we emerge with a percentage range of 4.5 to 7.4. Perhaps an average of 5 percent might be accepted as a conservative figure.

The Okinawans in Hawaii

Prior to World War II, the Territory of Hawaii was comprised of eighty-nine communities—cities, towns, and villages—a little more than half of which were plantations. In these latter settlements there was usually, in addition to the company buildings, a core consisting of a post office, store(s), barbershop, poolhall, gas station, and so forth. The various ethnic groups were segregated into camps or neighborhoods, and the Japanese areas were marked by separate family housing units, the inevitable community bathhouse, Buddhist temple (or Shinto shrine), and a language school (the latter sometimes a part of the temple). As noted before, the Japanese and Okinawans were often grouped in separate settlement areas.

Although there were some exceptions among the later arrivals (teachers, physicians, priests, students, housewives, and children), the overwhelming majority of pre-1924 migrants commenced their work careers on plantations. Despite abolition by the Organic Act of the binding three- to five-year contracts, theirs was not an easy life. As of 1900 an adult male could expect to receive $15 per month, perhaps as much as $20, for working twenty-six days. Field hands labored for ten hours, from 6 AM to 4 or 4:30 PM; and indoors, factory workers put in twelve hours. Housing and transportation (to and from the fields) were provided by the employer. Women received approximately $5 less than the men for the same number of hours. Despite a slow rise in wages up to World War II, as late as 1920 the average plantation wage was only $24 per month.

Given the low wage rates, the economic achievements of the migrants are all the more impressive. From their meager income they accumulated savings, much of which was sent back to Okinawa and/or invested in a *tanomoshi* so as to bring over wives, brides, and other family members. A not atypical example was an $18 income from which $7.85 was allocated for monthly expenses—food, laundry, bath, and tobacco (Miyagi, 1951). As much as $10 per month could thus be set aside for the *tanomoshi* (Asato et al., 1955) or sent home. During 1900, the Okinawans' first year in Hawaii, when they numbered twenty-six, approximately $240 in savings was sent back to Okinawa. But by 1910 the amount sent in that year surpassed more than a quarter of a million dollars (Ishikawa, 1977). Obviously, this was accomplished only by the exercise of great diligence and frugality.

In order to obtain additional income, some of the more energetic worked extra shifts, putting in the equivalent of as much as forty days per month (Asato et al., 1955). Other sources of income could be provided by operating a bath, barbering, cooking and feeding, gardening and selling produce, laundering, and sewing and tailoring. These latter tasks were largely assumed by the women, but in the early days of the migration, they were carried out by men. Often the last man to arrive ("new man") was given the task of cooking and/or laundering by the other bachelors; so, the arrival of a wife often provided a rise in status, at least for the husband. Women also worked in the fields and mills, but the limitations of time placed on them by pregnancies and the demands of small children frequently forced them to concentrate on these other tasks; unless physically ill, however, a woman's labor efforts were equal to those of the man.

Through savings (kept in cans buried under the house) and *tanomoshi* funding, they gradually extricated themselves from plantation labor and pursued more rewarding activities. But, as has been pointed out, the Okinawans tended to select occupations for which they had special skills—for example, hog raising or sugar farming—or for which they could perceive some clearly advantageous opportunity. In other words, they were not inclined to go beyond their limits or indulge in recklessly speculative pursuits (Ishikawa, 1977). So, initially, many of them moved into contract farming, leasing acreage from the plantation and independently raising sugar, which was sold to the lessor on harvesting.

Most Okinawan businesses in Hawaii seem to owe their initial start to *tanomoshi* funding (Miyagi, 1951). Moreover, many of these were often interrelated in exchange networks; thus, the farms, piggeries, hatcheries, and dairy herds supplied the food processors, wholesalers, retailers (groceries, supermarkets, and restaurants), which in turn could send back their wastes to the pig farms. Within these networks and establishments, ties of family (and clan) as well as place of origin in Okinawa, figured importantly in uniting producer and distributor, workers and employers.

A notable characteristic of the Okinawans in Hawaii has been their propensity to organize into groups which retain a strong solidarity and persistence through time. Not surprisingly, soon after their arrival in Hawaii, they commenced to organize themselves into clubs and associations based on their places of origin; these are most commonly *son-jin-kai* ("district peoples' association") and are prefixed by the district name: for example, Kin-son-jin-kai. As a *son* may encompass, on the average, about twelve separate villages, the larger ones are often subdivided into smaller associations, or *aza-jin-kai* ("village peoples' association") organized on a single community basis.

Originally, these various *jin-kai* provided mutual assistance in time of crises (accident or injury, sickness, death) and helped in obtaining employment and raising money (organizing a *tanomoshi*). Gradually, as their economic lot improved, the *son-jin-kai* (and similar groups) added social and recreational features, including weddings, sporting events, New Year's parties, and picnics. Most enthusiastically supported by the first generation, these groups have persisted and now involve second and third generations as well.

In those instances where there were not enough people from a given area to form a viable association, two or more small groups would form a "friendship association" *(dōshi-kai)*. In the outlying areas where population concentrations were light, Okinawan identity provided the single organizing principle. This also occurred in the city among those of the second generation with similar interests.

The cultural and linguistic differences separating Okinawan and Naichi were referred to early in this chapter. An article appearing in *Ryukyu Shimpo,* 1 March 1906, reported that the Okinawans were not getting along well in Hawaii with Japanese from other prefectures. A common complaint of the Okinawans on the plantation, as last comers, was that the Hiroshima and Yamaguchi people appropriated the better jobs and left the dirty, undesirable jobs for them (Taira, 1953). According to one informant, however, the trouble started on the boat. Before leaving Japan, two groups formed and remained apart throughout the voyage. Because so many migrants could not speak standard Japanese (due to their lack of communication skills), they stayed close together and did not mix with the others. Most Japanese thought of Okinawans as a different race. Another factor was the high fertility rate of the Okinawans, who had larger families compared to those of other Japanese, who despised them for this. "Okinawa, Okinawa" was contemptuously applied to anything bad, which stung their feelings and left them feeling desolate (Miyagi, 1951).

The insults, invective, and unflattering stereotypes (real and imagined) used by both groups have been amply documented in various writings by Okinawans and others (Toyama and Ikeda, 1950). Needless to say, these were deeply wounding to the smaller group, who largely bore them in silence, for there was no one to turn to but each other. And, of course, the tightening of their ranks and increased mutual support only served to strengthen the stereotypic charge that "they always stick together." Because the Okinawans were subjects of discrimination, their own sense of ethnic consciousness is said to have developed, and both *issei* and *nisei* tended to have inferiority complexes (Kohatsu, 1951).

Children were expected to attend Japanese schools, and for the early years of primary school this was nearly universal among the American-born second generation, Naichi and Okinawan alike. Little effort appears to have been devoted to perpetuation of the Okinawan language among the second generation, many of whom became bilingual in Japanese and English. Some reported their parents used primarily pidgin mixed with Japanese in speaking to them and reserved Okinawan for their "secret" language, or for use with age mates from back home. The third generation, mostly born after World War II, are predominantly monolingual in English. Except for family names, they are nearly indistinguishable from others of Asian extraction in Hawaiian society. Although some of the first and second generation altered their names to acquire a more Japanese sound, many retain their Okinawan sound—Agena, Arakaki, Higa, Ige, Iha, Goya, Matayoshi, Oshiro, Sakima, Shimabuku, Shiroma (Gusukuma), Tamanaha, Tamashiro, Tengan, and Yogi being typical examples.

World War II and its aftermath witnessed the beginning of a dramatic change in the Okinawan-Naichi relationship. At the outset, the attack on Pearl Harbor brought an abrupt and lasting termination of *issei* dominance in local Japanese society. Not only had the *nisei* come of age to assume their new role, they were also the products of the American public school system and, consequently, had been exposed to a more democratic view of ethnicity than had their parents. Okinawans and Naichi had come to know one another in the schools and commonly saw military service together during the war. Their beliefs and values gradually gained ascendency, while those of the *issei* were looked down upon as backward and discrediting.

During World War II most of the Okinawan occupations and businesses flourished. The once disdainfully regarded pig farmer who had collected garbage from restaurants and hotels was now viewed as working in a vital war industry, and his sons (and most others in Hawaii in food production, processing, and even sales) could be deferred from service for the important task of providing food for victory. Moreover, unlike some of the Naichi, the Okinawan leaders were not interned, nor were they able to send their money to Okinawa; so, as their savings accumulated, they invested in other businesses and property, further increasing their prosperity.

In postwar Hawaii, it is sometimes said that "there are no poor Okinawans." While that statement may be somewhat exaggerated, it nonetheless reflects a common stereotypic view that the Okinawans rose significantly in economic status after the war. Many had become rich; wedding, birthday, and the special sixtieth birthday observances became extravagant and conspicuous. It is estimated that perhaps two million dollars had been spent on such events in the years 1949–1950 (Wakukawa, 1951). Apparently, these escalated to the point where the United Okinawan Association publicly requested that people cooperate in curbing extravagance. The effectiveness of this request remains a matter of conjecture; however, it is readily apparent that wealth was not recklessly squandered and that considerable expenditures were also devoted to the enhancement of matters relating to education, welfare, and the arts.

The history of the Okinawans in Hawaii has been divided into three time periods, each characterized by a predominant theme or activity: 1900–1920, migration; 1920–1940, family building; and 1940–1950, economic expansion (Wakukawa, 1951). To these could be added a fourth—1950–1970, cultural florescence. One informant, born and raised in Hawaii, returned home in the early sixties after an absence of over a decade. His mother, in briefing him on events during the interim, remarked that the Okinawans had really come out for their culture, referring to the flurry of activity in music, dance, and the arts presented through public performances, radio, newspaper, and other media.

Prior to World War II there had been neither the money nor the time for active pursuit of cultural matters, but with the new affluence, *issei* retirement, and the ascendency of the *nisei* to power in the community, schools devoted to Okinawan dance and music *(koto* and *shamisen)* emerged and flourished. In September 1947 the first regular radio programming of Okinawan music in Hawaii commenced; by 1955 there was a regular exchange of programs with the Ryukyu Broadcasting System in Okinawa. So extensive were the Okinawa activities in local programming that rumors circulated in the Japanese community that the Okinawans were about to establish their own station. In addition to the musical programs, there were poetry presentations, and during 1962 a series of programs lasting more than two hundred hours covered Ryukyuan history and folklore (Oyakawa, 1974).

These important events for the community were matched by *nisei* achievements in higher education, science, the professions (law, dentistry, and medicine), business and politics (the state legislature in 1962 contained twelve persons of Okinawan ancestry). Indicative of the recognition of Okinawans in Hawaii was the establishment of Honolulu and Naha as sister cities in 1960, as well as Hilo and Naze. Symbolic of the change and of the close ties with the homeland was the 1966 election of former plantation worker and American college graduate, Seiho Matsuoka, as governor of Okinawa.

In a sensitively written account, Professor Masanori Higa (1972) describes the formal symbolization of Okinawan-Naichi rapprochement. The event occurred on 14 May 1972 at a party which ostensibly was held to observe the formal reversion of Okinawa from US military administration to Japan occurring on that date, but Higa demonstrates that the real significance was social and psychological, not political. Following World War II things had changed in Hawaii; prejudice diminished, intermarriage occurred, Okinawans obtained leadership in organizations such as the Hawaii Japanese Ancestry United Association, and a new generation of Japanese learned to enjoy pork. Many Japanese had come to regret the earlier discrimination; yet there was no way to make up easily. The Okinawan leadership, therefore, decided on this party as a means of clarifying their status vis-à-vis the Naichi, to start a new life as equals to other Japanese. In addition to state leaders in government, politics, education, and business, the Japanese consul general and many Hawaii Japanese organization heads were invited. Not more than eight hundred were expected to attend, but more than twelve hundred showed up. Formally, the party observed the political reunification of Okinawa and Japan, but locally it signified "burying the hatchet" and the unity of Naichi and Uchinanchu. Higa concludes that third and fourth generation Okinawan Americans know little of the bitter prewar conflict between Okinawans and Naichi in Hawaii, that they will live as Americans, and that gradually the terms "Naichi" and "Uchinanchu" will disappear from the local scene.

Mental Health

The favorable impressions made by Okinawan character on nineteenth-century visitors to the prefecture evoked, in particular, comments on the gentle nature, hospitality, and friendliness of the islanders. Statistical records in Japan and Okinawa show low incidences for Japan (1900–1940) of suicide and homicide among the Okinawans; obviously, whatever their frustrations, they seldom sought relief through the extremes of intro- and extrapunitive aggressions. Although standards of health care were below that of Japan's home prefectures, the people were noted for their longevity, and to this day the longest-lived Japanese are to be found in the Ryukyu Islands. Mental hospitals and psychiatric medicine were unknown in pre-World War II Okinawa, but there was also little evidence that mental health problems were regarded as pressing issues by any of the authorities.

Although Okinawa was the scene of some of the most intense combat during World War II, the people, many of whom lost a family member, seemed to exhibit surprising psychological stamina despite the ugliness and sorrow they witnessed. One American psychiatrist found the Okinawans to be a people with little tendency toward psychosis and other mental disorders (Moloney, 1945) and suggested that child-rearing practices of the society are "conducive to a healthy psychological maturation" which enables the individual to cope successfully throughout life with any trauma encountered, however severe.

Detailed research on child rearing in a northern Okinawan village during the 1950s, as part of a comparative study of children in six cultures, provides us with some ethnographic conclusions as well as analytical perspectives (Maretzki, 1966). Okinawan children were raised in an environment that stressed nurturance and disvalued aggression. On a comparative basis, Okinawan mothers appeared highest on personal warmth and lower than average on instability (Minturn and Lambert, 1964). They were the highest in reliance on the use of praise to train children and low on the use of physical punishment. Heavy reliance on praise in socialization apparently encouraged in children an eagerness to assume new responsibilities. Although they were rather moderate in reaction to aggression toward themselves from their children, they did, however, react somewhat more severely to the aggressions of sons than daughters, suggesting to the authors some cross-sex hostility. (It might also be viewed as reflecting the cultural disapproval of overt aggression, and especially on the part of the potentially stronger male.) Fellow villagers were depicted as gentle and sociable; despite some underlying tensions, quarrels were infrequent and fights rare.

In summary, the general impression of Okinawans in their homeland prior to the 1960s is that of a gentle, friendly, hospitable people, averse to crime and to violence in any form. Children of both sexes were cherished and socialized for mutual interdependence. Child training involved liberal use of praise and relatively little physical punishment; children were eager to assume new responsibilities. Both sexes were apparently early socialized to a work ethic. For both sexes there was considerable sexual freedom and marital choice; those born out of wedlock were not stigmatized. There was a strong tendency toward gregariousness, and the group approach to task solution was often favored. Cooperation and compromise were prized; social life was relatively placid. There was little evidence of hypertension and other degenerative disease; senility came late and longevity was (and remains) the highest in the nation. More recent evidence emerging in the last twenty years has presented some contradictions to this perhaps overly idyllic impression.

In contrast to earlier findings, contemporary studies in Okinawa, conducted by psychiatrically trained doctors and their colleagues, have tended to show a high prevalence of psychosis and, in particular, schizophrenia in remote rural communities as well as in urban centers (Hirayasu 1969; Yoshimura 1968). A broad survey in the

1960s suggested that the prevalence of psychosis in Okinawa might run as high as twice the national figure; moreover, schizophrenia appeared to exist in a frequency three and a half times greater than that in Japan (Nakagawa et al., 1969). Although these same figures were still being used by the Mental Health Association as late as 1973, they remain tentative and subject to verification by further research; however, the number of beds for mental patients now exceeds the national average (Shima, 1975).

In Hawaii, among the patients admitted to Queen's Hospital in 1947, the Okinawans had the highest rate, of the ethnic groups in Hawaii, for nonorganic psychosis (with schizophrenia high) (Wedge, 1952). Hawaii Territorial Hospital data (1945–1951) showed the Okinawans also had the highest admission rate for schizophrenia (Ikeda et al, 1962). Both findings are attributed to the minority status of the Okinawans within the Japanese community and to the very severe social discrimination they experienced, which contributed to their feelings of inferiority. Moreover, the Okinawans, when compared with Naichi Japanese, were overrepresented not only in schizophrenia but in virtually all other mental illness categories. But there was the clear indication that within Hawaii's Okinawan population the first generation *(issei)* were overrepresented and the second generation *(nisei)* underrepresented (Ikeda, 1955). Assuming the correctness of the explanation that the migrants suffered extensive prejudice as a minority group, then there may be a predictable decline in successive generations as the *nisei* data suggests (interestingly, the reverse was obtained for the Naichi).

Minimally, it would appear that schizophrenia is a more common diagnostic category among Okinawans than among Naichi Japanese, both in Hawaii and Japan. Okinawans have also been shown to display a significantly greater readiness to recognize mental illness, to seek psychiatric help, and to accept hospitalization for a family member who is mentally ill (Terashima, 1969). The Japanese family, in contrast to the Okinawan, is more likely to conceal a member from public exposure and/or to deny hospitalization for treatment. For this reason, it is difficult to assess the "true" incidence of Japanese mental illness (Kitano, 1970). Thus, the discrepancy in the rates for the two groups may be partially offset by this factor. (Parenthetically, a higher success rate has been found in the detection of mental illness among Okinawan public health personnel than among their counterparts in Japan [Nakagawa, 1969].) In addition, it should be recognized that the Hawaii Okinawan population base could possibly have been calculated too low, which would account in part for the higher incidence. Notwithstanding these reservations, the Hawaii Okinawan rate for schizophrenia, in particular, still appears significantly high, and in need of explanation.

In Okinawan culture there was (and remains) a considerable tolerance for drinking and drunken behavior. The traditional drink, *awamori*, contained about 40 percent alcohol, and illegal varieties were even more potent. Any festive event provided the occasion for drinking and, not uncommonly, the older women as well as the men drank sufficient quantities to produce inebriation. Inevitably, such parties were accompanied by music *(shamisen)*, singing, dancing, whistling, and clapping, often continuing into the early hours of the morning. In fact, some Okinawans have been quick to point out how much more fun their parties are than the more staid affairs of the Naichi. In general, consumption of alcohol required a social context, but solitary drinking might be done at the conclusion of a day's chores by a farmer, if he could afford it. According to Steiner (1946), who performed a large number of necropsies and interviewed native physicians, cirrhosis of the liver was common in men and women past forty. Most certainly drinking did not generate guilt feelings in the individual. There are findings which indicated that Okinawans were more likely to recognize alcoholism as a mental illness than their Naichi Japanese counterparts (Terashima, 1969). Yet the percentage of those ready to connect alcoholism and mental illness was less than half of those viewing schizophrenia as a mental illness. A Hawaii Territorial Hospital study (Ikeda, 1955) showed the Okinawans overrepresented in alcoholism as compared with the Naichi.

In both Okinawa and Hawaii the incidence of mental illness in women is consistently below that in men in all categories. In accounting for the lower female incidence of schizophrenia among Hawaii Okinawans, it has been suggested that this may be due in part to their escape from the larger Japanese community and the associated stresses resulting from social discrimination, through a disproportionately high rate of out-marriage. However accurate this explanation may be for the Hawaii scene, the lower female incidence is also true of Okinawa proper. Quite likely the persistence of certain religious beliefs and practices further contributed to the lower frequency of mental illness in women.

In traditional Okinawan thinking mental disorders discernible at birth were regarded as incurable. Those mentally retarded and others not prone to violence were quite free to roam about, but those who were excessively troublesome or dangerous were confined to cages constructed within the houselots. Behavioral deviations appearing after childhood, especially when suggesting or simulating the behavior of others, were taken as evidence of spirit possession. Similarly, hallucinatory experience was regarded as communication with the spirit world, most commonly the ancestral spirits. Women in particular were considered more susceptible to these.

In the home culture, all major religious functionaries were women, and the major social institutions—state, community, clan, family-household—constituted ritual groups. Priestesses of the state and community obtained office through inheritance, and within the family the oldest woman presided ritually. But the priestesses of the clan, as well as the shaman, were believed to be summoned through divine notification. Such women were regarded as predestined to serve. Thus, the hereditary priestesses and potential shaman were visited by a supernaturally imposed illness or misfortune, called *taari* or *kami-daari* (Lebra, 1969).

The somatic symptoms of *taari* might be quite diffuse, including one or more of the following: generalized stomach disorders, prolonged headaches, pounding noises, asthmatic-like symptoms, pain or stiffness in the limbs (especially the lower portion of the legs), skin problems, and occasionally impairment of vision. These are usually accompanied by physical weakness or lassitude precluding normal work roles and, not infrequently, sex functions. Disturbing dreams often occur, but the critical symptoms of this syndrome are hallucinatory experience (auditory, visual, tactile) and/or fuguelike periods of dissociation. The duration of *taari* may range from months to several years or more. It is believed that unless the person so afflicted accepts her role, death is the only alternative. If the woman recognizes her destiny, believes she has identified her spirit helper, and remission of these symptoms takes place, then it is assumed that she has the powers to help others as well as herself. Not insignificant in the recovery is the knowledge that all previous failures and misfortunes can now be explained away in terms of having been supernaturally imposed; moreover, additional satisfaction can be derived from the knowledge that her spiritual service renders protection to her family. Female shaman derive from such backgrounds and figure importantly in the treatment of misfortunes, especially those which are health related and have not readily yielded to medical treatment. Okinawan shaman types, *yuta,* may be found practicing in Hawaii.

Prior to World War II women thought to be afflicted with *taari* frequently returned to Okinawa permanently. Since that time there has tended to be greater ambivalence as to how it might be handled, some holding that it is a supernatural gift and others viewing it as requiring medical treatment. Complete denial of *taari* as a mental illness should not be unexpected. A common tragedy of the folk-diagnosis of *taari* is not the case of successful remission of symptoms and commitment to serve in a religious role, but those cases where an exclusively religious solution is pursued and the patient, unable to muster sufficient resources to meet expectations, further deteriorates. Locally, among those not Okinawa born, this disorder may not be referred to as *taari,* and the patient might be described as "gifted" or by some similar term.

A psychiatrist in Japan, familiar with both Naichi and Okinawan patients, remarked on the decided contrast in symptom manifestation. In his experience the Okinawans tended to be characterized by a sudden, rather abrupt, display of symptoms, whereas among the Naichi there was a more gradual buildup. The former were frequently hysterical, the latter more often hypochondriacal and depressed. In Hawaii two outstanding variant personality patterns have been suggested among Okinawan patients (Wedge, 1952). The first type was a shy, sensitive, suspicious, withdrawn, "schizoid" personality; the second, a strident, pushing, aggressively intrusive, "overcompensating" personality. A Japanese psychiatrist, describing his patients in Okinawa (predominantly male schizophrenics), referred to many evidences of symptoms of aggressive violence (Yoshimura, 1968). Another survey of Japanese and Okinawan attitudes toward mental illness found that the Okinawans had greater expectations of violence if the patient was not hospitalized (Terashima, 1969). Given the traditional Okinawan abhorrence of violence, it should not be surprising that overt aggression and violence are not uncommon symptoms of those put in mental hospitals.

The incidence of crime by Okinawans in Hawaii, including juvenile delinquency and other asocial activities, has been low. According to a wartime US Office of Strategic Services study (1944), the only "crime" associated with the Okinawans in Hawaii was that of bootlegging, and, of course, violation of Prohibition was virtually a national avocation for Americans during the "dry years." Interestingly, that same account indicates that it was more frequently a female violation; however, one informant suggested that the women commonly "took the rap" on the assumption that judges were more lenient with women and especially with mothers.

For some, acknowledgment of Okinawan origin or descent may not be readily admitted, and a considerable ambivalence may be expressed regarding Okinawan culture. In particular, this may be characteristic of those who have extensively assimilated Japanese culture, as, for example, persons with greater than average Japanese education. Similarly, those who have experienced very severe discrimination in an earlier period may have found less stress and frustration in concealment. Others may maintain a facade of silence and indifference toward things Okinawan in the presence of outsiders, but may nonetheless preserve all proper affiliations and reap the rewards of their identity within the group.

For those working with Okinawan patients, there are a number of factors which may help facilitate recovery. Foremost among these is the strong allegiance to the family system, nuclear and extended. Within the Hawaii Japanese community, the Okinawans have been noted for large families and for observing a greater range of kin ties. Another factor would be the organized groups, not only those like senior citizen organizations and the various *son-jin-kai,* but also some businesses and cultural associations (music, dance, poetry) which have tended to preserve a strong inner core identity of Okinawanness. Beyond this, there is the evidence that Okinawans tend to have a greater readiness to seek help, to accept hospitalization, and to expect favorable outcomes from therapy. This, in combination with family and group support, if skillfully utilized by the therapist, might augur well for a favorable prognosis.

References

Asato, Sadao et al. Round table discussion on the first and second generations. (In Japanese.) *Okinawa,* 1955, 45:32–48.
Glacken, Clarence J. *The great Loochoo: A study of Okinawan village life.* Berkeley: University of California Press, 1955.
Higa, Masanori. Hawaii's Okinawans. (In Japanese.) *Okinawa Keiken* (The Okinawan Experience), 1972, 4:18–26.
Hirayasu, Tsunetoshi. An epidemiological and socio-psychiatric study of mental and

neurological disorders on an offshore island of Okinawa. (In Japanese.) *Psychiatrica et Neurologica Japonica*, 1969, 71:466–491.

Ikeda, Kiyoshi. A comparative study of differential mental illness among Okinawan and Naichi Japanese in Hawaii. M.A. thesis, University of Hawaii, 1955.

Ikeda, Kiyoshi; Ball, Harry V.; and Yamamura, Douglas. Ethnocultural factors in schizophrenia: The Japanese in Hawaii. *American Journal of Sociology*, 1962, 68:242–248.

Ishikawa, Tomonori. The development of overseas migration. (In Japanese.) *Okinawa Prefecture History*, 1974, 7:207–420.

————. A socio-geographic study of migration from Kin-son, Kunigami-gun, Okinawa. (In Japanese.) In Ryukyu University, *Law and Literature Faculty Annual: History and Geography Section*, 1976, 19:55–92.

————. An historical-geographic study of the first generation Okinawan migrants in Hawaii. (In Japanese.) *Shigaku Kenkyū* (History studies), 1977, 136:57–84.

Kimura, Yukiko. *Social-historical background on the Okinawans in Hawaii*. Romanzo Adams Social Research Laboratory, University of Hawaii, Report 36, 1962.

Kinjo, Isaō. The social background of the migrants. (In Japanese.) *Okinawa Prefecture History*, 1974, 7:88–204.

Kitano, Harry H. L. Mental illness in four cultures. *Journal of Social Psychology*, 1970, 80:121–134.

Kohatsu, Koshu. Okinawan nisei education in Hawaii. (In Japanese.) *Okinawa*, 1951, 10:26–27.

Lebra, William P. *Okinawan religion: belief, ritual, and social structure*. Honolulu: University Press of Hawaii, 1966.

————. Shaman and client in Okinawa. In William Caudill and Tsung-Yi Lin (eds.), *Mental health research in Asia and the Pacific*. Honolulu: East-West Center Press, 1969.

————. Ancestral beliefs and illness in Okinawa. In *Proceedings of the 8th International Congress of Anthropological and Ethnological Sciences, vol. 3*. Tokyo: Science Council of Japan, 1970.

Maretzki, Thomas W., and Maretzki, Hatsumi S. *Taira: An Okinawan village*. New York: John Wiley, 1966.

Minturn, Leigh, and Lambert, William W. *Mothers of six cultures: Antecedents of child rearing*. New York: John Wiley, 1964.

Miyagi, Iei. The hardships of the early Okinawan immigrants. (In Japanese.) *Okinawa*, 1951, 10:4–6.

Moloney, James Clark. Psychiatric observances on Okinawa Shima: The psychology of the Okinawan. *Psychiatry*, 1945, 8:391–399.

Nakagawa, Shirō et al. The knowledge and attitude of public health officials in the detection of mental patients: From the experience of an epidemiological investigation in Okinawa. (In Japanese.) *Seishin Igaku* (Psychiatry), 1969, 11:147–152.

Nakasone, Kamasuke et al. Round table discussion on Hawaii Okinawan enterprise. (In Japanese.) *Okinawa*, 1954, 36:26–37.

Oyakawa, Kiye. Past and present of Okinawan radio programs in Hawaii. (In Japanese.) In Taro Thomas Higa, *The immigrants are living*. Tokyo: Nichibei Jiho, 1974, 280–282.

Ryukyu Government. *Okinawa prefecture history, vol. 19*. (In Japanese.) Naha: 1966.

Shima, Shigeo. Social change and treatment of the mentally ill: My personal experience in Okinawa. (In Japanese.) *Psychiatrica et Neurologica Japonica,* 1975, 77:449–455.

Steiner, P. E. Necropsies in Okinawa. *Archives of pathology and laboratory medicine,* 1946, 42:359–380.

Taira, Gyusuke; Tamayose, Houn; Higa, Seikan; Kohatsu, Koshu; Kinjo, Chinyei; Yamazato, Jikai; and Tengan, Hoei. Round table discussion on change in Hawaii. (In Japanese.) *Okinawa,* 1953, 33:1–7.

Terashima, Shogo. The structure of rejecting attitudes toward the mentally ill in Japan. In William Caudill and Tsung-Yi Lin (eds.), *Mental health research in Asia and the Pacific.* Honolulu: East-West Center Press, 1969.

Toyama, Henry, and Ikeda, Kiyoshi. The Okinawan-Naichi relationship. *Social Process in Hawaii,* 1950, 14:51–65.

US Office of Strategic Services. *The Okinawans of the Loo Choo Islands: A Japanese minority group.* Honolulu: Research and Analysis Branch, 1944.

Wakukawa, Ernest K. *A history of the Japanese people in Hawaii.* Honolulu: The Toyo Shoin, 1938.

Wakukawa, Seiyei. Fifty-year history of the Okinawan immigration. (In Japanese.) *Okinawa,* 1951, 10:12–23.

Wedge, Bryant M. Occurrence of psychosis among Okinawans in Hawaii. *American Journal of Psychiatry,* 1952, 109(1):255–258.

Yamamoto, George K. Some patterns of mate selection among Naichi and Okinawans on Oahu. *Social Process in Hawaii,* 1957, 21:42–49.

Yamazato, Jikai. Notes on the Okinawan migrants, 6 pts. (In Japanese.) *Hawaii Hochi,* March 7–12, 1960.

Yamazato, Yūzen. *The Okinawans in Hawaii.* (In Japanese.) Honolulu: Nippu Jijisha, 1919.

Yoshimura, Tadashi. Personal experience in mental health treatment and diagnosis in Okinawa. (In Japanese.) *Seishin Igaku* (Psychiatry), 1968, 10:515–519.

CHAPTER 8

The Koreans

Young Sook Kim Harvey
Soon-Hyung Chung

Introduction

Today, seventy-five years after their first arrival in 1903, the Koreans in Hawaii number about ten thousand, accounting for 1.3 percent of the state's total population. Because of their small number, they were, until recently, customarily included in the "all others" category of most comparative ethnic studies. As a result, their distinctiveness as an ethnic group was generally overlooked.

According to recent studies (Hong and Shin, 1975), more than 90 percent of the Koreans in Hawaii live in urban areas. They have the highest median family income, $16,621 as compared to $11,650 for all ethnic groups, and nearly half the families make between $15,000 and $24,999 yearly. Not surprisingly, the Koreans have the highest proportionate representation in the work force, with nearly two-thirds of the men and one-half of the women older than seventeen employed. In terms of occupations they are again conspicuously over-represented in the combined category of professional services and public administration, about 36 percent as compared to 26 percent for all ethnic groups. In postsecondary education, the Koreans rank third. They have the highest proportion of households headed by women, with the men leading all other ethnic groups in divorce rate and the women following close behind in second place. They also have one of the highest rates for interethnic marriage. During one four-year period, 1960–1964, 80 percent of the Korean brides and grooms married non-Koreans, as opposed to about 40 percent for all ethnic groups during the same period. Parenthetically, the out-marrying brides tended to acquire Caucasian grooms whereas the out-marrying grooms generally married Japanese brides. As for Korean representation in state institutions, the rate has remained proportionate to or slightly higher than their ratio in the general population (Joun, 1977; Lee, 1976; and Yang, 1977).

While these statistical data suggest a profile of today's Koreans in Hawaii, they are somewhat misleading in that they do not reflect the bimodal pattern of distribution that occurs within the Korean population on almost every dimension mentioned above. There is a clear separation between the pre-1924 immigrants and their native-born descendants and the new, post-1965 immigrants. Almost equally divided in number, these two subgroups within the Korean ethnic population in Hawaii mirror their history of immigration to Hawaii.

History of Immigration

At the turn of the century, just when the Hawaii Sugar Planters Association (HSPA) was searching for new sources of cheap labor, Korea was experiencing a high degree of political instability and social disorganization, as well as widespread famine resulting from droughts in successive years. Despite these predisposing factors which prompted the Korean emperor to encourage emigration to Hawaii, initial recruitment efforts by Deshler, the agent for the HSPA, were a complete failure. Ultimately, it was the American missionaries, such as the Reverend George Heber Jones, who successfully persuaded impoverished members of their congregations to emigrate: nearly half the first shipload of 101 Koreans to sail for Hawaii in 1902 came from the Reverend Jones' congregation. In subsequent shiploads, which by 1905 brought nearly 11,000 Koreans to Hawaii, 673 women among them, the pattern of a predominant Christian majority persisted. Christianity was a key factor not only in the selection of emigrants, but also in the shaping of their lives in Hawaii (Gardner, 1970; Sunoo, 1977; and Yun, 1974).

The majority of the early immigrants came from the provinces of Hwanghae and P'yŏngyang in what is today North Korea, a region long regarded by Koreans as a seat of nontraditionalism and rebellion where Catholicism took its first Korean roots in the eighteenth century and where, in the late nineteenth century, American missionaries of the fundamentalist and revivalist denominations found their greatest success. In terms of occupations, only about 15 percent of the immigrants were farmers, the rest being day laborers, low-grade government officials, ex-soldiers, students, house servants, unemployed mine workers, and political refugees from urban backgrounds. Their motives for emigrating were diverse, but almost without exception, they saw it as a temporary measure. They came to Hawaii as sojourners.

On their arrival in Honolulu, the immigrants were dispatched to plantations on every major island, the heaviest concentrations occurring on Kauai and Hawaii. Unaccustomed to agricultural work, they found plantation life exceedingly difficult and many moved around in search of more favorable conditions as they had no contract restrictions. Some two thousand left the islands for the United States before a 1907 presidential executive order banned further Korean and Japanese immigration (Gardner, 1970; Sunoo, 1977; and Yun, 1974).

Under the direction of Christian ministers and lay leaders, as well as of the political leaders among them, the immigrants who remained on plantations organized themselves, forming four types of organizations. The *tonghoe* ("village council") and the swornbrotherhood, traditional organizations in Korea, dealt with practical, immediate issues that impinged upon their survival and maintenance. Each plantation *tonghoe* was represented in the district assembly of the island, and each district assembly in turn was represented in the general assembly of Koreans which met annually on Oahu. This hierarchical organization of plantation *tonghoe* acted almost as a government within a government and effectively controlled the public behavior of Koreans throughout Hawaii. The swornbrotherhoods were covert organizations that cut across plantation boundaries and provided members with collective protection against non-Koreans.

By contrast, the religious and political organizations, emergent types with a brief history in Korea, served the less urgent needs for education, for supporting Korea's independence movement, and for maintenance of ethnic distinctiveness. Historically, these proved more important in shaping the immigrant and ethnic experience of Koreans in Hawaii. Sunday worship was "an almost universal feature of plantation life for the Koreans, and drift of non-Christian immigrants to these well-organized activities was so constant that through the years virtually all Koreans came to be identified with the Christian faith" (Gardner, 1970). These church gatherings provided the immigrants with weekly opportunities to be "culturally at home," to establish networks of mutual aid and public assistance, to acquire religious values consistent with the Protestant work ethic, to feel a sense of shared identity with Christian Americans, and most important, to foster a faith that insisted upon hope where little was warranted.

Organized by the same leaders as those in the churches and paralleling them in structure, the political organizations so successfully mobilized the compelling urge of Korean immigrants to do something to free their mother country from Japanese control that they supported the activities of the independence movement for more than forty years, despite recurring factionalism, and gave the immigrants an abiding sense of ethnic cohesiveness that generated "nationalist sentiment out of all proportion to their number in the new land" (Gardner, 1970) and, one may add, out of all proportion to their economic resources.

By 1919 a number of events in Hawaii, Korea, and the world coalesced to force upon the immigrants the realization that permanent settlement in Hawaii was their most reasonable and viable option, as well as a recognition of their ability to achieve it. The military bases World War I created in Hawaii, mainly on Oahu, and the recruitment of strike breakers, made it possible for many Koreans to leave the plantations for better paying jobs and to send for "picture brides" from Korea. Between 1921 and 1925 about 800 brides arrived from Korea, more than doubling the number of women and transforming the nature of the ethnic community here. Ranging in age from seventeen to twenty-five, the brides came principally from the southeastern region of Korea, which is noted for its sharp cultural and linguistic contrast to the northwestern region from which the majority of the men had come. Like their husbands, however, most of them came from the economically and socially deprived strata; they were also predominantly Christians. Some of the women had been political activists and had chosen marriage to "picture grooms" in Hawaii as a way of escaping oppression by the Japanese police and of continuing their political activities. Still others deliberately took this route because they rejected the traditional role of Korean women. By and large, the women were a progressive, determined, and resilient lot who coped resolutely with initial disappointments and subsequent hardships in Hawaii.

Much to their dismay, many women discovered that the grooms

who came to claim them upon arrival were not the "picture grooms" they had selected in Korea. Some grooms, as much as a generation older than the women, had sent pictures of younger and more handsome men to insure successful recruitment of wives. Naturally enough, many of the "picture brides" were widowed young, with small children to support. Even though women were in high demand because of the skewed sex ratio, five men to one woman, many widows refused remarriage, preferring to raise their children without interference. They looked to community leaders like Syngman Rhee for their children's career guidance and, having pointed the children's feet accordingly, devoted themselves single-mindedly to their success. For these women, no cost appears to have been too high for the education of their children, including girls. Many second generation Koreans, whose success was fueled by the unrelenting determination of these women, recall them with a sense of awe. These immigrant women found in Hawaii the social channels, cultural sanctions, and personal strategies that would enable them to achieve the traditional Korean dream of attaining the *yangban* (gentry status) and the new dream of women of entering the public domain; and for these goals they were not afraid to work. The children through whom many of these women realized their delayed dreams could not always fully appreciate either the source of their mothers' dreams or the significance of their realization.

Excluded from community organizations in Hawaii as they would have been in Korea, these women formed their own and dedicated it to encouraging the education of Korean children, boycotting Japanese commodities, assisting churches and other organizations established by men in Hawaii, and rendering relief to Koreans in distress wherever they were found; these women successfully entered the public domain, at least within the ethnic community of Koreans.

In the meantime, the Japanese colonial regime in Korea worsened, the great powers in the world, including America, grew increasingly indifferent to the cause of Korean independence, and the 1924 Oriental Exclusion Act cut off any further emigration from Korea. Under the circumstances, Koreans in Hawaii felt compelled to escalate and intensify their political activities, although, given their small number and economic status in Hawaii as well as their inexperience in international politics, their efforts must have seemed mad to all but the Koreans. So possessed were they by their passion to liberate

Korea that, after a full day's work, young men assembled in the pine-apple fields of Kahuku to train for military combat against the Japa-nese in Korea at some future point! As their sense of political urgency mounted, factions emerged among the leaders, each of whom felt that he had the best plan for achieving Korean independence, their common goal. They competed bitterly for the allegiance and "blood money" of the immigrants. Rhee emerged as the ultimate victor from this struggle (Kimm, 1977), but not before their frequently ug-ly disputes earned for them some enduring stereotypic ethnic traits. They came to be perceived as hot-tempered and quick-fisted; per-snickety, loud, and aggressive; proud and stubborn; hardworking and tenacious; and, above all, prone to factionalization. That these are traits likely to emerge among any ethnic group under similar cir-cumstances was not generally recognized; nor was it recognized that the Koreans remained always single-minded about their goal for over forty years. The stakes were very high for these Koreans caught in their factional struggle: they were trying to influence the course of their nation's fate in an indifferent world, on resources literally squeezed out of their blood and pittance. Moreover, coming as they did from a society where maintaining one's face is a culturally in-grained moral imperative with a forgotten history, but where they had had little or no personal experience in political decision making, they were ultrasensitive to maintaining face without knowing the fine points of successfully operating in a prestige economy based on *ch'emyŏn* ("face" or "reputation"). Maintaining one's face, losing it, saving it, regaining it, or gambling it—all were deadly serious transactions among the Koreans in Hawaii, for they had few or only frustrated opportunities for participating in the prestige economy of the wider society.

In any event, the accomplishments of the early immigrant Koreans are believable perhaps only in retrospect. They raised a generation of children whose place in Hawaii has already been described, while playing the key role in liberating Korea from Japan in 1945, thirty-five years after its annexation by Japan. The immigrant and ethnic experiences of Koreans in Hawaii between 1903 and 1945 were domi-nated by their political preoccupation, Christian churches, concern for the children's education, and the active and public role of women in these areas of Korean life.

By contrast, in the intervening years between the end of World

War II, when Rhee and his independence workers returned to Korea, and the start of the new wave of post-1965 immigrants in 1969, the Koreans in Hawaii underwent a period of anticlimatic ethnic dormancy. Many second and third generation Koreans married non-Koreans and/or entered occupations dominated by Caucasians and learned to live privately with a more or less nagging sense of bicultural dissonance in their experiences. Still others lost themselves in the multiethnic shuffle of Hawaii, without any stable cultural anchorage, or overcompensated in favor of the dominant Caucasian culture.

After World War II, many surviving immigrant women returned to South Korea to visit families and were dismayed by the poor economic and educational conditions of the nation. With their characteristic decisiveness and determination, they signed affidavits of support for their relatives and brought them over to study at the University of Hawaii. These newcomers were later joined by a more sizable number of Korean women who married American servicemen during and after the Korean War and came to settle in Hawaii. Together, they constituted the first significant infusion of immigrants from Korea to Hawaii since the 1924 Oriental Exclusion Act, but they were not able to revitalize the Korean community. In fact, most of the young war brides found it difficult to integrate themselves into the social structure of the Koreans here. Moreover, many were also finding their interracial, intercultural marriage a difficult water to navigate and were soon being separated, deserted, or divorced from their American husbands, often with young children and no support. Destitute and despondent, they sought employment in bars and cocktail lounges as waitresses and hostesses, these jobs being the most easily obtainable and most quickly rewarding monetarily. They thus inadvertently created the nucleus of a subculture that has since grown conspicuously, and has become perhaps the most definable source of tension between the old-timers and the newcomers in the last ten years.

Since President Lyndon Johnson signed the new immigration bill into law in 1965, there have been rapid increases in Asian immigrant groups, the Koreans being the fastest growing group. Hawaii alone has received approximately six thousand Korean immigrants between 1969 and 1974, the new immigrants more than doubling the Korean population and greatly magnifying their visibility. Since the rate of Korean immigration to Hawaii has increased in subsequent years, the new, post-1965 immigrants today clearly outnumber the pre-1924 immigrants and their native-born descendants by a significant margin. The implications are many and important; for, although they share the same ethnic identity, they are culturally, socially, and historically divergent groups, with different kinds and ranges of personal experiences. They cannot be thoughtlessly lumped together and treated as homogeneous.

Recently there has been a resurgence of ethnic activity and pride among the Koreans in Hawaii as a result of the growing number of new immigrants. There are, on Oahu, some fourteen Protestant churches, one Catholic church, one Buddhist temple, a shaman, a weekly television program, and a more frequently broadcast radio program, as well as two daily newspapers from Korea with news of Los Angeles and the local Korean community added—all new since 1965 with the exception of three of the Protestant churches. In addition, there are numerous restaurants, grocery stores, and other businesses run by the new immigrants. For the first time in decades it is commonplace to hear Korean spoken in public places. In schools, hospitals, and social agencies it is the new immigrants who are the focus of special attention and are thought of as the Koreans in Hawaii by others. With more than thirty Koreans (most of them new immigrants) on the faculty of the University of Hawaii at Manoa alone, the new immigrants have an articulate leadership which can ably demand and gain respect for the ethnic integrity of the Koreans when necessary from those in established sources of power, such as the media.

The surviving early immigrants, mindful of their dwindling number, seem genuinely pleased by the reinforcement of the new immigrants and are helpful to them. The second generation Koreans watch the newcomers with a kind of nostalgic recognition from their youth that gives them a better retrospective understanding of their parents and makes them empathic to the new immigrants, especially the children. The third and fourth generations look on with curiosity for clues to the cultural heritage for which they lack an intuitive sense.

Adjustment and Adaptation: The Post-1965 Immigrants

Because of their brief history in Hawaii, there is relatively little written about the new, post-1965 immigrants from Korea, although their increasing number makes better understanding imperative.

Unlike the early immigrants, the new immigrants come to Hawaii by choice and almost always in family units, with the intention of staying permanently. They come believing that Hawaii offers them better economic opportunities and their children better education. As a group, they are the most educated in Hawaii, including the early Korean immigrants and their native-born descendants. Their occupations range from skilled labor to professional services, with the majority in the managerial category. Most of the immigrant families are young, with half the immigrant children under eighteen. Nearly half of the families arrive in Hawaii without funds, but with promises of help from sponsoring relatives. Almost a quarter of the families are headed by women. Within the first six months of arrival, 90 percent of the household heads find employment, although they suffer drastic occupational devolution in doing so. Only about 8 percent find work in some way related to their preimmigration jobs, training, and experience. The resulting occupational mental distress is reflected in the rate of job change among them, which averages twice a year (Hong and Shin, 1975) and is a serious concern for preventive mental health care.

The average annual income per immigrant household is $6,475. The low wages of the primary wage earners force previously unemployed members of the immigrant families, usually wives and mothers, to seek outside employment with the inevitable consequences for child care and family life. About a third of the new immigrant households receive public assistance in the form of public housing, medical care, and/or food stamps (Hong and Shin, 1975).

For about 90 percent of the immigrants, Korean is the only language in which they have any facility, which causes underemployment among adults and underachievement among children in school and has serious implications for the mental health of immigrants as they undergo acculturation here. The language barrier not only intensifies their experience of culture shock, but also impedes their successful transition through the various stages of it. It keeps the immigrants ignorant of the basic values and modes of life that shape America and involves them in the logical consequences resulting from such ignorance (Hong and Shin, 1975). The new immigrants themselves regard their inability to speak English as the most serious difficulty facing them in making a new life here. Language barrier notwithstanding, they are eager for full participation in their new society: half of the immigrants obtain American citizenship within six years of arrival, the highest rate among Asian subgroups (Kim, 1977).

The immigrants face other, less obvious difficulties in adjusting and adapting to life in Hawaii. The spatial arrangement of American houses and apartments is a case in point. In typical Korean houses there are clearly demarcated, though not necessarily structurally divided, spheres which are sexually segregated and permit the practice of avoidance relationships that minimize potential interpersonal conflicts and keep them under manageable limits when they occur. The American custom of designating each room in terms of a single primary function forces unexpected complications on the new immigrants. It suddenly becomes inappropriate to entertain guests in one's own (bed)room because in America that carries certain cultural connotations. What is more, in America guests are generally entertained in the living room and sometimes in the kitchen, an unthinkable place, incidentally, for that purpose in Korea. The seemingly simple act of a family eating around a common dining table in a designated area, as American custom demands, is a radically new experience for many immigrants, for Koreans do not usually eat together. The older men eat first and generally alone, often in separate rooms, and the younger women eat last after older women and children have been served (Lee, 1967). The kitchen, which in Korea is off-limits to men under normal circumstances, intrudes conspicuously in Hawaii into the living room, which must be shared by all members of the family. The new immigrants might have had considerable experience in living in crowded space, but in all likelihood very little experience in living in space unsegregated by sex or generation.

Most immigrant families leave the grandparents in Korea, so their immigrant life often coincides with their first experience of nuclear family living. Although most couples say they prefer the nuclear family, they are not infrequently confused and distressed by the intense interpersonal demands it places on them. These demands are apparently more distressful to the men, not only because they have had less experience than women in intense domestic involvement, but also because these demands come at a time when they feel extremely vulnerable. In Hawaii they have neither the institutional support that accords special privileges to men in Korea nor the financial means for cultivating the all-male friendship networks that in

Korea serve as the anchorage of men's emotional health. Moreover, Korean cultural expectations of men do not make it easy for them to admit any inadequacies, least of all to their wives and children. Hence, their feelings of helplessness and the resulting depression are not likely to receive attention until they become crippling. Under these circumstances it becomes difficult for some immigrant fathers to be convincing role models for their children, particularly sons. If, in addition, they are challenged in their authority by their now working wives, they can be intimidated into losing control over their children as well. And if they respond to these challenges by autocratic demands for obedience, a common traditional coping pattern among Korean men, they are likely to further alienate family members. Alcoholism becomes a real threat to some of these men.

The impact on the children of fathers with badly frayed self-images and of mothers anxiety-riddled under the multiple pressures of working both in and out of the home has apparently been adverse for many. During 1975 Korean immigrant students accounted for half of the total suspensions meted out by a public high school. The counselors and teachers see the students' inability to communicate effectively in English and their lack of parental guidance at home as their major sources of problems. On the whole, however, immigrant students find schools in Hawaii academically easy, the language barrier notwithstanding, and the social environment in school far freer than in Korea. They are excited by their unprecedented freedom and autonomy, but are no less frightened by them. Accustomed largely to externally generated constraints on their behavior, they feel uncertain in attempting to direct their own behavior in terms of internalized guidelines. And until they become experienced in American culture they are frequently confused by behavioral cues given to them by their teachers and classmates. As their acculturation proceeds, some come to feel "culturally orphaned" and are disturbed by what they perceive to be their ineptitude in both Korean and American culture.

There is a minority of immigrant Korean women who, by the standards of the Korean immigrants, are extremely fortunate, but who themselves feel tremendous distress as a direct consequence of immigration. They are the wives of successful professional or businessmen who provide them with a comfortable living. Still, these women experience in their immigrant life a drastic downward mobility in status as well as a severe constriction in their sphere of authority, influence, and movement. In Korea these women had live-in servants, their own social network of kinswomen, and friends independently of their husbands, and had complete autonomy in the management of their households and child rearing. In Hawaii they find themselves suddenly having to assume a number of roles which were, except in a supervisory capacity, outside their domain in Korea. They must cook, wash, and clean house themselves. They no longer have a power base within their own domain at home. Their distress is further compounded if they do not speak English or drive, for then they are totally and personally dependent on their husbands in discharging their duties. Dislodged from their traditional roles, and unaccustomed to open and frank negotiations in role improvisations, couples frequently grow resentful under these burdens and grow apart emotionally.

As immigrants begin their new life in Hawaii, they shy away, adults and adolescents alike, from penetrating the larger society in Hawaii, relying instead almost exclusively on relatives and friends within the Korean community for information and assistance. Although the language barrier is undoubtedly a factor in this behavior, it may also be a carry-over of institutionalized shy behavior in public. In finding housing, for example, two thirds of the immigrants rely on relatives and/or friends, about 20 percent on classified ads, and only 11 percent on government referral service agencies, although knowledge of such agencies is fairly widespread among them. Even in emergencies requiring outside financial assistance Korean immigrants strongly resist getting help from the government. In one survey half of those sampled indicated they would solicit help from friends and relatives, 42 percent from the bank, and none from the government. Such abiding and negative attitudes toward government prevent many eligible immigrants from making use of available services (Hong and Shin, 1975).

In part, underutilization of available public services by Korean immigrants stems from their lack of sophistication about such concepts as preventive medicine and medical insurance, as well as from deeply rooted folk beliefs that to prepare for catastrophies is to invite them. Many who have medical insurance and desire to use it, do not however, because they do not know how to make appointments and otherwise use services available to them. And even those who learn to make use of health care services are reluctant to return for follow-up or additional treatment, for they find health care delivery personnel by and large intimidatingly impersonal and sometimes even humiliating in their style of interaction. The underutilization of health care services not only interferes with the welfare of the Korean immigrants, but also is a source of concern to the larger population, as the Korean immigrants have a high rate of infectious disease. They have the second highest admission rate for tuberculosis, for example.

Given the difficulties that face the new Korean immigrants, and the fact that they are the ones with whom members of the helping professions most frequently experience problems in providing services, it may be useful to set forth a psychiatric profile of contemporary Koreans in Korea as further background information.

Korean Culture and Mental Health

Koreans living in Korea continue the tradition of regarding mental illness as a form of deviant and harmful behavior the causes of which are variously attributable to supernatural sources, such as the displeasure of ancestral spirits, spirit intrusion, somatic-natural conditions, and psychological distresses originating in interpersonal disharmony (Harvey, 1976/77/78; Kim 1973/74).

About half the population regard mentally ill persons as sources of potential danger and of extreme shame to their families. Koreans rarely regard psychosomatic symptoms or neurotic symptoms as psychiatric problems if they are not acted out in ways dangerous to others. As long as they lead a calm and withdrawn life, the mentally ill, or those who would be so diagnosed by Western psychiatry, are well tolerated by both the family and the society. Alcoholism, for example, is perceived as a form of mental illness by only a fifth of the population and is well tolerated as long as it does not lead to disruptive behavior. Because Koreans find mental illness in a family member a source of shame and believe the cause to lie in interpersonal disharmony in the family, they consider family care, usually in the form of radically reduced occupational and social demands on the patient, the most logical and effective treatment. They will consider hospitalization of the mentally ill only when the patient becomes unmanageably aggressive in behavior. Koreans consider mentally disordered behavior as temporary; hence, it is difficult to convince them that mental illness may become progressive unless treated.

Some culturally inherent sources that may give rise to mental distresses in Koreans are the vertical nature of the social structure and the high degree of interdependence programmed into all social roles. These characteristics make emotional continence a culturally valued personal trait and the individual highly vulnerable to social pressures. They make the Korean's "face" not only his most vital possession, but also his most precarious (Goffman, 1967). Given the additional cultural emphasis on group orientation that draws the eyes of the society to every individual's role performance, it is naturally easy for individual Koreans to become hypersensitive to the opinions of others, to feel as helpless as pawns, and to project the blame or praise for one's fate onto external sources, including the supernatural. In emotionally disturbed persons the necessity for maintaining one's face can cause them to portray themselves as abused, injured, or falsely accused parties and to put the blame on their families, friends, and/or employers. Healthy Koreans seek relief from difficult situations by ventilating to friends or families, with the aim of having someone important to them acknowledge the feasibility of their mental and/or behavioral predicament.

Implicit in this strategy is a plea, easily understood and responded to among the Koreans, that others in one's environment create a climate that would be conducive to one's mental health. This accounts for the use of go-betweens, not only to arrange marriages, but also to settle interpersonal misunderstandings. And it makes good sense in Korean culture in which self-reliant and individualistic behavior is regarded as antisocial and dangerous. To be spontaneous is equally unacceptable because it introduces unpredictability into social intercourse. Hence, although freedom and spontaneity are deeply cherished personal goals among the Koreans, they must be carefully suppressed except in approved places, occasions, and manners. In a culture which also insists upon the superordination of one and the subordination of the other in every social relationship except friendship, friendship bears a heavy burden of the flooding of repressed emotions originating in other relationships; this is recognized in the institutionalization of friendship, especially among men. The ideal friendship in Korea is one in which there exists no firm boundaries between the friends and is exclusive of all others, including spouses and children. It is this kind of friendship the absence of which Koreans, again especially men, report as the single most painful emotional experience associated with immigrant life. In their longing for such friendship, Koreans sometimes misread the superficial friendliness of Americans and eventually come to feel angry and humiliated by the false promise they had read into it. No American can know the depth or the scope of such injuries that Koreans experience in the early phases of their immigrant life.

As to the types of mental disorders, the most common is schizophrenia, of the paranoid type. Anxiety neurosis is on the increase in women in urban areas and conversion hysteria is still quite prevalent among rural women, perhaps owing to poor popular knowledge of medicine, traditional repression of sexuality, and inhibition of verbalization and emotional expression. Depression is becoming more common, especially in situations involving intergenerational conflicts of values, the most conspicuously involved relationship being that of mother-in-law and daughter-in-law. Depression in its incipient stage is most difficult to detect, however, as in nearly all cases (75–85 percent) the symptoms are somatized as headaches, indigestion, fatigue, palpitation, or respiratory difficulties, and patients generally seek relief from internists. Among the young, obsessive compulsive neurosis and identity crisis are on the gain and are found in all social strata whereas they used to be found mostly in the upper strata. Many Korean youths feel caught in a cultural double-bind; they have internalized traditional values but want to live their own lives through emerging values which often contradict the old. Senile psychosis, too, is on the increase as Korea industrializes rapidly, disrupting traditional family structure. Although fully three quarters of the adult population use alcohol and 13 percent are habitual users, alcoholism is rarely seen as a psychiatric problem (Kim and Rhi, 1976).

Koreans seldom seek psychiatric help as the initial step, preferring to exhaust other, more traditional modes of treatment first. The most popular and effective of these is shamanistic healing which incorporates such therapeutic processes as ventilation, persuasion, suggestion, transference, group support, and symbolic use of culturally defined trance. Shamanistic healing also emphasizes deep interpersonal empathy, peaceful resolution of hostility rather than confrontation, and ritualized, collective sharing of suffering in an empathic milieu. The single most negative feature of shamanistic healing may be its extensive use of projective mechanisms which hinder development of personal insights; however, projective mechanisms work well in the context of Korean cultural psychology. Furthermore, Koreans regard suffering as a necessary experience in achieving full human maturity and do not look upon it or symptoms of neurosis as abnormal unless they become socially disruptive.

The reluctance with which Koreans in Korea seek psychiatric service probably explains the clinic rates for Koreans in Hawaii which have been and are low. Their Hawaii State Hospital admission rate has been consistently proportionate to or only slightly higher than their representation in the general population. But their reluctance also means that their treatment plan is likely to be lengthy when they finally seek help. Clinical experience in Hawaii has shown that Korean patients tend to be intractable and resistant to their initial treatment plan and no less unwilling to follow long-term institutional treatment regimes. It is, therefore, critical that therapists working with Korean patients be sensitive to their culturally unique proclivities, in order to gain and retain their cooperation.

Koreans are a proud people who tend to be ultra sensitive to the opinions of others; they are, therefore, prone to suspiciousness and competitiveness, particularly in the realm of social prestige. Their need for interpersonal nurturing is exceptionally great when compared with the Americans' need. Role gratification is a core value among the Koreans, so they are most vulnerable to guilt when they perceive themselves to be role failures. Therapists need to be delicate and subtle as they probe into these areas in the course of treatment, as they need also to be in discussing matters of sex, especially with women patients. Interethnic comparisons of Koreans are probably best avoided unless patients bring up the subject themselves. A fairly long period of supportive approach in therapy is generally needed before a trusting therapeutic relationship can be established and retained with Korean patients. In coping with uncooperative adult patients, the particular sensitivities of the Koreans may be used to advantage if done with wisdom. For example, therapists may successfully appeal to recalcitrant patients to modify their behavior for the sake of children or parents.

Traditional Culture: Some Folk Values

In considering what may be economically said about the traditional culture of Korea that would enhance the understanding of the culture and behavior of contemporary Koreans in Hawaii, one is faced with two possible choices: 1) give an overview of the Yi Dynasty

(1393–1910) which is generally considered the traditional period relevant to modern Korea, or 2) selectively focus on those folk values that have threaded their way in relatively unbroken lines from their origin in the remote past of Korea to the present, undergirding and guiding the behavior patterns of Koreans in Korea and in Hawaii. For the purpose of this book, the second approach seems more suitable, because it would give a more practical cultural framework for understanding both the new immigrants and the old immigrants and their native-born descendants in Hawaii, and because there have already been numerous references in passing to traditional cultural traits in this chapter. Furthermore, there is ample literature on the traditional culture of Korea.

P'alcha ("destiny") and *chaesu* ("fortune") are concepts used daily by the Koreans to deal with the supernatural forces that shape their lives but remain beyond their control. Because Koreans believe that supernatural ordination of human affairs is not revealed to humans but is discoverable by human efforts, their belief in these concepts does not make them passive; rather, it gives them both comfort and hope when their earnest efforts do fail. The failures may not have been their fault and their fortune may yet change.

The Korean word for human is *in'gan,* literally the "connectedness between persons." The central folk concept that governs all human affairs is *chŏng,* meaning emotions and circumstances of man. *Chŏng* is the substance that gives human life its affective quality, and it has a satellite of subconcepts that the Koreans use daily in discussing their affairs. They are:

inchŏng "tender heartedness"
mujŏng "indifference"
sunchŏng "pure emotion," as perhaps in first love
onchŏng "charity"
naengchŏng "cold heartedness"
mojŏng "mother's love"
ujŏng "friendship"
pakchŏng "emotional miserliness"
maejŏng "cold heartedness" bordering on hatefulness

Koreans tend to interpret nearly all their experiences in terms of these concepts and thus frequently appear to others as having a strong propensity for "taking things too personally."

Some folk concepts deal with interactional strategies that focus more on prescribed role obligations and privileges than on emotions. Similar to the Japanese concepts of *amae, on,* and *giri,* which are better known in the West, they are:

ŭji   to depend on others for support

ch'emyŏn-sang   for the sake of face

myŏlsi or *musi*   to be refused in one's request to have one's face upheld

sinse or *ŭnhe*   moral indebtedness

put'ak   to entrust another with something and to expect him to be benevolent in his discharge of it

Because to be human for the Koreans is to be interconnected to other persons, role gratification is vital to their emotional health. No experience is more ego damaging to the Koreans than to be refused in a request *(myŏlsi* or *musi)* made in the name of their "face" *(ch'emyŏn-sang),* for refusal is tantamount to having been denied in a plea to another for allowance to keep their pride as humans.

As Osgood (1951) observed, Koreans recognize as legitimate only to a point the demands of a highly stratified society and a restrictive culture, pointing out that even a worm will wiggle if stepped on. When Koreans feel pushed to a point where they are compelled to assert their human dignity regardless of consequences, they tend to do so explosively and abruptly and are under extreme mental distress. Needless to say, they are in desparate need of supportive counseling in such circumstances.

Understandably, Koreans rarely relax their *nunch'i,* the ability to detect and interpret subtle shifts and nuances in interpersonal relations. The key variables Koreans assess with their *nunch'i* are:

kibun "whim"

yŏmch'e "limit" or "restraint"

yŏyu "surplus," "generosity"

In assessing others' *kibun,* which usually comes into play in just those tense situations where the sense of human dignity is at stake, it is important to know what their tolerance for *yŏmch'e* and *yŏyu* is. Relationships that do not require constant *nunch'i* are described as *hŏmulŏpnŭn-sai,* or "true friendship," and are cherished. Koreans consider such relationships the ultimate experience of life.

For the Koreans, then, the greatest source of mental distress comes from feeling violated in their human dignity, as they perceive it. When such injuries have occurred, the most effective therapy, practiced daily by Koreans with one another, is to help the victim "unravel the knots in his heart" *(kasŭm-p'ulōjuda)* by allowing him to recount fully the history of his psychic injuries.

In circumstances that support their sense of human dignity and ethnic pride, the Koreans are generally a cheerful, gentle, and affectionate people who are easily given to romanticism. They are musically and artistically talented, with a tremendous zest for life. Hardworking and persevering, they place a tremendous value on social responsibility and achievement, as their past accomplishments in Hawaii testify. As one of the fastest growing ethnic groups in Hawaii, their future contributions to the state and America promise to be equally significant if not more so.

References

Gardner, Arthur L. *The Koreans in Hawaii: An annotated bibliography*. Hawaii Series no. 2, Social Science Research Institute, University of Hawaii. Honolulu: University Press of Hawaii, 1970.

Goffman, Erving. *Interaction ritual: Essays on face-to-face behavior*. New York: Anchor Books, 1967.

Harvey, Young Sook Kim. The Korean *mudang* as a household therapist. In William Lebra (ed.), *Culture-bound syndromes, ethnopsychiatry, and alternate therapies,* vol. 4 of *Mental health research in Asia and the Pacific*. Honolulu: The University Press of Hawaii, 1976.

————. "Sinbyong": the possession sickness of Korean "mudang." Paper read at the 76th Annual Meeting of the American Anthropological Association, Houston, 1977.

————. *Six Korean women: The socialization of shamans*. St. Paul: West Publishing Company, 1978.

Hong, Kay, and Shin, Myong-Sop. *The Korean immigrants in Hawaii, 1970–1974: A study of their problems*. Honolulu: Immigrant Service Center, 1975.

Joun, Richard Young Pyo. Economic history of Korean immigrants in Hawaii: 1903–1977. In L. Kim (General Chairman), *75th Anniversary of Korean Immigration to Hawaii, 1903–1978*. Honolulu: The Diamond Jubilee Committee, 1977, p. 58.

Kim, Hyung-chan. *The Korean diaspora: Historical and sociological studies of Korean immigration and assimilation in North America*. Santa Barbara: ABC-Clio, 1977.

Kim, Kwang-Iel. Traditional concept of disease in Korea. *Korea Journal,* 1973, 13:12–18, 49.

————. Psychodynamic study on two cases of shamans in Korea. *Journal of Cultural Anthropology*, 1974, 6:45–65.

Kim, Kwang-Iel, and Rhi, Bou Young. A review of Korean cultural psychiatry. *Transcultural Psychiatric Research Review,* 1976, 13:101–114.

Kimm, Richard C. Korean Christian Church. In L. Kim (General Chairman), *75th Anniversary of Korean Immigration to Hawaii, 1903–1978*. Honolulu: The Diamond Jubilee Committee, 1977, p. 30.

Lee, Dorothy B. Ethnic structures in Hawaii: A report based on the Hawaii health, surveillance program survey, 1969–1971. *Population Report,* no. 6, Honolulu: Hawaii Department of Health, Research and Statistics office, 1976.

Lee, O. Young. *In this earth and in that wind: This is Korea.* Seoul: Hollym, 1967.

Osgood, Cornelius. *The Koreans and their culture.* New York: The Ronald Press, 1951.

Sunoo, Harold Hakwon, and Sunoo, Sonia Shinn. The heritage of the first Korean women immigrants in the United States: 1903–1924. *The Korean Christian Journal,* 1977, 2:142–171.

Yang, Sara Lee. 75 Years of Progress for the Koreans in Hawaii. In L. Kim (General Chairman), *75th Anniversary of Korean Immigration to Hawaii, 1903–1978.* Honolulu: The Diamond Jubilee Committee, 1977, p. 16.

Yun, Yo-jun. Early history of Korean emigration to America. Pt. 1, *Korea Journal,* 1974, 14(6):21–25. Pt. 2, ibid., 14(7):40–45.

CHAPTER 9

The Filipinos

Introduction: The Philippine Background
Danilo E. Ponce

Filipinos are the fourth largest ethno-cultural group in Hawaii, numbering approximately one hundred thousand, and comprising over 11 percent of the total state population. Now in their seventy-third year as participants in Hawaii's heterogeneous and increasingly complex society, Filipinos, on the whole, occupy the lower strata of the state's social and economic life. In a paper that summarizes demographic and socioeconomic characteristics of Filipinos on Oahu (where 82 percent of Hawaii's Filipinos reside) Cariño (forthcoming) presents the following profile as drawn from a 1975 Office of Economic Opportunity (OEO) survey: The median income of employed Filipinos in 1975 was $6,554, much lower than the $8,396 for all Oahu residents, higher only than the median income of Samoans ($5,756) and Blacks ($5,554). This was true in spite of the fact that a larger proportion of Filipinos (59.2 percent)—as compared to Oahu residents as a whole (55.9 percent)—were in the labor force, and thus it reflected the concentration of Filipinos in more readily available, less prestigious, and lower-paying occupations. Filipinos had the smallest proportion of workers engaged in professional, technical, and management occupations, and the second smallest (after Hawaiians) in clerical and sales occupations.

The factors affecting Filipino status, as cited by Cariño, included recency of arrival, relatively slow urbanization, a large immigrant population, an imbalance in age–sex structure, low levels of education, and patterns of stratification and inequality that may exist across ethnic lines of participation in the occupational life of the host community. Important variations among subgroups of Filipinos were related to place of birth, place of residence, and recency of migration. Statewide implications of the preceding profile can be inferred from similar socioeconomic data in the 1970 census and income and literacy statistics from other islands (e.g., Kawaguchi and Jedlicka, 1975). Cariño observed that there is growing evidence that patterns of social stratification along ethnic lines are gradually diminishing. The study also noted that government policies with regard to the existing differences in wealth distribution, and the concentration of specific immigrant groups in certain occupations, are important in defining the situation into which immigrants move. "On the whole, however, [government policies] tend to ignore the reality of stratification along ethnic lines as well as the potential conflict among ethnic groups which have varying access to the economic resources of the host community."

This conclusion reflects in part a perspective that this chapter adopts as a starting point: that "issues tied to change in the macrosociety—whether defined racially, ethnically, medically, or legally—constitute the center ground in terms of community health."

An additional starting reference must be a description of the history and traditional culture of the Filipino homeland. The history of the country, including as it does a marked degree of exploitation, is especially significant in explaining the Filipino character of today.

The Philippines is a group of more than seven thousand islands bounded on the north by Formosa, on the south by Borneo, on the east by the Pacific, and on the west by the China Sea. The islands are scattered over 114 thousand square miles—an area twenty-eight times the size of Hawaii. Many of them are uninhabited, and many are mere specks in the ocean.

The Philippines became a colony of Spain in the early 1500s through the efforts of the well-known circumnavigator Ferdinand Magellan. His find proved a very costly one, for Magellan paid for it with his life; he was slain by a native chieftain, Lapu-Lapu, on the small island of Mactan, just across a narrow strait from the island of Cebu in the central Philippines.

Basically, the Filipino stems from the Malay race, but centuries of occupation by other ethnic groups, whether as rulers (the Spanish and Americans) or as expatriate entrepreneurs (Chinese, Germans, and others), has produced a genetic mixture. The modern Filipino suffers not a little confusion about cultural identity. Geographically, the islands are in the Asian region but the peoples of mainland Asia do not look upon the Filipinos as true Asians.

Spain ruled and exploited the Philippines for more than three hundred years and left an enduring imprint on the native Malay culture. Spanish rule was followed by nearly half a century of American occupation, during which the Americans sought to convert the Philippines into a democracy in their own image. The Americans failed. The vast differences in cultures and the absence of any sizable middle class, which is deemed necessary in order for democracy to thrive, had not been sufficiently considered. On the one hand, it had taken the British and the Americans centuries to develop democratic institutions which even today are imperfectly realized; on the other, Filipino culture is marked by a number of facets, including strong hierarchical relationships, that are sometimes seen as not hospitable to Western democracy.

A salient feature of Philippine culture, which has endured with pervasive strength throughout all the years of rule by outsiders and efforts to impose alien values, is the concept of the extended family. George M. Guthrie (1968) writes:

> If there is one aspect of Philippine life that impresses a western observer it is the role of the family in the life of the individual. Filipinos inculcate a strong sense of a family loyalty which spreads beyond the nuclear family of parents and children. Family obligations extend to cousins several times removed, to in-laws and to others who are made a part of the family by such ceremonies as sponsors at a marriage or a baptism.
>
> The ties are just as strong whether the kinship is through the male or female side of the house. This bilateral extended kinship system means ideally that each Filipino has many people to whom he can look for help and support and he will have demands from many for whatever help or influence he has available. A Filipino may reckon as many as 100 or more people as his relatives, although his feeling of obligation is not as strong toward the more distant ones and their demands are smaller and fewer.

The extended family is, in effect, the basic unit of Philippine society. Its concerns are largely turned inward and nonmembers are regarded as outsiders. The Filipino will readily share his labor and good fortune with his relatives but tends to a strong indifference toward those outside the family.

The respect for authority in the family does not imply blind authoritarianism as has been asserted in some of the literature on the Philippines. One Philippine anthropologist has shown in his studies that family supportiveness rather than authoritarianism is a primary value (Mendez and Jocano, 1974). Jocano draws on the excellent data base of his extensive anthropological research and in so doing agrees with others who have come to similar conclusions. A closer look at family interaction has led one researcher (Youngblood, 1974) to state that the structural authoritarianism of the Filipino family is evidently mitigated by other cultural mechanisms, such as the right of appeal for younger members of the family and the heavy duties and responsibilities of those in authority as these are lodged in a family atmosphere of warmth and solidarity.

The Philippines is divided into three major geographical areas: the large northern island of Luzon, on which Manila is situated, and the adjacent islands of Mindoro and Palawan; the central group, called the Visayas, including the major islands of Cebu, Negros, Leyte, Panay, Samar, and Bohol; and Mindanao, the largest and southernmost island of the entire group.

The primary language of northern Luzon is Ilocano; the language of the capital city of Manila and the immediate surrounding area is Tagalog; the Visayans speak a variety of related dialects, the chief ones being Cebuano, Waray-waray and Hiligaynon. On Mindanao one finds speakers of both Tagalog and Cebuano as well as other tongues. Altogether, however, there are seventy-five or more dialects and eight major languages. Language, then, is a hallmark of regionalism, and differences among Ilocanos, Tagalogs, and Visayans are more linguistic than cultural.

Of the three groups, the Tagalogs were most subject to the influence of Spain and consequently are more likely to think, feel, and behave in the Spanish tradition. They were the earliest immigrants to Hawaii and are likely to be better-educated, urban in outlook, and less enthusiastic about rural life.

The Visayans, although they adopted the orthodox Roman Catholicism of Spain, at the same time remained more festive and sensual.

Thus, they are a study in contrast. A standing joke is that Visayan men who enter the priesthood tend to be intense about their vocation to compensate for the uninhibited behavior of their earthy sisters. The Visayans followed the Tagalogs in migrating to Hawaii.

The Ilocanos were the last and by far the largest group to migrate, driven in part by the barren, unproductive soil of northwest Luzon. Due in large part to the poverty of their region, the Ilocanos tend to be more venturesome than the Tagalogs and Visayans. They also seem more quarrelsome, more prone to violence, and have been described as the "Irish" of the Philippines.

The three groups have their stereotypic views of one another. The Visayans are seen as colorful, sensual, internationally minded, and prone to spend money on dress and other emblems of affluence. The Ilocanos in turn are seen as austere, puritanical, work-oriented, at times parsimonious and at times spendthrift, and, in general, poor country cousins. The Tagalogs are considered more westernized, urban and nationalistic, and in some ways conservative.

The divisions in the Philippines go far beyond the Visayans, Tagalogs, and Ilocanos. Most Filipinos are Roman Catholics, but on the major southern island of Mindanao and in the Sulu archipelago, extending southwest almost to Borneo, is a large Moslem population which is hostile to the Christian Filipinos and has never fully integrated with them or submitted completely to rule from Manila. In addition, there are numerous ethnic and cultural minority groups throughout the islands, including, to mention only two, the former head-hunting tribes of the mountain region of northern Luzon and the pygmy Negritos of central Luzon. And, as already mentioned, there is the wide variety of languages and dialects.

Officially, the national language of the Philippines is Filipino, which is based on the Tagalog spoken in the Manila area. Filipino is the language of instruction in the public schools through the third grade, after which the language of instruction becomes English, although instruction in Filipino as a separate study continues into the higher grades. It is noteworthy that the ordinary provincial grade school pupil is thus exposed to at least three languages: his own, Filipino, and English.

One reason for the creation of the Filipino language was a hope that it would bring greater cohesion among the various groups and regions, but so far it has not achieved this purpose. Regional jealousies and dialects together with the fact that the majority of children in the rural areas drop out of school somewhere between the third and fifth grade, revert to their local dialect, and lose school contact with Filipino, have combined to frustrate efforts toward this goal. Furthermore, there is general resentment against the Tagalogs of the Manila area on the part of other groups for a presumed effort to impose their language on others. English is actually, if unofficially, the country's national language. This condition is more and more resented by nationalists in the Manila area, but nevertheless it is a fact and it remains to be seen whether Filipino can be made to supplant English.

Filipino Character—Traits in Contradiction

Three major factors have dominated the Filipino culture and character. First is the basic Malay influence. Next is the centuries-long rule by Spain, and last is the relatively brief experience under the Americans.

The ancient Malay influence strikes to the deepest core of the Filipino personality and accounts for the persistence of animism, belief in magic, fatalism, clannishness, and group affinity (the extended family).

The Spanish influence is discerned in the predominant religion, Catholicism, in the impact on language, in class consciousness, and in a profound respect for and obedience to authority.

The American influence is apparent in at least the lip service paid to democratic ideas, in the adoption of English as a major language, and in the emulation of American dress, music, art, and science.

The Filipino, then, can be extremely difficult to understand. On the surface he may behave like an American in dress and conversation, while in more personal moments the Spanish heritage takes over in the form of religous attitudes, acceptance of class differences, and a belief that anything foreign is automatically superior. In his more Malay moments, he becomes a superstitious, animistic, gambling fatalist.

As a result of these conflicting influences, which can operate simultaneously, the Filipino can be seen—even by other Filipinos—as inconsistent and contradictory.

A distinctive feature of Philippine society is that it is virtually impossible to have symmetrical, truly equal relationships. Almost always the relationships are complementary: leader-follower, teacher-pupil, boss-subordinate. It would be thoroughly alien to the Filipino mind, for example, for a physician to discuss a mutual approach with a patient. The physician is an authority who treats and cures and it is the patient's responsibility to do as the doctor expects—respond favorably to the treatment.

This characteristic is seen most dramatically in the schools. Teachers teach and pupils absorb by rote and recite back what they are told. Pupils are not expected to question what they are told by teachers nor are they expected to attempt to engage the teacher in any probing discussion of the subject matter. The pupil's role is quite passive. Similarly, teachers passively and even timidly bow to the dictates of principals and administrators. Each level of authority, in other words, behaves dictatorially and autocratically toward the subordinate level.

There are four distinctive and, to an extent, interrelated cultural characteristics of great value in understanding Filipino behavior. These are *amor propio,* or self-esteem; *hiya,* shame or embarrassment; *utang ng loob,* the debt of gratitude; and *pakikisama,* or getting along harmoniously.

Amor propio often exhibits itself as an exaggerated sense of personal worth which, underneath, the individual secretly recognizes to be overdrawn. As Guthrie puts it, it involves "the need of the Filipino to be treated as a person, not an object. His fragile sense of personal worth leaves him specially vulnerable to negative remarks from others and leads him to be vigilant to signs of status that will indicate how he stands in his group at the moment." Self-esteem, it should be added, is not to be confused with self-confidence, a fact that helps explain the Filipino's extreme sensitivity. As a working concept, it is probably closer to the Greek notion of hubris or false pride.

The concept of *hiya* has been described as shame, but the English word is inadequate to convey the full extent of the term's meaning. It is a form of self-deprecation, involving embarrassment, inferiority, and shyness all arising from having behaved improperly, and it is one of the more powerful sanctions operating to maintain the overall system of social relationships.

Utang ng loob is a debt for a voluntary favor that must be repaid at some time but cannot be repaid in money and perhaps never in full. Failure at some time to repay this moral obligation is shameful, and the individual who fails to meet the obligation is said to be *walang hiya* ("without shame"), as is someone who shows disrespect, brashness, and vulgarity.

Pakikisama underlies virtually the entire structure of social relationships. The Filipino, being sensitive, is aware of the sensitivity of others and consequently elaborate means are employed to avoid giving offense. There is, for example, the extensive use of the go-between in a wide variety of activities, ranging from requesting a loan, attempting to improve relations between associates or superiors and subordinates, and to proposals of marriage. At virtually all times there are deliberate efforts to avoid direct confrontation, disagreement, or criticism. This desire for frictionless relationships also leads to extensive use of euphemism in conversation, and the speech is loaded with metaphors that convey a message with minimum risk of offense.

The role of *pakikisama* in the experience and expression of hostility is much debated among Philippine specialists. *Pakikisama,* as a value, favors avoidance of direct confrontation that could lead to open and violent aggressive behaviors. Intermediate forms of aggression, expressed by various culturally shaped means, are common: metaphors or analogies in speech, humor, blaming of others, and gossip are some of the milder forms. Ostracism and sorcery are some of the more severe traditional ways. Lapuz (1973), a prominent Filipino psychiatrist, has given many examples of displaced as well as open expressions of hostility by patients and family members that are characteristic of general experiences in the society. There is much evidence in the Philippines that the emphasis on smooth interpersonal relations cannot prevent the occurrence of many forms of aggression —some quite violent.

One other characteristic which distinguishes the Filipino is called *Bahala Na,* meaning, in effect, leaving things to fate or God (Bathala). The Filipino is a fatalist, believing he has little or no control over his own destiny and that good fortune is simply good luck and will probably disappear.

In Hawaii there are a number of stereotypic attitudes among other ethnic groups concerning the Filipino. These include such characterizations as lazy, backward, withdrawn, envious, hot-tempered, flamboyant, hypersensitive, and self-important. As we have seen, there are kernels of truth behind some of these characterizations, but as with all stereotypes the error content is great. The vital thing is to better understand the cultural traditions behind the individual.

With this preliminary knowledge of the home culture of this immigrant group, the focus in the remainder of the chapter will be on their adjustment to their new environment. Other students of Filipino immigration have examined the influence of government policies, institutional practices, and general social conditions on Filipino responses to their lifestyle in Hawaii. In the sections which follow, the interaction between social system variables and individual/group behavior will be discussed in the context of existing descriptions of the nature and quality of Filipino life. Three periods, or waves, of Filipino immigration are found to be distinct and thus are utilized as frameworks for discussion: 1906 to 1932, 1945 to 1946, and 1965 to the present.

Hawaii's Immigrants from the Philippines
Sheila Forman

The First Wave

In 1898, the Spanish ceded the Philippines to the United States in accord with a proviso of the Treaty of Paris, which ended the Spanish-American War. At the same time, the United States was finalizing action against immigration from Asia culminating in the Chinese Exclusion Act of 1900 and the Gentleman's Agreement of 1907, which extended exclusion to the Japanese. The Hawaii Sugar Planters' Association (HSPA), which had been relying on China and Japan for plantation labor, shifted its recruitment efforts to the Philippines, whose people, as a result of annexation, were free to travel to the United States without restriction. Sporadic Filipino immigration to Hawaii took place between 1906 and 1909, but it was not until 1910, after the HSPA established a Manila office, provided fares to Honolulu, and three-year contracts to recruits, that Filipinos began to arrive in large numbers in Hawaii. Details of immigration are readily available (e.g., Alcantara, 1975; Melendy, forthcoming). Alcantara's

(1972) bibliography, however, mentions prominent gaps in the re-telling of the Filipinos' experiences. A later description of Filipino life in a plantation town (Alcantara, 1973, 1975) is typical of the ex-perience of most of Hawaii's Filipinos and exemplifies their attempts to pursue "the good life" in a new setting. In the Philippine cultural context this pursuit has been described by Nydegger and Nydegger (1966) as follows:

> The "meaning of life," semimystical, elusive, and compulsively sought in the West, is reduced to a homely, modest, and attainable set of goals, roughly in this "proper" order of importance: (1) to strengthen and ex-tend the bonds of neighborliness and make them secure, (2) to establish a family of which one may be justifiably proud, (3) to improve one's socio-economic position if possible, largely as a legacy for the next generation.

FIRST LIFE GOAL

"Neighborliness" translates as *panagkakadua* in Ilocano (Nydegger and Nydegger, 1966), which means "feeling and behaving with re-sponsibility and good will towards one another" (translation courte-sy, P. Espiritu, Indopacific Languages, University of Hawaii). In Waialua the first wave of migration resulted in "an aggregation of males with little stable basis for interaction because of individual re-cruiting, transient orientation and a high turnover rate" (Alcantara, 1975). Filipinos attempted to achieve the first life goal by "extensive use of such adaptive devices as fictive kinship, multiple sponsorship at weddings and baptisms, voluntary organizations, and familial schema in communal households" (Alcantara, 1975), in order to "extend bonds of neighborliness." Melendy (forthcoming) describes a similar adaptation: "The workers searched out friends and relatives from the barrio, and bunked and cooked and ate their meals together, producing the *cumpang,* a surrogate family of sorts, with the eldest person acting as head of household."

Life-cycle feasts became important occasions for reinforcing the values of neighborliness and increasing the number of participants in what eventually took the place of the all-important "alliance" sys-tem of the Philippines. This alliance is the Filipino basis for social in-teraction (Hollnsteiner, 1963). It is a sometimes nebulous and shift-ing, but generally long-lasting and identifiable network of relatives and friends bound by mutual rights and obligations (often referred to as *utang na loob* in the literature on Filipino values) (Lynch and de Guzman, 1973).

The HSPA often respected Filipinos' requests to join members of alliances at different plantations. Alcantara (1975) states, "After 1927, some Filipinos were able to arrive in Waialua because their passage fare was paid" by alliance members in the town.

SECOND LIFE GOAL

The second life goal, "to establish a family of which one may be justifiably proud," was practically beyond reach during this period. Alcantara (1975) explains, "The wages of a common laborer on the Hawaii plantations were adequate only for the needs of a single man. . . . The men who came with their families ended up always in debt at the plantation stores and, therefore, often sent their wives and children back to the Philippines."

The Filipino population at this time, then, may reasonably be said to have exhibited a pattern of familyless men. Those Filipino men who were married had to fear a practice known as *coboy-coboy*. This practice, the abduction of married women by other Filipinos, may be attributed to the highly skewed sex ratio (roughly 10 to 1 in 1910—improving slightly over the years [Melendy, forthcoming]) and to the lack of protection by large, well-developed alliance networks. Knowledge of the existence of this threat must also have served to dissuade other young men from marriage if it had been possible for them. Some intermarriage with non-Filipino women did occur, yet it may be noted that interracial marriages involving Filipinos showed the highest divorce frequencies as of 1927. Here again, we can see that experiences in the islands must have worked discouragingly against the impetus to fulfill the second Filipino life goal.

Despite the prevalence of familyless men, there were a few Filipino families that managed to stay together at this time in Hawaii. Since educational attainment is one of the manifestations of value in which a Filipino can take pride in the family, it would be useful to report on the educational attainments of members of those families. What was accomplished must be viewed within the context in which these families had to struggle.

Educational opportunities during this period were characterized by what Senator Daniel Inouye later called "subtle segregation" through tracking (Inouye, as cited in Wright, 1972). Beginning in 1924 children who could pass written and oral tests in standard English went to English Standard schools, and those who failed the tests went to "nonstandard" schools. The duality in the school system also reflected racial and social stratification. "There was a stigma in the non-standard school clearly recognized by those who attended them." In addition, "a major part of the [legislatively appropriated] money went to the English Standard Schools" (Wright, 1972). "Even so, some of the leaders of the business community thought the education being offered to public school students was excessive" (Daws, 1974). This dual system did not go unchallenged. Dr. A. L. Dean, then president of the University of Hawaii, took the position that the new system was not even democratic.

The data on Filipino literacy and school attendance, then, must be seen at least in part as an indictment of the educational establishment of the time.

> In 1930, three out of every ten Filipinos, including children, were illiterate. . . . Even among the youngest and strongest—those 15–19—nearly one out of four could not read or write. . . . 50 percent [of all Filipinos] were unable to speak English . . . only three teachers in the territory were Filipino . . . only 24.2 percent of the eligible 16 and 17 year old Filipinos attended school. (Fuchs, 1961)

The oft-repeated attempt at explanation, that Filipinos must not value education, simply does not withstand careful scrutiny. The noted sociologist of the Philippines, Hollnsteiner, during a recent visit to Hawaii, expressed shock at this stereotype when she discovered that it was common in Hawaii. She regarded it as evidence of a lack of local knowledge of Philippine culture. Probably more apropos of real explanation is the attitude expressed by Edward P. Irwin: "We are fond of saying that the children of America, of whatever parentage, are entitled to all the education we can give them. . . . They're not, of course; they're entitled to only such an amount as we think is best for them" (as quoted in Daws, 1974).

Literacy is one of the major sources of parental pride among Filipinos. "Competence in reading by a child is a source of parental delight. Parents often proudly relate how their children can read books" (Jocano, 1969). In the Philippines respect for learning is actually quite traditional. Before the Americans came to the Philippines the Malolos Constitution of 1898 provided that "popular education shall be obligatory and free in the schools of the nation" (Kuhn and Kuhn, 1968).

Where real lack of respect for schooling can be validly identified in the Filipino population of Hawaii, one is tempted to speculate that these Filipinos have been here long enough to recognize real limitations built into the extant system and to foresee that better chances for the good life may lie outside the schooling system.

THIRD LIFE GOAL

For the first wave of Filipino immigrants, the third life goal, that of improving one's socioeconomic condition, also was unattainable during the period. Plantation employment required ten to twelve hours of work a day under extremely difficult living and working conditions. The now familiar histories of immigrant laborers in general include the same list of grievances: no job security, the threat of arbitrary dismissal on petty and often unsubstantiated charges or for "insubordination," and the lack of formal channels for redress of grievances. Perhaps less well known is the fact that this lack of civil rights for Filipinos was aggravated by a decision made by Attorney General John A. Matthewman, legal spokesman for the territory, who stated that the imported Filipino field workers were "neither citizens nor aliens" since they came from a commonwealth then governed by the United States; as the Filipinos were not born on American soil, Matthewman declared that they were "subjects" while living in the Territory of Hawaii. This was "a rather unusual term in a democratic society" (Wright, 1972). Unlike the immigrants from China and Japan, Filipinos could turn neither to a representative at home nor to the Hawaii government for protection.

Lack of progress in their socioeconomic condition eventually led Filipinos to participate in at least nine labor strikes throughout the islands between 1909 and 1925, including the big strikes of 1920 and 1924 (Abbott, 1971; Sharma, 1975).

In 1920 the best known of the Filipino labor organizers was Attorney Pablo Manlapit, who, after repeated HSPA rejections of the Filipino labor movement's wage demands for $2/day wages for a forty-hour workweek, called his union out on strike. The Japanese union was making similar demands and joined this strike, which spread to six plantations. Although the strikers did not succeed in getting the wage changes they demanded, their agitation resulted in slightly improved attitudes and conditions in some plantations (Norbeck, 1959). The 1924 strike occurred when these demands were continually ignored. The strike, originally shrugged off as one involving "docile" Filipinos, lasted eight months and attested to the staying power of Filipinos determined to demand fair wages for their labor. Manlapit's leadership reflected the Philippine tradition of the "fiscalizer," a verbally adept opposition speaker. This role in a leader is little recognized in Hawaii because of a paucity of historical and cultural material on Filipinos available or utilized in Hawaii's schools (notable exceptions are the Philippine Studies Program and the Ethnic Studies Program at the University of Hawaii). Manlapit's efforts, however, are still mentioned with respect by elderly Filipinos (Reinecke, as cited by Sharma, 1975).

For Filipinos seeking higher socioeconomic status, the absence of opportunities outside plantation work compounded the problem of low wages in plantation labor. Some elderly Filipinos suggested that Honolulu firms blacklisted Filipinos who left plantation employment. Part of the problem was the 1900 Hawaii Organic Act which barred non-American citizens from public employment (Alcantara, 1975). Filipinos, as wards of the United States, not citizens, were generally not eligible for positions in public agencies. These conditions led a sizable number of Filipinos to seek opportunities in the mainland United States or in the Philippines. Out of approximately sixty-five thousand men, twelve thousand had returned to the Philippines by 1925. Twenty years later, only a handful of the Filipinos assigned to work for a sugar company between 1909 and 1920 could still be found in the plantation town (Melendy, forthcoming). Traditionally a highly mobile group (Smith, 1976), Filipinos again used migration as a response to job scarcity and lack of opportunities.

The declaration of Filipinos as aliens, and the restriction of their entry into Hawaii and the United States to an annual quota of fifty persons as stipulated by the Tydings–McDuffie Act in 1934, further limited their goals and achievements beyond a plantation existence. Even as conditions began to improve because of the strikes, few married Filipinos could send for their families in the Philippines because of the small quota. Ironically, the naturalization laws of the Philippines, applied by American authorities, allowed American citizens to enter the Philippines in any number with no restrictions or stipulations. In 1939 some nine thousand Americans were living in the Philippines, most of whom had business or professional interests there, owning some sixty-three thousand acres of land (McWilliams, 1943).

The Second Wave

In 1945 the HSPA and the Pineapple Growers Association declared a labor shortage and invoked Section 8 of the Tydings-McDuffie Act, which provided exemptions for demonstrated labor needs. An exemption was granted and the governor of Hawaii authorized the importation of new Filipino workers for the plantations. This led to the arrival in 1946 of approximately 7000 workers, 450 wives, and 900 children.

FIRST LIFE GOAL

During the 1946 recruitment, plantation workers pursued an opportunity to increase their alliance networks by requesting recruitment of male kin between the ages of eighteen and forty. Many more requests were made than were granted. Waialua, for example, had a quota of only 207 workers, far below the 368 male relatives requested (Alcantara, 1975).

SECOND LIFE GOAL

In addition to the local exemption, the federally determined annual immigration quota was raised from fifty to one hundred persons in 1946. This quota too was far below the number of Filipino petitions for entry of immediate family members. When naturalization became available that same year, which could have enabled some of the workers to get their families outside the quota, few of them could fulfill the literacy requirements. A later regulation, the McCarran–Walter Act of 1952, left the one hundred persons quota intact, gave preference to immigrants with special skills or training, and thus further reduced the immigration of family members.

This second period, however, saw some improvement in opportunities for educational advancement, which we have already argued was a major factor contributing to family pride. The dual school system was struck down in Hawaii. Department of Public Instruction figures in 1947 showed that Filipinos comprised approximately 10 percent and 7 percent respectively of students in public and private schools (Hormann and Kasdon, 1959). In spite of the individual accomplishments of Filipino students, however, group images and thus purportedly inherent traits continued to plague Filipinos as a whole, as a 1962 interview of a member of another ethnic group suggests (Samuels, 1970):

> *Samuels (S):*   What is the picture that you have of Filipinos? When you think of them, what comes to your mind?
>
> *Respondent (R):* They are moody and quick-tempered. It is in their blood.
>
> *S:*   How did you form this image of them?
>
> *R:*   From the papers, the things people say.
>
> *S:*   Have you ever known any Filipinos personally?
>
> *R:*   Yes, one. He was our class president at Iolani.
>
> *S:*   Did he fit the picture you painted of Filipinos?
>
> *R:*   No, he was calm and pleasant.
>
> *S:*   Then the moodiness and quick temper could not have been "in his blood" could they?
>
> *R:*   *(Pause; then a shy smile)* He was an exception.

THIRD LIFE GOAL

During the second wave period, pursuit of the third major life goal, improvement of one's socioeconomic condition, was aided by federal legislation that provided for collective bargaining. The first union contract for sugar workers was finally signed (Melendy, forthcoming). In 1946 the ILWU unionized all plantation workers in Hawaii, finally securing for them job tenure, seniority benefits, a formal pension plan, strict job classifications, formal arbitration of worker grievances, and universalistic standards for job accession and promotion. Medical and recreational facilities were being established, mechanization had eased some of the work, and, most important for socioeconomic security, in 1953 workers were offered the opportunity to buy plantation homes (Alcantara, 1975). Housing options varied widely among plantations. In some the option to buy was not offered; in others unwritten agreements for lifelong use were substituted; in still others former written agreements were relinquished or not honored in the transfer of plantations from one owner to another. In spite of continuing difficulties in the economic sphere and in establishing solid family and alliance ties, Filipinos by the end of the 1950s were increasingly inclined to stay and call Hawaii home.

The Third Wave

The 1965 Immigration Act mandated abolition of the national origin quota system, which had discriminated against eastern hemisphere countries outside northwestern Europe. The Philippines' quota increased to the per country limit of twenty thousand set by the new act (not counting exempt classes such as spouses and children of US citizens).

FIRST LIFE GOAL

Filipinos in Hawaii, almost immediately aware of the implications of this liberalized law for their major life goals, petitioned for the entry of extended-family kin. Between 1970 and 1976, 26,626 Filipinos were admitted to Hawaii, and they now represent an estimated 54 percent of all immigrant aliens in the state (Hawaii Commission on Manpower and Full Employment, 1978). The current geographic distribution of Filipinos on Oahu suggests the continuing vitality of the pursuit of the first life goal. Data show that Filipinos are concentrated in the adjacent areas of Kalihi-Palama and Upper Kalihi, and in Waipahu and Ewa-Makakilo. Almost half of all Filipinos on Oahu lived in these districts in 1975. More than one-third of all Kalihi-Palama residents and approximately one-fourth of Waipahu and Ewa-Makakilo residents were Filipino. This strong concentration in a few districts suggests the persistence of ethnic and kinship networks, as well as of the occurrence of the "phenomenon of chain migration." Indications are that this concentration is continually increasing (Cariño, forthcoming).

In support of the order of priorities for life goals adopted as a framework for this paper, it is interesting to note that the most organized and publicized Filipino movement (called *Makibaka*) during the third-wave period involved a successful two-and-one-half years (January 1972–June 1974) attempt to relocate an entire community facing eviction to a new site. Numerous government agency roadblocks threatened the community's efforts to stay together as a group, but the residents, with the help of a volunteer lawyer and several sympathetic community groups, utilized media, demonstrations, and clever monitoring of county versus state politics to build a resident-planned housing project featuring important elements of Filipino community life.

There are other illustrations of the strength and importance of these alliance networks among Filipinos. Data were collected which supported a community's preference to remain in their town when given the option of moving to another, newer Molokai town. They were convinced that their community alliance network was more intact than that of the newer community, with its larger houses and lots. The statistics taken showed a lesser tendency toward sharing of services and consumer goods in the newer community. In the older community 65 percent of the residents shared services compared to 37 percent in the newer community; 53.3 percent of the first group shared consumer goods compared with 37 percent of the second group. Similar studies were also done with communities on Oahu and Kauai with comparable findings (Anderson and Pestaño, 1975).

Personal communication with residents of the Ewa Beach community suggests the presence of alliance networks across ethnic lines utilizing the same baptismal and wedding sponsorship devices found in the older alliances in Waialua. Full-scale goods-and-services sharing functions appear to characterize these alliances in Ewa. Such cross-ethnic alliances were not evident in Maunaloa in 1975, and it would be interesting to explore the factors (e.g., major ethnic groups involved, religious ties, household distances, camp grouping by ethnicity) involved in the Ewa alliances. It is possible that cross-ethnic alliances as adaptive strategies reflect changing attitudes on the part of the host society.

SECOND LIFE GOAL

The goal of family reunification was explicitly embodied in both legislative and administrative changes as a result of the 1965 Immigration Act. The law allocated 74 percent of all visas to the relatives of American citizens and permanent residents. These features of the law helped numerous Filipinos to realize two previously unattainable objectives: (1) bringing in immediate family members originally left behind, and (2) acquiring new brides from the Philippines. Many elderly Filipinos, although already retired or nearing retirement, had not given up their second life goal of establishing a family, despite the long wait. In Maunaloa, for example, approximately 44 percent of all immigrants arrived after 1965, and the large majority of these post-1965 immigrants were young women who had met and married elderly Filipinos from the plantation while these men were visiting the Philippines (Forman, 1976). In most of these cases, the men had returned to the Philippines for the express purpose of marrying. In at least two cases, two unrelated men had married sisters. All but a handful of the women have since borne several children. While problems of unmet expectations, disagreements regarding child rearing, and other difficulties do exist within these marriages, a considerable number are stable and relatively harmonious. The birth and baptism of a child to one of these couples is one of the most important celebrations in the town.

In the past few years highly placed government officials have raised opposition to Filipino immigration. In 1974 an article in the *Honolulu Star-Bulletin* (February 26, 1974), headlined "High Costs of Immigration Questioned," reported that a committee headed by the director of Hawaii's Department of Social Services and Housing was investigating the national immigration policy for possible changes to relieve those states with "severe alien problems." The director cited costs for welfare, medical care, education, housing, and "displacement of possible employment to local citizens" as reasons for concern.

Several Filipinos as individuals and in associated groups reacted to this threat to the reunification of families; firm statements of opposition were voiced.

Recent studies provide some information on the status of Filipino families during the third-wave period. One study suggests that traditional families (as opposed to those headed by women) characterize Filipino, Hawaiian, and immigrant groups in Kalihi-Palama (Sybinsky, 1977). Another study (Higginbotham and Marsella, 1977) cites separation from family (among some immigrants in the same area—Kalihi-Palama) and the incidence and threat of divorce as sources of stress. Filipinos feel keenly the burdens and expenses of child rearing. Some cannot afford to buy things children need for school. They are saddened by the absence of caretakers (who in the Philippines are numerous among extended kin) when both parents work.

Future educational and economic opportunities for children, as with most groups, are topics of intense concern and planning. During field work in Maunaloa, a Molokai community, the author found that most Filipinos thought that educational opportunities for children were better in the United States, yet a few still intend to send (or have already sent) their children back to prestigious schools in the

Philippines. One motivation for this is to spare them the discrimination arising from stereotypes of Filipinos in Hawaii's schools. It is also felt that an education in the Philippines might instill in children some of the values taught to their parents which, in turn, might reduce serious intergenerational problems that some parents feel are characteristic of too many Filipino households in Hawaii. There is also some concern about bilingual/bicultural education in the schools. To some Filipino groups this would be both a desirable educational approach in a multicultural community and a means of preserving the integrity of families. Administration and curriculum specialists within the school system, however, constantly debate the type of bilingual/bicultural education which should be taught and the objectives and expected outcome of the various possible programs. It appears as though bilingual education exists in Hawaii schools only as a concession to federal pressures.

How do Filipino children fare in the Department of Education? Data from the Hawaii Association of Asian and Pacific Peoples (1974) show that Filipinos are found in greater numbers in schools with low achievement scores; that in 1970 39.4 percent of Filipinos sixteen years and older completed high school compared to 65.1 percent of the Chinese and 61.3 percent of the Japanese.

A 1971 study on Kauai showed Hawaiian and Filipino children at age ten to have the largest percentage of Ds or Fs in reading, writing, or arithmetic. "One child out of every two Hawaiian and Filipino children had such problems" (Werner, Bierman, and French, 1971). Filipino respondents to a recent survey expressed a strong desire to make up for educational deficiencies (Higginbotham and Marsella, 1977).

The Oahu Filipino Community Council, an umbrella organization for more than sixty Filipino civic organizations on Oahu, has addressed itself on numerous occasions to what it sees as barriers to equal educational opportunity, including disproportionately small numbers of Filipino teachers and administrators in the Department of Education, disproportionate placement of Filipino children in special education classes, disproportionate expulsion of Filipino students, and language discrimination.

Although Filipinos represent approximately 11 to 12 percent of the state's population, 17 percent of the students in the Department of Education are Filipino. Because of these large numbers of Filipino children continuing efforts to increase educational opportunities will probably characterize Filipino strategies to achieve their second life goal.

THIRD LIFE GOAL

The unemployment rate for Oahu Filipinos as a whole in 1975 was 7.3 percent, lower than that of Oahu residents as a whole (7.9 percent) (Cariño, forthcoming). Unemployment rates were higher, however, among third-wave immigrants than those for immigrants in the first two waves (Cariño, Table 2). The unemployment level among the nonmigrant Filipino population (10.5 percent) was much higher than that among the foreign-born (6.5 percent, see Cariño, Table 12), suggesting that the immigrant population has "accepted lower-paying, servile types of jobs when compared with the non-migrants."

There are other recent studies of socioeconomic status indicators for Filipinos, particularly in Kalihi-Palama, the area of largest concentration. The following data summarize recurrent findings: Filipinos, Hawaiians, and immigrants as a whole cluster together in what Sybinsky's (1977) factor analytic study labels "the underprivileged minorities dimension." (These groups are explicitly targeted by federal and state authorities as "underprivileged.") Filipinos report job dissatisfaction and difficulties seeking employment—problems they react to with anger, unhappiness, and discouragement. Lim (1971) reports that, in her sample, in attempting to find solutions to some of these problems 33 percent of the Filipinos go to relatives and friends, 34 percent do not know where to go, 17 percent go to banks, 10 percent to agencies, 3 percent to counselors, and 3 percent to churchmen, but the latter only for advice. Higginbotham and Marsella (1977) report that Filipinos cite the slowness, inefficiency, and negligence of public agency assistance; to these they react with anger and impatience. They are "torn between persistently confronting the system with their needs and requirements and simply giving up by avoiding further direct dealings with the agencies."

Compounding such socioeconomic difficulties, Filipinos face further endangerment just when they are most vulnerable from constraints on employment, such as earlier citizenship requirements, and from intermittent public announcements from high-ranking government officials who want to enact such measures as "a constitutional amendment permitting states to establish residency requirements for new arrivals for publicly supported programs such as welfare assistance, public employment and housing (Governor Ariyoshi, State of the State Address, January 25, 1977).

The Ninth State Legislature passed Act 211 which imposes durational residency for public employment in Hawaii. This was challenged by the American Civil Liberties Union (ACLU) in behalf of four plaintiffs, and a federal judge issued a temporary injunction restraining the act's enforcement.

A state administration attempt to impose similar requirements for welfare recipients died in the House Committee on Public Assistance and Human Services when the committee chairman claimed that the proposed bill was "capricious and punitive" and that the administration should explore "other approaches which are more equitable and would save the State money" (*Honolulu Star-Bulletin*, April 5, 1977).

Third-wave Filipino immigrants have responded both as individuals and in groups to such recent threats to their third life goal.

In 1972 an employee sued for reinstatement when she was fired from her job with the Model Cities Outreach to the Elderly Project on the ground that she was not a United States citizen. Mrs. Domingo was reinstated and the Honolulu City/County deputy corporation counsel noted that the agreement reached in the case meant an effective end to the citizenship requirement for city and county employment, although the matter would have to be considered on a case-by-case basis (David and King, 1972).

The Interagency Council for Immigrant Affairs (IAC) position on residency requirements for immigrants on welfare and for public employment states that it constitutes inequitable, unjust treatment of a small minority of the actual state welfare caseload and actual number of public employees (IAC Legislative Packet, 1978 Session).

Filipino individuals and groups are also participating in current efforts to ensure compliance with the Civil Rights Act of 1964 in the state departments of Health (*Mangrobang* vs. *Yuen*, 1976) and Social Services and Housing (HEW citation for noncompliance, November 1968).

Conclusion:

The brief overview of Filipino immigration presented in this section suggests a cultural context from which to view specific stresses that may arise as a result of socioeconomic problems. Filipinos feel they are better able to function normally when they have developed extensive alliance systems which involve regular and predictable exchanges of goods and services among many households, in an atmosphere of responsibility and good will. Their coping behaviors over the years reflect this value. There have, no doubt, been violations of behavior norms associated with the value, and the value, in its specific manifestations, is likely to undergo continual change. Stresses associated with these changes are themselves interesting subjects for mental health research. Parents in Maunaloa, Molokai, explicitly articulated their concern that they were not successfully passing on their own notions of the good life to their children. Their older children, they claimed, were succumbing to the pressures to adopt life goals which were ranked in reverse order to the parents—economic productivity and financial status first, family and pride next, and neighborliness last, if at all. Their younger children needed to be disciplined constantly for disrespectful behavior towards alliance members—failing to acknowledge their relationships by appropriate kin terms of address when meeting these people in the streets, in their homes, or at social events. The parents attribute these failures to what they call growing ''immorality'' among second generation children, which they associate with lack of concern for the elderly who are integral and revered members of alliance systems in the Philippines, and which they see manifested in the decreasing evidence of helping behaviors among their siblings and peers. Whiting and Whiting (1973) may be seen as providing support for the Maunaloa parents where they find in their study increased altruism in societies that are kin-oriented and depend on reciprocal services (as opposed to cash economies) for social welfare. In this cross-cultural study Filipino children in an Ilocano barrio in the Philippines scored 63 percent on a measure of altruistic behavior as compared to 8 percent for children of a New England town in the United States.

An increasingly individualistic and materialistic society reduces the chances of accommodating group goals to extend affiliative networks. This same concern is most eloquently advanced today by leaders of Hawaiian movements. It is this similarity between Hawaiian and Filipino notions of human dignity and accomplishment, with identical emphases on affiliation and interpersonal harmony, that suggests that the passage of time alone will do little more for

Filipinos in Hawaii than it has done for Hawaiians. The "wait your turn" theory of adaptation that sometimes appears to characterize the host society's attitudes toward Filipinos is gravely flawed when scrutinized from this Hawaiian perspective.

Assimilation strategies of many Filipinos (as of Hawaiians as well) have increasingly challenged the viability of affiliative approaches to the good life. The lack of a larger host-society commitment to biculturalism creates an either/or atmosphere that is at least partly responsible for intragroup as well as intergroup conflicts.

In Hawaii it is increasingly unfashionable to discuss ethnicity at all, on the grounds that it is divisive (existing chasms among groups notwithstanding). There is cause for optimism, however, in the work of a few individuals: teachers, counselors, members of ethno-cultural organizations, agency workers, and others who work directly with the large numbers of young Filipinos in the state, encouraging them to understand and evaluate their heritage, to recognize the people who shaped and gave dignity to it, and to determine and realize their life goals.

A great deal of research remains to be done, perhaps by some of these young Filipinos. Much of the literature dealing with purported Filipino characteristics is based on concepts generated in the American academic community. As Sechrest, Fay, and Zaidi (1972) observed, certain popular concepts (i.e., aggression, hostility, and authoritarianism) are not necessarily salient in the Philippines, or defined in the same way in the Philippines as in America. These concepts and their correlates seem to be brought into the field by American researchers wherever they go. Unless the concepts are validated, their use in the human and social services may simply result in substituting new stereotypes for old.

There has already been much criticism regarding the uselessness of these concepts for explaining behavior in the Philippines. Ethnographic data, in particular, present evidence contrary to the behavior predicted in the more psychologically oriented literature. The range and variability of behavior as described by ethnographers make the psychological concepts and propositions appear simplistic.

In Hawaii, where the multicultural setting as well as the specific social and institutional factors discussed in this section can be expected to alter behavior in significant ways, it is all the more important that psychological concepts invoked in working with Filipinos be based on systematic observation of actual behavior.

Mental Health Implications
Danilo Ponce

A 1974 HEW report on alcohol, drug abuse, and mental health in Hawaii provides a sample of community opinions and definitions of cross-group mental health in Hawaii. Respondents who were interviewed gave the following items as important concerns relevant to a definition of mental health:

land ownership
land use
needed social services
federal funding
in-migration
increase in tourism
low-paying jobs
residency requirements
unequal distribution of resources
mechanization
automation
the educational system (bilingual/bicultural immigrant grouping in classes for the metally retarded)
civil service rules which often eliminate immigrant applicants
emotional and learning problems of children
problems of elderly, including housing
competition, hostilities, and conflicts among ethnic groups
lack of systematic needs assessment

These are concerns that indicate the salience of socioeconomic variables.

Specific references to Filipinos in the report include statistics on their usage of state hospitals (2.8 percent of all users), in-patient (4.3 percent) and out-patient (6.4 percent) services, intragroup conflicts, plantation shutdowns affecting older Filipinos, Filipinos' acceptance and tolerance of "abnormal" behavior, their relative comfort with nurses and paraprofessionals as opposed to psychiatrists and psychologists, and their concern with regular health services as opposed to mental health services.

Some approaches to these problems can be suggested: first, it is neither fair nor wise to lump all Filipinos into a single category. The clinician must discover where they came from originally, when, whether they are immigrants or Hawaii-born, their education and training, and their socioeconomic status. "Typical" Filipinos may have difficulty recognizing and acknowledging emotional factors as a basis of problems. For them it is easier to present "a touch of the flu," or a "headache," or "punishment from God," or from "spirits," rather than depression touched off by problems with anxiety, anger, or self-esteem. They may feel that to acknowledge emotion is a sign of weakness, and for a man a lack of manhood. It may be difficult for them to comprehend how such intangibles as emotions could result in very tangible somatic manifestations such as loss of appetite, loss of weight, and sleeplessness.

Filipinos may view the mental health worker with alarm or confusion—alarm because the presence of the mental health worker may reinforce a belief that they are insane or weak, and confusion because they honestly may not understand why they should be seeing a mental health worker. The first task, then, may be to clarify the reason for the appointment, not dwelling on emotional considerations, but not ignoring them either. Secondly, the patient may wish to see the mental health worker as an expert and the clinician may need to take on the role of an authority, at least at the beginning. To do this involves an authoritative explanation of what is wrong, directions and advice as to what is to be done about it, what the intervention entails and for how long. Clinical experience suggests that it is wise to avoid, at least until a solid relationship has been established, emphasis on such Western approaches as communication, interpersonal relations, introspection, and so forth. Instead, efforts should be directed toward pragmatic, problem solving strategies through which results can be demonstrated. Examples are: concentration on not drinking too much, helping find the patient a job, or ironing out youngsters' school problems.

Finally, the clinician is advised to be satisfied with achieving limited goals. Indeed, working with Filipino children and adolescents is even more difficult because the clinician must contend with the cultural attitudes and the prescribed role of children and adolescents. The child may not speak unless spoken to and even then the response may be very brief, limited at times to mere nodding or shaking the head, so that a good deal of patience and tolerance is essential. A most effective way to establish a trusting relationship is to help the youngster deal with concrete problems, serving as a spokesman with teachers and parents or teaching him how to do things better, such as to achieve a better command of English. Once the relationship of trust has been established, it is possible with either child, adolescent, or adult to move into further explorations of feelings, hopes, ambitions, and attitudes.

References

Abbott, William L. Filipino labor struggles in the islands. *Hawaii Pono Journal,* 1971, 3:56–68.

Alcantara, Ruben R. The Filipino wedding in Waialua, Hawaii: Ritual retention and ethnic subculture in a new setting. *Amerasia Journal,* 1972, 1:4:1–12.

———. The Filipino community in Waialua. Ph.D. thesis, University of Hawaii, 1973.

———. Filipino adaptation in a Hawaiian plantation setting. Paper read at the Conference on International Migration from the Philippines, East-West Center, Honolulu, 1975.

Alcantara, Ruben R.; Alconcel, Nancy S.; with Wycoco, Cesar. *The Filipinos in Hawaii: An annotated bibliography.* Honolulu: The Social Science Research Institute, 1972.

Anderson, Robert N., and Pestaño, Rebecca Y. Computer printout from 1975 survey. University of Hawaii, College of Tropical Agriculture.

Ariyoshi, George, Governor of Hawaii. State of the State Address. Honolulu, January 25, 1977.

Cariño, Benjamin. *Filipinos on Oahu.* Honolulu: East-West Population Institute, forthcoming.

David, Kenneth H., and King, William L. *The immigrant study.* Honolulu: Office of Social (Human) Resources, 1972.

Daws, Gavan. *Shoal of time: A history of the Hawaiian Islands.* Honolulu: University Press of Hawaii, 1974.

Forman, Sheila Maria da Silva. The social-psychological context of planning in response to industrial withdrawal: A case study of a Filipino plantation town in Hawaii. M.A. thesis, University of Hawaii, 1976.

Fuchs, Lawrence H. *Hawaii pono: A social history.* New York: Harcourt, Brace, and World, 1961.

Guthrie, George M. *Six perspectives on the Philippines.* Manila: Bookmark, 1968.

Hawaii Association of Asian and Pacific Peoples. *A shared beginning: An Asian and Pacific perspective of social conditions in Hawaii.* Proceedings, Statewide Mental Health Conference, Honolulu, June 14–15, 1974.

Hawaii Commission on Manpower and Full Employment. *Immigrants in Hawaii.* Honolulu: Immigrant Services Center, 1978.

Higginbotham, Howard N., and Marsella, Anthony J. Immigrant adaptation in Hawaii. Unpublished manuscript, 1977.

Hollnsteiner, Mary R. *The dynamics of power in a Philippine municipality.* Quezon City: Community Development Research Council, University of the Philippines, 1963.

Honolulu Star-Bulletin. "High Costs of Immigration Questioned." February 26, 1974.

Hormann, Bernhard L. and Kasdon, Lawrence M. Integration in Hawaii schools. *Educational Leadership,* 1959, 16:403–408.

Interagency Council for Immigrant Affairs. Legislative packet, 1978 session.

Jocano, F. Landa. *Growing up in a Philippine barrio.* New York: Holt, Rinehart, and Winston, 1969.

Kalihi-Palama Interagency Council for Immigrant Services, Inc. Annual Report, 1977.

Kawaguchi, Paul T., and Jedlicka, Davor. *A study of the illiteracy provisions of the federal voting rights act and its application to the Hawaii electorate.* Hawaii Dept. of Health, Research & Statistics Office Report, no. 6, 1975.

Kuhn, Delia, and Kuhn, Ferdinand. *The Philippines yesterday and today.* New York: Holt, Rinehart and Winston, 1966.

Lapuz, Lourdes V. *A study of psychopathology.* Quezon City: University of the Philippines Press, 1973.

Lim, G. Kalihi area needs survey undertaken by the Maryknoll Sisters: Final composite report. Unpublished manuscript, 1971.

Lynch, Frank, and de Guzman, Alfonso. *Four readings on Philippine values.* Quezon City: Ateneo de Manila University Press, 1973.

McWilliams, Carey. *Brothers under the skin.* Boston: Little, Brown and Co., 1943.

Melendy, H. Brett. Filipinos. *Harvard encyclopedia on American ethnic groups.* Forthcoming.

Mendez, Paz Policarpio, and Jocano, F. Landa. *The Filipino family in its rural and urban orientation: Two case studies.* Manila: Centro Escolar University, 1974.

Nader, Laura, and Maretzki, Thomas W. (eds.). *Cultural illness and health: Essays in human adaptation.* Washington, D.C.: American Anthropological Association, 1973.

Norbeck, Edward. *Pineapple town, Hawaii.* Berkeley: University of California Press, 1959.

Nydegger, William, and Nydegger, Corinne. *Tarong: An Ilocos barrio in the Philippines.* New York: Wiley, 1966.

President's Commission on Mental Health. *Task panel reports.* Washington, D.C.: US Government Printing Office, 1978.

Samuels, Frederick. *The Japanese and the Haoles in Honolulu.* New Haven: College and University Press, 1970.

Sechrest, Lee; Fay, T.; and Zaidi, S. Problems of translation in cross-cultural research. *Journal of Cross-cultural Psychology,* 1972, 3(1):41–50.

Sharma, Miriam. Pinoy in paradise: Environment and adaptation of the Filipinos in Hawaii 1906–1946. Paper read at the East-West Center Conference on International Migration from the Philippines, East-West Center, Honolulu, 1975.

Smith, Peter C. The social demography of Filipino migrations abroad. East-West Center Population Institute Reprint No. 82. *International Migration Review,* 1976, 10(3).

Sybinsky, Peter A. *A multivariate study of social indicators for the Kalihi-Palama catchment area.* Kalihi-Palama Community Mental Health Center Branch Research Report No. 2, 1977.

US Department of Health, Education, and Welfare; Alcohol, Drug Abuse and Mental Health Administration, Minority Advisory Committee. *Alcohol, drug abuse, and mental health in Hawaii: A Pacific Asian perspective.* 1974.

US Department of Health, Education, and Welfare; Office of Civil Rights. Letter from Floyd L. Pierce, Director, to Andrew Chang, Director, Hawaii Department of Social Services and Housing, 1968.

US District Court, District of Hawaii. *Mangrobang* vs. *Yuen,* 76–0365, filed September 3, 1976.

Werner, Emmy; Bierman, Jessie M.; and French, Fern E. *Children of Kauai: A longitudinal study from the prenatal period to age ten.* Honolulu: University Press of Hawaii, 1971.

Whiting, John W., and Whiting, Beatrice. Altruistical and egoistic behavior in six cultures. In Laura Nader and Thomas W. Maretzki (eds.), *Cultural illness and health: Essays in human adaptation.* Washington, D.C.: American Anthropological Association, 1973.

Wright, Theon. *The disenchanted isles: The story of the second revolution in Hawaii.* New York: Dial Press, 1972.

Youngblood, Robert L. The political socialization of high school students and their parents in the city of Manila, 1972. Ph.D. thesis, University of Michigan, 1974.

CHAPTER 10

The Samoans

Richard A. Markoff
John R. Bond

The Samoan Islands are divided into two political entities: American
Samoa and Western Samoa. American Samoa is a territory of the
United States, and Western Samoa is an independent kingdom with
close ties to New Zealand, having been formerly governed by New
Zealand under a United Nations mandate.

The two Samoas are disproportionate in size and population.
Western Samoa has much the greater land area and much more of its
land is arable. The population of Western Samoa is about 150,000
compared with approximately 28,000 in American Samoa. Nevertheless, American Samoa has a higher standard of living and considerably more social services, as a result of American technical and financial support. During most of this century, American Samoa was a US
Territory under the administration of the Department of the Navy,
which used it as a coaling station. Gray (1960) has given a detailed
history of the naval administration of the islands. During the past
several decades, American Samoa has been administered by the
United States Department of Interior under a governor appointed by
the president. In November 1977, after years of declining to do so,
the American Samoans elected their own governor for the first time.

Culturally, the two Samoas are similar. At one time, they were
united politically, although the union was always relatively loose.
Thus, there are important cultural and family ties between the two
Samoas; and there is a certain amount of migration to the United
States from Western Samoa, via American Samoa. Most of the Sa-
moan population movement to both Hawaii and the mainland
United States, however, has been from American Samoa. It began in

a fashion very different from that of any other ethnic group coming to Hawaii, that is, via the United States Navy.

Samoans have come for a variety of reasons: some in search of greater economic opportunity; some to escape the somewhat restrictive social environment of Samoa; and some, no doubt, are drawn by the prior migration of relatives. The family is a most important element in Samoan social organization, and the choice of Hawaii or the US mainland by migrating Samoans may depend as much on where other family members live as on the specific ideas and aspirations of the migrants. Many young Samoan men have enlisted in the American armed services during the last two decades, and their experiences in the course of military duties outside Samoa have provided a powerful stimulus for their own migration and that of their peers. Moreover, Samoan life has been changing, especially during the last decade, in ways which may tend to favor migration.

Traditional Culture and Recent Developments

The Samoan economy has traditionally been based on subsistence agriculture, and, in many important respects, it remains so. The unit of social organization is the extended family or *aiga*. The *aiga* contains several nuclear families related by blood or by marriage, and it may also contain members who are adopted. The *aiga* will possess several houses in a village, agricultural lands, and material goods.

At the head of the *aiga* is a chief or *matai*. A chief enjoys high status and carries out a considerable range of judicial, executive, and ceremonial functions. But a chief's rule is not absolute. Rather, the chief rules as an influential executive who must nevertheless keep an ear carefully tuned to the sentiments of the *aiga,* and who must depend upon agreement and consensus within the *aiga* on important issues. Chieftainship tends to be hereditary, but the rules of inheritance are somewhat elastic.

A Samoan village is made up of several *aiga.* The village is governed by a council or *fono* composed of the chiefs of the *aiga.* The process of decision within the *fono* is one of consensus, and important matters require unanimity. There are status differences among the *matai* who make up the village *fono,* and the *matai* with the highest status represents the village at a district *fono.* The most influential district *matai* form still another government level. Social and political organization is thus hierarchic, and involves several levels and many gradations of status. Moreover, the relationships among titles with respect to status are many and complex, and the possibilities of social mobility are correspondingly complicated.

Given such a social organization, it is not surprising to find that the dominant values of the culture include the primacy of the *aiga* in nearly all matters. The concerns of the *aiga* are to be placed above the concerns of any of its members. This translates, in many instances, into obedience to the wishes of the *matai;* and, of course, the ideal case of such a system would be one in which the needs and concerns of the *matai* coincide precisely with those of the *aiga*. Obedience has therefore been a consistent, major theme in the education of children. Because the hereditary principle with respect to titles is not strictly adhered to, and the elective element is considerable, it is not usual for a man to come into a title for which he may be eligible much before middle age. The value of respect for and obedience to the *matai* thus takes on a generational aspect: the contrast between the wisdom of experience and maturity and the comparatively limited wisdom of untried youth is a factor. This tends further to strengthen another important social value: respect for one's elders.

As a corollary to the primacy of the *aiga*, persons outside the *aiga* may very well be regarded with suspicion, or even as potential enemies. In traditional Samoan culture each individual belongs to some *aiga;* thus, relations between people of different *aiga* are greatly influenced by the relations between their *aiga*. Relations of hostility and distrust do not always exist between people of different *aiga*. There are relatively close ties between *aiga* within a given village, and friendships between their members are common. Different villages may have specific relationships with one another. A good deal of ceremony attends and mediates these interfamily relationships.

A further corollary of the primacy of the *aiga*, taken together with the potentialities for upward movement, is the importance of status. Essentially, status serves to locate an individual within the social fabric. Thus, the concern with status translates into a concern with personal ambition in a society which is highly group oriented.

Other important values in Samoan culture emphasize cooperative effort in economic affairs and attitudes of resignation and stoicism with respect to those aspects of nature which seem to be beyond possibility of human control.

The measures used by a society for social control and discipline are quite relevant to mental health. In Samoan culture they tend to be direct and overt, and often involve physical punishment and public exposure or "shaming." These methods are employed both in the education of children and in the control of the deviant behavior of adults. The ultimate measure of social control, however, has always been banishment from the *aiga*.

The subject of social control leads immediately to the related matter of education and child rearing. That association is particularly relevant in any discussion of Samoan culture, for social control is a very prominent, explicit element of the traditional Samoan educative process. The Samoan view is that the goal of education is wisdom, which involves comprehension of the complexities of the social structure, and leads to correct social behavior. Wisdom develops with time, and the "bad" behavior of children meanwhile is to be discouraged and controlled by punishment. Punitive measures are regularly employed by age three, when children first begin to be involved in the work of the household, and continue through mid-adolescence.

Small children past infancy are placed in the care of older children, who see to it that they do not interfere more than is absolutely necessary with the lives of the adults. Adults, of course, continue to be active in matters of discipline and training. The *matai* of the *aiga* and his wife are often as important as the biological parents, if not more so. The functions of parenthood, and the corresponding filial relationships, if compared to the American pattern tend to be diffuse in Samoan culture.

In a social order as closely structured as the Samoan there would seem to be little room for the expression of aggressive feeling—especially when such behavior might be seen as rebellious. A Samoan in a rebellious frame of mind could turn for support to the several peer organizations that exist in the traditional community; or he could displace his aggressive behavior "downward"—in the social sense. But the ultimate response would be to remove himself and associate with a different *aiga*, a symmetrical counterpart to the traditional, ultimate sanction of the *aiga* against the individual.

No description of Samoan culture would be complete without some consideration of the role of Christianity. The largest aggregate membership belongs to the London Missionary Society (LMS) Church, which is Congregational. Lesser, but still substantial Roman

Catholic and Mormon congregations make up the bulk of the remainder. Christianity was introduced into Samoa during the first half of the nineteenth century and has acquired great importance over the years. Ministers are highly respected and have the status, although not the political power, of *matai* even when they are untitled. They perform important educative as well as religious functions and may exercise considerable influence upon village life and public policy. They do not, however, traditionally occupy the role of pastoral counsellor as Western society defines that function. Organized Christianity remains a considerably more direct and immediate moral and ethical influence in Samoa than it is in many Western cultures.

There have been a number of forces at work in American Samoa that have tended to introduce changes or to weaken the traditional culture and social organization. One of these has been the imposition of control by institutions of the US government. Thus, for example, there has grown up a legal system for the adjustment of disputes. This system, however, much as it attempts to take cognizance of the traditional institutions and standards of social control, nevertheless tends to weaken those traditional institutions. Then there is an educational system, heavily subsidized by the United States and influenced by American culture—although definite efforts are made to integrate these influences with traditional *fa'a Samoa*, the "Samoan way of life." The effect is to intensify generational conflicts within the fabric of Samoan life and to promote attitudes and behavior that are viewed from the standpoint of *fa'a Samoa* as disrespectful.

The educational system makes extensive use of television and has brought entertainment programming, as well as educational programming, to American Samoa. This has had a powerful impact upon Samoan culture. Television programs present a vivid, compelling, and often attractive view of life outside Samoa—especially in the United States. News broadcasts tend to diminish the Samoan isolation from external events. The result, again, is to weaken the hold of traditional culture, to encourage change, and to encourage emigration.

There are other forces, perhaps less immediately apparent, but even more powerful. One of these is the shift toward an increasingly youthful population which occurs wherever Western public health technology is applied. Emigration, also, has served to produce this same result. This again intensifies implicit generational conflicts.

Finally, during the past decade there has been considerable growth, especially in terms of complexity, in the Samoan economy. The development of hotels, fish canneries, air traffic, and recently, some light industry have provided greater opportunities for the earning of wages, as has the continued development of the governmental bureaucracy. There also are more opportunities to shop for consumer goods. The shops, although they cater to the *papalagi,* or Caucasian population, demonstrate very concretely to the Samoans what money can buy.

All of this has led to pressures upon the traditional subsistence agriculture and economy, and a general weakening of the traditional organization of society. *Matai* and *aiga* still continue to be of central influence, though traditional values are no longer so controlling; but by the same token, neither traditional institutions nor values are as effectively supportive as they once were.

The Position of Samoans in Hawaii*

Residents of American Samoa are US citizens and may travel freely between their islands and all the states of the Union. Hawaii and California are the most common destinations, although Samoans are also settling in other parts of the country. It should be noted that the number of Samoans outside the Samoan islands far exceeds the population at home. The movement of Samoans to Hawaii and elsewhere began during World War II. The US Navy, which used Samoa as a wartime base, and the general ferment of the war made Samoans much more aware of the outside world, the United States in particular. A number of young Samoans enlisted and came to Hawaii where some of them settled after the war. Migration increased from a few hundred soon after World War II to several thousand in the mid-seventies. In 1976 the Lieutenant Governor's Survey, done by the Hawaii Department of Health, counted 4537 Samoans in Hawaii. The estimate in 1978 is more than 6000. Only a small number, less than 15 percent in 1976, are members of the armed forces and their dependents. The majority of Samoans live on the island of Oahu. They come from both titled and untitled classes.

---

*Portions of the remaining sections of this chapter were written by the editors, who wish to acknowledge the assistance of medical student Louie Fiatoa without implicating him in responsibility for the statements made.

Growing up in Samoa is not an effective preparation for life in Hawaii. Even the considerable changes in Samoa, especially on the island of Tutuila, in no way approximate contemporary Hawaii. The capital of Pago Pago and its surrounding areas can be compared with one of the neighbor islands twenty years ago. Yet a small rustic airport with a single runway that accommodates the largest passenger airplanes is the takeoff point for Samoan travelers who come as migrants.

Samoans move to Hawaii in search of economic opportunities and to join relatives who have preceded them. It is only a flight of a few hours, but the cultural distance between the relatively traditional Polynesian setting in which communally and kinship-based Samoan culture continues and the modern Americanized setting in Hawaii provide a sharp contrast which no Samoan arriving for the first time can escape. How Hawaii appears to a Samoan who for the first time leaves his native islands can probably not be appreciated by anyone else, except through a general realization that it must be a remarkable experience. The journey begins at one of the outer islands or on the main island, from which travelers converge on the terminal at Pago Pago International Airport; there they are surrounded by a large group of relatives who come to wish them farewell, showing their concern and affection, and sharing their good wishes while hanging shell leis around their necks. A few hours later, the plane deposits the Samoan migrants at the busy Honolulu airport, which must seem confusing with hundreds of people milling around who make the few relatives or friends who have come to welcome the migrants the only familiar sight. Traffic confusion, impersonal encounters, the neatly arranged houses and apartment buildings which all reflect the individualism and relative isolation of American families, and most of all the English language which is spoken everywhere are evidence of the tremendous psychological distance covered across a relatively narrow segment of the Pacific Ocean.

Samoans are residents in some rural districts on the North Shore and Waianae, as well as in parts of central Honolulu. In areas such as the Mormon community of Laie and the surrounding small communities, the patterns of extended families living together continue, and in some ways the lifestyle there may be more reminiscent of the home islands. Those who are residents of the urban areas, notably Kalihi-Palama, live in small apartments in which a father, mother, and their children are crammed together in limited space, with hardly any opportunity to grow food in a garden. Obviously, the length of time spent in Hawaii is a significant factor in the adjustment and activities of each Samoan when it is considered that some have been in Hawaii for thirty years and others have arrived very recently.

The work experience of Samoans varies widely. While the number of Samoans entering college increases steadily, it generally lags proportionally in comparison with other ethnic groups in Hawaii. A few Samoan men are preparing to become physicians or have entered residency training. Almost no women of Samoan background at this time are in educational or training programs leading to licensed professional positions in the health or welfare services in Hawaii. A few Samoans who have finished college are in appropriate positions in the community, but it seems that for cultural and other reasons Samoan women are more disadvantaged in that respect than are Samoan men. Nurse's training in American Samoa leads to a practical nursing diploma which is not recognized in Hawaii, therefore professional transfer from Samoa to Hawaii is precluded.

Among the most important leaders in the Samoan community are ministers of the various churches who often assume the functions of the traditional *matai,* although they themselves are not titled. Those Samoans who have a title or a status position are not expected to work in common jobs, such as labor or menial activities.

Because of their recent arrival, language difficulties, inadequate training, and for reasons of insufficient cultural adjustment, job opportunities are particularly limited for many Samoans. Men will engage in a variety of activities, menial or semiskilled, until better opportunities arise. Contrary to a common stereotype of Honolulu residents, however, only a small number of Samoans are employed at agrarian jobs, such as tree trimming and yard work. Very few Samoan women are employed because there is in Samoan culture no demand on them to find outside employment and their proper role is considered to be mother and housekeeper, no less and no more. Given the cultural preference of Samoan women toward not working, the presence of many elderly relatives living with their families, and the large numbers of young people, it may seem as though unemployment is high. Coupled with the role of the extended family in Samoa, and the difficulties in providing for a large family in a total cash economy such as that in Hawaii, there are a number of adjustment problems which are often judged inappropriately and without knowledge of the factors that characterize the Samoans' situation.

The figures for Samoan employment, unemployment, and the use of the welfare system must, therefore, be interpreted in terms of several sensitive factors, such as cultural preferences, compatibility of values, existing traditions, and other factors that take into consideration the Samoan as well as the dominant population's point of view. This, for most Hawaii residents, is not easy because there is indeed a significant cultural gap. There is a general view that Samoans are less inclined to engage in individual work because in Samoa the American government is running a benign welfare program which supports able-bodied adults or supplies goods at nominal costs. This is a very one-sided and even false interpretation of the situation, one in which families have lived off the land and their own labor for countless generations, long before the changes took place that dislodged a good deal of the native culture.

Where the extended family is responsible for mutual support, and where there are limited goods for cash purchases as in American Samoa, people's needs and consumption habits develop in a different way than in an all-cash economy where the individual family is responsible for providing income from paying jobs. This raises conflicts which are common to immigrant situations in parts of the world where similar circumstances prevail, and where the cash flow is so small; the amounts earned and spent in Hawaii seem far beyond the realities of anything known at home. The *aiga* cannot support its members in Hawaii as it does in contemporary Samoa for it controls no land. A newly arrived migrant in Hawaii is an additional mouth more than an additional pair of hands. Houses in Hawaii are differently built, different in size and in interior arrangement; thus ordinary occupancy standards, in Samoan terms, often turn out to be violations of housing codes and zoning laws here.

Given the contrast of lifestyles and other cultural differences which distinguish Samoans from the middle-class Americans whose values permeate life in Hawaii regardless of ethnicity, it is obvious that there are conflicts and misunderstandings. Unlike other immigrants to Hawaii, Samoans seem in no hurry to adopt middle-class patterns with the same speed and by the same mechanisms which have spelled such success for several groups from Asian countries that came to Hawaii. There are specific differences to which Samoans have to adapt. For instance, in Samoa there is a different concept of property: the *aiga* rather than the individual has rights over land and its products. The lack of an authority structure and the confusing or conflicting stimuli in Hawaii may affect some young Samoans shortly after their arrival. From the Western perspective Samoans are often seen as not conforming to the rules; from the Samoan perspective other factors seem of greater importance. What is lacking are sufficient numbers of leaders, sufficient preparation of migrants, adequate support systems to help Samoans who have settled in Hawaii learn to adapt to a different life, and tolerance.

One puzzling and significant difference between Samoans and the majority culture of Americans is their concept of discipline and child abuse. There is clear evidence that in disciplining their children Samoan parents consider physical punishment appropriate, and their ideas of severity or threshold seem to differ from those of the American majority and from the accepted standards of professionals. As a result many Samoans seem to be caught in the official wheels of the Children's Protective Services and other social services that try to assist them. Samoans are also found to be resistant to or lack understanding of health care matters. That this is again a function of cultural differences and preferences is intellectually understood, but raises many problems in the absence of adequate numbers of knowledgeable intermediaries. This must be a matter of considerable anguish to Samoans, but the complaints seem to come more consistently from the majority group, unless acting out in a variety of ways is considered a reaction. But this is in no way the sole response of some Samoans.

In sum, Samoans are the butt of many criticisms, stereotypes, misunderstandings, and cultural conflicts. The resulting stereotypes may be a powerful negative influence on the course of their adjustment. In this respect, the important role of churches in supporting Samoans and helping them to adjust and retain a sense of community is often overlooked. But most important, the violations of a few persons of Samoan background in no way diminishes the fact that the greater part of the Samoan community has been guided by principles of "the Samoan way," which stresses respect and courtesy, and has remained free of many of the difficulties that a minority encounters in altered life circumstances.

Mental Health and Psychological Treatment

A number of terms in the Samoan language, if glossed into English, reveal the concepts which Samoans hold about unusual behavior. There is no verification from clinical studies in Samoa, however, and no parallel studies for Samoans in Hawaii, so it is not certain what terms are used by Samoan residents of Hawaii, or to what extent meanings may have shifted.

A few examples based on interviews by Clement (1974) follow. The term *valea* covers different conditions that would be considered psychotic in Western psychiatric usage and includes those that have an organic base as well as those that do not. In a general sense this is insanity, usually a permanent condition of the individual so designated, although there are exceptions. Temporary conditions which are refractory can be brought about by unusual stresses such as excessive concern over something, too much acquisition of knowledge, or too harsh family discipline. (Note once more that these are interview statements, not clinical impressions.)

Ma'i ita covers angry outbursts or rage which is thought usually to respond to treatment at home. In this behavior, as in others, the notion that people can control their own behavior, but may at times need help to do so, governs the thinking of those others who are affected by a person with angry outbursts.

Fiafia valea can be glossed as "foolish happiness," a fit of good feeling usually associated with traditional ceremonies or ritualized situations, which may suddenly assume manic proportions to the point where the individual becomes destructive.

The term *ma'i popole* and related terms describe anxiety; lack of confidence related to the anticipated loss of an object, health, or person; unwanted pressure; or other stressful problems. This term covers deep despondence and may therefore be glossed as "depression." Unlike the perception of depression in the Western setting, however, Samoans see this condition as transient; if it takes a chronic character it then changes to *valea*.

Given these examples of terms and their meaning and behavior ranges in Samoa, there are obvious implications for migrants to Hawaii. Worry, anxiety, and depression are not uncommon reactions to the unfamiliar conditions awaiting new arrivals in Hawaii. Family support here can make some or all of the difference. But how mental health conditions change for Samoans as migrants to Hawaii in relation to what they experienced at home is not clear at this point.

Clement also comments on certain beliefs about the causes of disturbance and the handling of disturbed persons in Samoa. Some of these beliefs continue to be prevalent in Hawaii.

For example, someone seen as *valea* seems more easily aggravated and more difficult to calm down, and it is felt that such a person should not be provoked or teased by others (as contrasted with behavioral phenomena which are thought to be under the control of the individual, and, therefore, the individual has to be helped—even forcibly—to control them).

Some conditions of insanity are thought to be caused by supernatural forces, supernatural spirits, and/or specific ancestral spirits *(aitu)*. Initially, at least, individuals who know remedies for spirit possession, persons called *foma'i aitu* and *foma'i vaiaitu,* may be called for therapy. Such beliefs in spirit possession are very common, although they are discouraged by the Christian churches in Samoa. If someone is not believed to be truly possessed by a spirit, the person may be beaten in order to force the individual to drop the pretense.

Spirit-possession beliefs continue to be held by Samoans who are afflicted in Hawaii and may therefore be relevant to the explanation of causes in the diagnosed mental illness of a Samoan in Hawaii.

Among those seen as providing help in case of mental disturbances are pastors of churches. This is of specific relevance to the situation in Hawaii where members of the family or pastors are those most easily consulted. The pastor may be seen as more appropriate for conditions associated with spirits.

Since Western disbelief in spirits is clearly recognized in Samoa, and even more so in Hawaii, spirit-possession beliefs may be less likely to surface in immigrant patients and their families. Mental illness is very vaguely defined and even less so acknowledged in the Samoan social framework. Comparable labels for persons with any disorders are often plainly interpreted as "strange," "funny," or "unbecoming." What may seem a serious illness to a Western specialist is regarded with little concern by the Samoan. The illness may exist, but the alarming unconcern and sometimes wildly childlike and often malicious treatment of deviant members is done as routinely as the disciplining of a child. For this and other obscure reasons, the only term appropriately applied is *valea* which can be taken to mean any of several qualities: stupid, dumb, crazy, retarded, slow, or childish. The truth is that Samoans do not identify mental illness per se; they either look away and ignore it, or laugh it off.

Little of a general nature can be said about characteristic Samoan behavior patterns that are expressive of psychopathology or evoked by stress. The Samoan under stress goes through denial, suppression, regression, withdrawal, and other defense mechanisms. He may appear stoic in public, but the pain is there inside, the anger is pent-up, there are unseen scars still marring and degrading such an individual.

The tendency of Samoans to express directly or indirectly hostile and angry feelings is a fact of life. Often the anger is directed from the older toward younger members of the group. They also react aggressively to anxiety. There is no one available in most families to sit and counsel or help to control intrapersonal conflicts. The emphasis is on maintaining and improving interpersonal bonds.

To what extent psychological pressures are greater for Samoans in Hawaii than in their home islands is not known objectively at the present time. The high suicide rate of several Pacific populations also holds for American Samoa with an estimated thirty-four per one hundred thousand, one of the highest (Murphy, 1978). There does not seem to be a parallel high suicide trend among Samoans in Hawaii.

Recent studies show that Samoans in Samoa, as well as in Hawaii, are at high cardiovascular risk. An analysis of lipid profiles and anthropomorphics indicates that acculturation rather than migration per se is a significant factor. Recent arrival from Samoa does not seem a sufficient cause. Instead, the nature of relationships and support from the established family structure, the *aiga,* may initially ease migration pressure and help reduce the impact of coping with new cultural demands. As individual Samoans advance economically in Hawaii, the traditional family, previously a source of support, becomes a drain on resources, thereby contributing to stress as the acculturation of Samoans progresses (Hanna and Baker, 1979; Hornick, 1979). The complexity of interacting factors suggested by available data and related speculations will be clarified in future research.

From all that has been said so far, it would seem quite apparent that Western psychiatric approaches to mental disturbance may present problems in the counselling of Samoans who still closely identify with their home culture. In general, supportive and directive approaches in such situations would appear to have the greatest utility. It is obvious that for those Samoans who have little command of English, a Western therapist without an interpreter cannot be effective. Even nonverbal communications present serious problems where there are quite diverse implications or meanings attached to physical or nonverbal expressions. Therefore, the presenting symptoms have to be very carefully checked, and standard examinations, including the mental status examination, need to be administered with care and with cultural differences constantly in mind. Unfortunately, there are few other positive and helpful suggestions available at this time which would assure a better match between Western psychiatrist and Samoan patient.

The implication of all these observations is that one should be cautious about inferring mental or emotional states from behavior, especially when the behavior seems incongruous or out of place. A stoical response to physical illness should not lead to the assumption that the patient is experiencing no psychological complications or distress. The reason for stating this principle as a generality, rather than calling attention to specific behavior, is the lack of an adequate catalog of specific behavior.

Many of the problems faced by Samoans in Hawaii relate to problems of acculturation, lack of preparation, limited opportunity, and stereotyping. It follows from this that many of the problems encountered among Samoan patients may have strong social elements; they may in effect be more related to the specific social difficulties under which Samoans in Hawaii labor than they are to intrinsic psychopathology. The psychopathology one sees may often be secondary to environmental factors.

In such situations psychotherapeutic approaches alone may be insufficient. It is necessary to institute measures that directly alter the environmental situation, or that improve the ability of the individual to cope with the environmental factors involved. In a great many instances this means the provision of a specialized kind of education dealing with the issues which confront the Samoan patient. This education consists of discussing and clarifying for the patient the pertinent social and economic aspects of Hawaiian American life that seem to be poorly understood. The task is difficult and subtle, and in most cases the educational efforts need to be an integral part of a program of supportive psychotherapy rather than distinct from that program. Such a program may be carried out more effectively by one of the few trained social workers among the Samoans than by Western physicians.

One also must guard against assuming that the patient understands when he appears to understand or readily acquiesces in what is said. Repeated, careful questioning to check that the patient does in fact comprehend will often be necessary. Role playing and similar devices would probably not be helpful. A particular therapeutic task is to deal with the effects of negative stereotyping on the Samoan patient. This involves some provision for the ventilation of anger and frustration. Repeated discussion, with a goal of desensitizing the patient to the operation of stereotyping, may form part of the treatment. Later, rehearsal of specific situations and employment of a problem-solving approach in an effort to develop new and more effective responses will probably be useful.

One must be particularly on guard against the error of viewing the patient simply as a "character disorder" or perhaps an "antisocial personality." The objection is not so much that these labels are pejorative. Rather, it is that they represent opaque diagnoses, which obscure rather than clarify underlying social and psychological dynamic factors. Furthermore, they represent therapeutic dead-ends. In the case of Samoan patients the parsimonious as well as useful diagnosis is one which takes specific account of the pertinent social factors leading to apparent asociality or antisociality.

References

Alexander, John F. Samoans in the labor market. *Proceedings: Samoan Heritage Series.* University of Hawaii, 1972.

Bond, John R. Acculturation and value change. Ph.D. thesis, University of Southern California, 1967.

Clement, Dorothy, C. Samoan concepts of mental illness and treatment. Ph.D. thesis, University of California, Irvine, 1974.

Gardener, Louise C. Gantavai: A study of Samoan values. Ph.D. thesis, University of Hawaii, 1965.

Gray, John Alexander Clinton. *Amerika Samoa: A history of American Samoa and its U.S. Naval Administration.* Annapolis, Maryland: U.S. Naval Institute, 1960.

Hanna, Joel M., and Baker, Paul. Biological correlates to blood pressure of Samoan migrants in Hawaii. *Human Biology,* in press.

Hawaii Department of Health, and Department of Planning and Economic Development. Population characteristics of Hawaii, 1976. *Population Report,* no. 9. Honolulu: 1977.

Hollingshead, August de Belemont, and Redlich, Fredrick C. *Social class and mental illness: A community study.* New York: Wiley, 1958.

Hornick, Conrad. Heart disease in a migrating population. Ph.D. thesis, University of Hawaii, 1979.

Jessor, Richard; Graves, Theodore D.; Hanson, Robert C.; and Jessor, Shirley L. *Society, personality, and deviant behavior: A study of a tri-ethnic community.* New York: Holt, Rinehart and Winston, 1968.

MacDonald, James A. Substance abuse in Samoa. Unpublished manuscript, 1973.
Murphy, H. B. M. *Mental health trends in the Pacific Islands: Report on a tour of Pacific Territories, September 1977–March 1978.* Noumea, New Caledonia: South Pacific Commission, 1978.
Walters, William E. Community psychiatry in Tutuila, American Samoa. *American Journal of Psychiatry*, 1977, 134(8):917–919.

The People of Indochina

Introduction
Cheryl Tack

The people of Indochina in Hawaii comprise for the most part a refugee rather than an immigrant population. Unlike emigrants who voluntarily leave their homeland in search of better opportunities, or for reunification with their families, refugees are uprooted by an intolerable situation, usually political or religious persecution. The emigrant's departure is anticipated and planned, whereas the refugees escape, often fleeing with only the clothes they wear. Exiled and displaced, the refugees face the unknown cut off from their homeland.

Among the refugees from Indochina in Hawaii the Vietnamese are the largest and best known group, but Hawaii has also become a destination for refugees from Laos and Cambodia. Ethnically, the refugees in Hawaii are Vietnamese, Chinese from Vietnam, Lao, and Hmong from Laos. The Vietnamese have the largest number, with about 3500 people (Nguyen, 1979), but of the recent arrivals from Vietnam more have been Chinese. Hawaii is also one of the few states with a substantial community of refugees from Laos, who have come since the evacuation began in 1975. In May of 1979 there were 534 ethnic Lao in Hawaii (Sananikone, 1979), and an estimated 600 Hmong. At times there have been up to a thousand Hmong, but many have moved on to the mainland (Bliatout, 1979). There are only about a dozen Cambodian refugees in Hawaii.

All Indochina refugee arrivals share the plight of adjustment in a new country, no matter how diverse their cultural background in the home countries. Each group comes with its own cultural identity. Although there are many Chinese influences in Vietnamese culture, the Vietnamese and the Chinese from Vietnam remain distinct. There is a marked difference between the refugees from Vietnam and those from Laos, although the Vietnamese and ethnic Lao generally share a common background in terms of a dependence on wet rice agriculture, a culture shaped by Buddhism (for many), and education influenced by French colonialism. In contrast, the Hmong are mountain dwellers who depend on slash-and-burn agriculture, a group which enjoyed tribal unity and an education essentially based on maintaining native cultural traditions. In brief, the refugees come to Hawaii with a varied and rich cultural heritage.

The initial refugee evacuation began in April 1975, as new governments took control in Indochina countries. The refugees from Vietnam today continue their exodus by boats and, after dangerous voyages, reach refugee camps throughout Southeast Asia, with variable fortune. It has been estimated that about one half of the attempted escapes by sea have ended in death for the ''boat people,'' who head for the coasts of Thailand and Malaysia, and even the Philippines and Indonesia. Peoples from Cambodia and Laos continue to flee across the Mekong River into Thailand to await resettlement in camps.

More than 205,000 refugees from Indochina have been admitted to the United States since 1975 and nearly that number will enter during 1979–1980 (*U.S. News and World Report*, 1979). Approximately 12 percent of those who have come to this country have settled in Hawaii (Kavanagh, 1979).

While many of the earlier refugees who came from urban areas were professionals with advanced education, subsequent waves consist of more individuals with rural backgrounds. All come with varying skills, educational achievements, customs, and needs, and require different strategies of adaptation to life in the United States. The Vietnamese, as the best known of the refugees, will be given a major focus in this chapter. The Hmong will also be described, to illustrate a contrasting lifestyle and background and to exemplify the diversity among the people of Indochina whose history as refugees in the United States is still developing with their continued arrival.

The Vietnamese
Nguyen Dang Liem
Dean F. Kehmeier

Historical and Cultural Overview of Vietnam

It is not possible to begin to understand the Vietnamese in Hawaii without a knowledge of what life was like for them in their homeland, both traditionally and more recently in the conflict of the past thirty-five years.

"The Vietnamese live on rice and legends," says an old proverb. Legend has it that the race was born of the union of a Dragon King and a Fairy Queen—thus they are sometimes called "sons of dragons, grandsons of spirits." The best scientific evidence, while inconclusive, suggests that the Vietnamese were indeed formed of a fusion of nationalities. For centuries Vietnam has been a center of meeting and amalgamation for large Austro-Asiatic migrations; the two prevailing elements have been the Indonesian and Mongoloid. Almost from its birth this race of people was threatened with extinction by absorption into other civilizations, particularly the Chinese. Though willing to learn Chinese skills, customs, and ideology, the Vietnamese resisted from the very beginning the great assimilative power of Chinese civilization, and formed a distinct Vietnamese culture which has survived to the present day.

A dozen times in the thousand years of Chinese domination, the Vietnamese rose up against their conquerors. Once free of the Chinese, Vietnamese independence was marred by several civil wars. With the coming of the French in the nineteenth century, nine hundred years of independence ended and the traditions and beliefs of the culture were challenged with the technology and ideas of the West.

For more than a century the Vietnamese have attempted to harmonize a basically rustic culture with the materialistic civilization of the modern world. During this process clashes have occurred between their traditional values and the requirements for technological mod-

---

We are grateful to Barbara R. Ferguson and Doris W. Viola for their valuable comments on the first version of this paper, but we are entirely responsible for the views expressed.

ernization. These clashes may be the basis of the recent conflict in Vietnam.

Life in Vietnam is based on a rice culture attuned to the rhythms of the seasons of planting and harvesting. For a thousand years the technology of the water buffalo was stable. One's ancestors—the source of one's life—had planted and reaped on this land. Their graves stood in the rice fields, and their spirits continued to watch over the family. Individual death did not mark an end. Here the past and present merged, and there existed the sense of a natural harmony between man and the land, between the living and their ancestors.

The cradle of Vietnamese society was the village. Enclosed behind a tall hedge of bamboo, each village was a separate entity, complete with its own population, customs, even its own deity enshrined in the communal house—a tiny world within the world of Vietnam.

The village provided the individual Vietnamese with security in a potentially hostile environment. Within its web of social relations one's place and duties were exactly defined. Happiness consisted of fulfilling the obligations to one's family, to one's village, and to the nation. In the past, few people left the village of their birth, for to do so was to leave one's place in the world, to lose touch with one's past and one's ancestors' interactions, and to enter a moral, legal, and spiritual void.

The Westerners considered these settlements rustic, but it was within the encircling hedges of the villages that the Vietnamese found the strength to carry on a covert resistance to foreign invaders and occupations.

The Americans who attempted to influence Vietnam were generally not prepared to understand the land, its villages, or its people. They did not fully understand the importance of the village to the Vietnamese, hence mass evacuations and resettlement programs resulted in half the population of South Vietnam becoming refugees within their own land. With the old system of values under intense, prolonged pressure and without emerging values of comparable strength, it is small wonder that many people adopted the ethics of survival. "Getting by" became a way of life, especially for the dislocated and underprivileged in the cities.

In Vietnam the family rather than the individual is the basic unit of society, and harmony in personal relationships is valued more than personal achievement and competitiveness, which are equated with selfishness. Intelligence, scholarship and, by extension, wisdom, are valued more than physical prowess or bravery for its own sake. Physical beauty and grace are important attributes for both men and women, but virtue is praised most highly.

Filial devotion, brotherly love, and conjugal fidelity are also highly valued. Marriages formerly were arranged by the family; second wives and mistresses have been an institution reluctantly tolerated by the first wives. In contrast to China, however, women have enjoyed a measure of influence and freedom.

Profile of Vietnamese Character and American Misconceptions

Western observers have often been intrigued with the grace, charm, intelligence and apparent friendliness of the Vietnamese. They have also come to realize that the Vietnamese character is more complex than initially suspected.

Long experience with foreign domination has taught them a wariness of all strangers, never entirely nullified by the desire for friendship and mutual understanding. One must never be in a hurry to explain oneself. They have their own ways and will discover the truth for themselves in time.

The Vietnamese possess an inwardness, a well-developed ability to keep their true feelings hidden. Desires are expressed by indirection, by hinting and talking around the subject. American straightforwardness is considered at best impolite, at worst brutal. In Vietnam one does not come directly to the point. To do so is, for an American, a mark of honesty and forthrightness, while a Vietnamese sees it as a lack of intelligence or courtesy. Falsehood carries no moral stricture for the Vietnamese. The essential question is not whether a statement is true or false, but what the intention of the statement is. Does it facilitate interpersonal harmony? Does it indicate a wish to change the subject? Here one must perceive the heart of the speaker through his words.

In Vietnam one thinks very carefully before speaking. The American style of speaking one's mind is thus misunderstood; meanings not present are looked for and perhaps found. On the American side, meanings present are missed, leading the Vietnamese to regard Americans as unintelligent. Many Westerners may view the Vietnamese as suspicious or paranoid. Again, in Vietnam, multiple levels of meaning and covert intentions are often present and always sought. To take a statement at its face value is, for them, simply naive.

To many, the Vietnamese are seen as clannish. Obviously, in a foreign environment one wishes to associate with others of similar cultural background, and it must be remembered that in Vietnam the family commands one's first loyalty.

Sometimes the Vietnamese are seen as dependent or without individual initiative. This is generally true, but should be viewed in the context of their culture. To an American the ability to "go it alone" is seen as a strength, whereas such a posture is, for the Vietnamese, an act of selfishness. The concept of individuality is not present in the traditional Vietnamese mental framework. Strong individuals, moreover, have an automatic obligation to the weaker members of their family and their society.

The Vietnamese have a well-developed "inner life"; much emotional and mental effort may take place in a quiet individual. Passive resistance has been developed to a fine art, leading to flexibility and adaptability in the face of many years of occupation and political domination. This may be misinterpreted by some observers as indecisiveness or being "two-faced."

Francis Fitzgerald has remarked in *Fire in the Lake* (1972), "In order for the Americans and the Vietnamese to understand each other, each would have to recreate the world of the other entirely." Vietnamese adjustment to the American way of life will be accomplished more easily when each group is able to overcome its misconceptions of the other.

Vietnamese Migration to the United States

Since World War II there has been continual warfare in Vietnam. The Japanese occupied the country from 1940 to 1945, and at their surrender the French returned. A resistance movement spread in the country and defeated the French colonial forces at Dien Bien Phu in 1954. Vietnam was then divided into two countries. In the South the Republic of Vietnam came under the leadership of Ngo Dinh Diem from 1955 to 1963. The country enjoyed relative peace until 1960 when the National Liberation Front began to wage guerilla warfare. Duong Van Minh, succeeding Nguyen Van Thieu, surrendered to the advance of the North Vietnamese forces on April 29, 1975. With the sudden fall of South Vietnam, some 125,000 Vietnamese were hurriedly evacuated to Wake Island, Guam, and the Philippines. The first groups left by airplane from Tan Son Nhut Airport, the last ones by helicopter or small boats from Saigon, and then by ships off the coast of Vung Tau. From the Pacific Islands, the people were sent to refugee camps in California, Arkansas, Florida, and Pennsylvania, and to countries such as France, Canada, and Australia.

A high percentage of the evacuees in April 1975 were people who had been affiliated with the former South Vietnamese regime or the Americans. Most of them lived in urban areas, chiefly Saigon. They could trace their rural origin, however, either as first or second generation urban settlers. Many of them were among the million people who fled the North in 1954 when the Communists took over. Although they had lived in cities, deep in their hearts the evacuees still felt a very strong attachment to their native village and their ancestors' tombs. Unlike the other groups who have come to Hawaii, these refugees were engaged in a forced migration. They had no choice but to flee and no time to prepare themselves emotionally for the separation and culture shock involved.

In a survey of three hundred Vietnamese refugees by Chuoc Nguyen (1977) in Honolulu in late 1976, one third of them had college education, almost half had secondary education, and about one fifth had elementary education. Perhaps because of the Confucian influence, which favors the education of men over women, there was a much higher proportion of college-educated men than women. The same survey indicated that 51 percent of the people were Buddhists, 24 percent Roman Catholics, 6 percent Protestants, and 19 percent claimed to be of other religions, such as Confucianism, Hoa Hao, and Cao Dai. In the religious framework of Vietnam, composed as it is of Confucianism, Taoism, Buddhism and more recently, of Catholicism and the unique fusion of Cao Daism, the element of paradox is again seen. What at first glance appears to be religious pluralism, or perhaps religious tolerance, is in fact a more difficult achievement. Whatever their religious affiliations, the influence of Buddhism, Confucianism, Taoism, and the Cult of Ancestors shapes the thought and behavior of the Vietnamese.

Life in camps in Wake Island, Guam, the Philippines, and in the United States was hard and full of uncertainties. Everything was new and strange: the food, the camp life, the lack of medical assistance, the search for sponsors, the burning heat, and the chilling cold. Camp authorities wanted to move the refugees as soon as possible, but sponsors were scattered throughout the nation, and the usually large families of the refugees were often split up, with members separated from one another by thousands of miles. This situation and the fact that more than 75 percent of the refugees still had members of their immediate families in Vietnam, increased the tendency to fatalism and the search for guidance in their behavior from Buddhism and Taoism. The many refugees who arrived directly in Hawaii from the Pacific islands were those who had relatives or sponsors in the state; others went to the camps in the mainland United States before coming to Hawaii.

Since April 1975, people have continued to flee Vietnam in unseaworthy fishing boats and rafts. It has been reported by news media that more than half of them never make port. The more fortunate ones reach the shores of Thailand, Malaysia, Singapore, or the Philippines. Those who reach the Philippines are generally better treated than those who arrive in other countries, where they have sometimes been chased back to the open seas after being given food and water. At best, they are kept in crowded refugee camps. Recently, the US Congress has passed a law accepting more Indochinese refugees, particularly those presently in camps in Southeast Asia. Hawaii is continuing to receive its share of these people.

Vietnamese Adjustment in Hawaii

For the Vietnamese in Hawaii the cultural forces that dictate their mode of living and adjustment in this new environment are molded in many ways by the moral and religious framework within which the people have lived for hundreds of years.

As was mentioned earlier, there seems to be a harmony of religions in Vietnam in that the religions coexist as a pool of wisdom that guides the behavior of a Vietnamese whether he is primarily Buddhist, Confucianist, Christian, or Taoist.

THE INFLUENCE OF BUDDHISM

According to Buddhism, life is a vast sea of suffering in which man wallows hopelessly. In effect, the vicious circle of existence is renewed in the course of endless reincarnations. The cause of suffering is desire: desire for life, happiness, riches, power, and so on. If desire were suppressed, the cause of pain would be destroyed. The essence of Buddhist teaching is contained in the concept of Karma, the law of causality: the present existence is conditioned by earlier existences and will condition those to follow. Thus, the virtuous man should strive constantly to improve himself by doing good deeds and by renouncing sensual pleasures, so that he can become conscious of the existence of Buddha, who is present in every living being. Consequently, desire first must be overcome; a pure heart is necessary to break the chains binding man to an earthly existence.

Thirty-five years of almost continuous warfare have greatly affected the psychology of the Vietnamese and have strengthened their belief in the concept of Karma. In fact, the sudden changes during the war, the loss of property and position by many of them, the tragic deaths of their relatives and friends, the massive movements of people from one place to another, and the hasty and random departure from their native land, seem to defy any logic and seem to be explained only by fatalism, or Karma, or by some supernatural law of punishment and reward that man cannot know. This concept of Karma explains why some Vietnamese refugees are not enthusiastic about trying to move forward, to strive for success, or even to make the most out of life. Instead, these people try to renounce earthly pleasures and aim at religious deeds in order to get to the state of Nirvana, or bliss, after their present lives. It also explains why some Vietnamese seem to be quite content with their seemingly substandard housing, modest clothes, and even jobs that have no promise of advancement.

THE INFLUENCE OF CONFUCIANISM

Whereas Buddhism teaches the Vietnamese to strive for Nirvana, Confucianism, as understood by them, addresses social problems. Confucius founded his doctrine on the basis of etiology, that is, on a theory of causes or origins. He said that the stability of a regime depends on an ideal, and this ideal can have value only if it is based on great examples from the past.

From this concept, Confucius instituted the Cult of Ancestors, which places the spirits of the dead relatives in the very heart of the household. Since that time, the family has been required to respect this tradition, because no one would dare to offend or provoke the dead. In traditional Vietnam, the tombs of the ancestors are well cared for by the descendants. In order to care for their ancestors' tombs, the Vietnamese remained in their native villages generation after generation, which explains their strong attachment to their villages. In their homes, ancestors' altars occupy the place of honor. It is in front of the ancestors' altar that ceremonies, such as weddings and new year's celebrations, are performed, and it is in front of the altar that the family (extended family) meets to make all the decisions that affect its members. Because the ancestors are ever present among their descendants, they are consulted on any major matter through prayers, and they give advice via dreams and other forms of enlightenment. Because of this, attempts at dialogue with the dead, or reports of such contacts by a Vietnamese, should not be considered abnormal psychological signs.

The Cult of Ancestors, the attachment to the native site of their tombs, and the dialogue with them in front of their altars are missing in Hawaii. This explains much of the loneliness, guilt, and incapacity felt by many Vietnamese. They feel lonely because they cannot have contact with their ancestors, guilty because they cannot care for their tombs, and incapable of making any decision because they do not receive the ancestors' advice. The Cult of Ancestors also explains the intergenerational conflicts: parents feel that their children, raised in this environment, will not worship them after their death and will not worship their ancestors. In the traditional Vietnamese family the wife belongs to her husband's family and helps him in his duties toward his ancestors. When her husband passes away she becomes dependent upon her son. The economic situation in Hawaii, however, often means the wife has to work outside the family and has no time for the traditional activities directed toward the husband's ancestors.

Another concept of Confucius that influences the behavior of the Vietnamese is a belief in the innate goodness of man. In order to preserve this quality, it is only necessary to keep passions in check. If one does not live up to one's potential goodness, it is because of neglect of the intellect, which atrophies in the humdrum routine of everyday life. Wise people, in contrast to ordinary ones, improve themselves through study. They know themselves and are the masters of their passions. For this they will be honored by their heirs and their souls will have peace in the hereafter. In sum, those who are good are rewarded, and those who do evil must suffer the consequences.

The Vietnamese, imbued with Confucian ideas of the innate goodness of man and self-improvement through study, appreciate education. It is not unusual for a father to sacrifice everything else for the education of his children, particularly his sons. For this reason, it is not surprising that the majority of Vietnamese students are doing well in their studies despite some initial difficulty with the English language. Presently, there are no Vietnamese language classes taught in Hawaii's public or private schools.

The Vietnamese desire to have their children succeed academically may explain some adjustment problems being experienced by students. When their parents' expectations are high and when, for one reason or another they cannot meet them, students may react by withdrawal and give up their struggle to get to the top in their classes. There are some Vietnamese who used to be excellent students in Vietnam, but who have abandoned their classes and studies here because the pressure for success from their parents was too overwhelming and unrealistic.

The Confucian idea of improving oneself through study may also be the reason behind the choice made by a fairly large number of Vietnamese to go back to college instead of taking entry level jobs. This attitude has been misinterpreted by some as an indication of the unwillingness of the Vietnamese to work. It may also be related to their lack of enthusiasm for vocational training programs here; many of the refugees would prefer a more challenging educational opportunity.

Another concept of Confucianism that has been integrated in the normative behavior of the Vietnamese pertains to social relations. Confucianism is a doctrine of social hierarchies the effectiveness of which has been demonstrated by history; the status quo was better maintained by the application of this doctrine than it could have been by the use of force. Confucianism defines, by rigid rules, the attitudes that each member of society should have, and it prescribes the formula for three all-important sets of social interaction, called *Tam Cuong*. These interactions are between ruler and subject, between father and son, and between husband and wife. It also dictates a moral code for the man of virtue who should be a living example of the five cardinal virtues: humanity, equity, urbanity, intelligence, and honesty. The man of virtue should also follow a path of moderation; exaggeration in any direction is to be avoided and equanimity is to be cultivated. This moral perfection may be progressively attained by going through four steps: the improvement of oneself, the management of the family, the government of the country, and finally, the pacification of the world.

Ruler and Subject. The first set of social interaction, namely be-

tween ruler and subject, explains the success or failure in the relationship between the Vietnamese worker (in the role of subject) and the
employer (in the role of a ruler), as well as in the relationship between the refugee and the sponsor or the assisting volunteer agency.

Vietnamese employees consider their employers as mentors. As
such, the latter are expected to give guidance, advice, and encouragement, while the former execute orders, perform their tasks quietly,
and do not ask questions or have doubts about the orders. Because of
their concept of the relationship, Vietnamese employees do not voice
opinions to their bosses, but just listen to their orders. This seemingly passive and unimaginative attitude is aggravated by a linguistic
difference between Vietnamese and English. The Vietnamese literal
equivalent of the English word *yes* is *da* (pronounced /ya/ in the
Southern Vietnamese dialect). However, whereas the English *yes*
means unequivocally "yes," the Vietnamese *da* means a variety of
things. In the final analysis, it can mean "yes," but in general usage,
it merely means "I am politely listening to you," and it does not at
all mean that "I agree with you." The listener may disagree with
what is heard but, due to politeness and deference to the boss, cannot say "no." His English "yes" conveys the polite and noncommit-
tal Vietnamese *"da,"* but to the American it can carry only its
English meaning. Thus, the Vietnamese may appear insincere, or
even stupid, to the American.

Another factor that can contribute to strain and misunderstanding
between the Vietnamese and the American is the enigmatic Vietnamese smile. The Vietnamese smile when politeness prevents con-
tradiction of the interlocutor. They also smile when they do not completely understand what is said and yet, also out of politeness, do not
want to ask for clarification.

At the same time, the Vietnamese expect the employer to be paternalistic, kind, and soft-spoken; the latter's direct and straightforward
speech may sound rude to them. And because they are not supposed
to retort or talk back, the only alternative is to try to swallow their
frustration until they cannot bear it anymore. At that time, their last
recourse is to resign and to look for another boss who would be more
understandable and kind by Vietnamese standards.

While a very small number of Vietnamese refugees had sponsors
who were their relatives or friends, the majority had to wait in camps
for sponsors whom they had not known before; sponsors were solicit-
ed by volunteer agencies, known as volags, which, in the interim,

provided immediate assistance for essential needs, such as housing and food. Similar to their concept of their relationships with employers, the Vietnamese associate the role of sponsor, or volag, with that of the ruler and their own role with that of the subject in the Confucian ruler-subject relationship. Hence, they expect the volag, or sponsor, to do everything for them. This gives the appearance that they are taking things for granted, are demanding, or even lazy. The problem is aggravated by the fact that they are in a strange environment and in most cases do not speak English well enough to communicate; hence, the Vietnamese do not know what to do.

Father and Child. The second set of social interaction influenced by Confucianism, that between father and child, is governed by the rule of total obedience of the child to the father. Owing life and everything else to the father, the child is supposed to venerate him, to do whatever is asked, and to continue the father's task in the Cult of Ancestors. The rule of order may create conflict between the father and his children in this country. The father adapts more slowly, if at all, to the American culture where his relationship to his children is less formal and restrictive than what he is used to. He expects them to conform to the Confucian order just as he himself did in his relationship to his own father. But the children are socializing with their own age group here and tend to act in the American way. Also, in most cases, if not in all, the children speak English better than their father. Thus, the father resents this reversal of roles, his children feel it, and the situation becomes explosive. On the other hand, the children may conform to the traditional norm of relationship with the father. In that case, they may feel some difference or conflict with their peer group.

Husband and Wife. The third set of social interaction, that between husband and wife, is based upon the idea that the woman should, in all circumstances, conform to the three obediences: obedience to her father until she is married, obedience to her husband after she leaves her father's house, and obedience to her eldest son should she be widowed. Further, the model wife should possess the four essential virtues: skill with her hands, pleasant appearance, prudence in her speech, and exemplary conduct.

It is quite apparent that the role of the traditional Vietnamese woman and her relationship to her husband, according to the Confucian norm, may clash with the reality of the American environment.

In most cases, the husband's salary alone is not sufficient to meet the high cost of living in this state. The wife may then have to work to supplement the family's income and often is able to get a more lucrative job than her husband, though not necessarily a desirable one in traditional terms—for example, as a waitress (Liem, 1977). Furthermore, women seem more adept in second language learning and the wife may make better progress in speaking English. Again, there may be role reversal and the husband may feel, either consciously or subconsciously, threatened. On the other hand, the wife, because of her work and interaction with the outside world, may not have enough time to perform her traditional role in the family. Being exposed for the first time to the ideas of freedom, self-sufficiency, and equality for women, the Vietnamese woman may react more strongly against the traditional role than her American counterpart. This conflict between her husband's conservative expectations and the role of women in American society may precipitate breakdowns in the family structure. All this may cause marital problems. In the past, the expectation of the four traditional virtues for women limited their education to the high school diploma, in the majority of cases. In Hawaii, where the job market is tight, openings for the Vietnamese woman most often are found in jobs related to the tourist industry and often require them to work at night. This may be another source of marital conflict.

THE INFLUENCE OF TAOISM

Another cultural force influencing the conduct of the Vietnamese, no less important than Buddhism and Confucianism, is Taoism. Vietnamese Taoism is derived from the teaching of Lao Tzu, which is essentially a vision of the participation of man in the universal order. This harmony depends on the equilibrium of the two elements *yin* (negative) and *yang* (positive), which represent the constant duality of nature: rest and motion, liquid and solid, light and darkness, concentration and expansion, material and spiritual. The material world is imbued with these two principles, according to Taoist belief; whoever is able to act according to these principles can become the master of the world. This belief, in turn, has promoted interest in the magical practices of sorcerers who appear to possess the secrets of the universe. Taoists refrain from disturbing the natural order; on the contrary, they conform to it in every circumstance. They consider the taking of initiatives to be vain, and thus disdain the active life; this is the basis of the Taoist doctrine of passivity and absence of care. These doctrines are summed up in the Taoist maxim "Do nothing and everything will be accomplished spontaneously."

Whereas Buddhism teaches the Vietnamese to seek happiness after life in the form of Nirvana, free from the circle of life and death, Confucianism and Taoism both teach them to seek happiness in their present life. The former essentially recommends dynamism, activity, and advancement by means of self-improvement; the latter essentially advocates stillness, blending oneself with nature, and remaining in harmony with oneself, one's fellow creatures, and the universe. Thus, one could picture the Buddhist way toward happiness in Nirvana as a vector pointing upward, the Confucian trajectory toward happiness as a horizontal arrow pointing forward, and the Taoist road toward happiness as a horizontal arrow pointing in a direction opposite to that of the Confucian one. From this picture, it is possible to see how the Taoist influence brings about a neglect of material possessions, success, worldly power, and social activities. It directs the Vietnamese to look for pleasure and contentment in the enjoyment of nature, in quietude, and in the depths of a peaceful mind. Especially when faced with apparently insurmountable difficulties, such as those of a refugee, the Vietnamese may adopt a fatalistic attitude toward the outside world.

THE INFLUENCE OF CHRISTIANITY

In comparison with the other religions, Christianity was introduced to Vietnam relatively recently. It was not until the sixteenth century that Christian missionaries began preaching the Gospel in Vietnam. The dominant Christian influence in the country was Catholicism. In 1965, in the South, Catholics comprised 10.5 percent of the total population. As mentioned previously, however, a survey in late 1976 in Hawaii showed the Catholics accounted for 24 percent of the sample. This may have been because the Catholics were better organized than other religious groups and because many of them originally fled Communist domination in the North in 1954 and feared the prospect of again living under that regime. Protestant religions got a much later start in Vietnam and, as a result, have not achieved the same popularity as the Catholic faith. Since the end of World War II, however, Protestant missionaries have taken an increasing interest in Vietnam, and their influence has steadily, if slowly, increased.

THE INFLUENCE OF GEOGRAPHY AND HISTORY

Not only do the religious beliefs of Buddhism, Taoism, and Confucianism affect the way of life and the pattern of thought and behavior of the Vietnamese; their country's geography and history also play an important role in their world view.

Despite more recent moves to the cities, the Vietnamese have kept their roots in the villages where agriculture dictated the mode of life. Perhaps for this reason, the Vietnamese peasants face natural catastrophies stoically. Knowing how to cope with the inevitable disasters, they exemplify Pascal's "thinking reeds" which bend but do not break under strong winds. This flexibility in the face of difficulties may have helped the Vietnamese endure through long years of war, the trauma of exodus, and resettlement. But on the other hand, attachment to their native land may contribute to their nostalgia, loneliness, and even lack of stamina.

The system of intensive agriculture in Vietnam required a large pool of laborers, so that the Vietnamese appreciated large families with numerous children and three or four generations living under the same roof. This arrangement enabled the grandparents to take care of the children, the men to work in the rice fields, and the women to assist the men during planting or harvest time and to do the various chores around the home. The extended family constituted a mutual network of assistance, counseling, and comfort. The Vietnamese refugees in the United States tend not to have the kind of family support they used to have and, depending on their individual stiuations, they may miss this support to varying degrees, a matter to be discussed below.

The thirty-five years of civil war have conditioned the Vietnamese to be suspicious of anyone other than members of their family. The classic example of this reliance on one's family was seen in the government of Ngo Dinh Diem where the key positions were occupied by his brothers, sisters-in-law, and other members of his family. Such a mistrust of outsiders hinders cooperation and mutual assistance within the Vietnamese community. Fractionalization has proved to be all too common.

The Vietnamese refugees can be classified into different categories according to their family situation in the United States. There are the elderly who came as dependents of their adult children, the nuclear family units of husbands and wives who came with their children only, and finally, the unaccompanied children. Each of these categories face individual adaptation problems, as well as those common to all.

The elderly, in general, have come to the United States as dependents of their adult children, who were themselves evacuated because of their connection with the previous Vietnamese regime, or with the United States military or civilian installations in their country. These elderly Vietnamese were usually members of the upper social class and were either professionals, high ranking civil servants, or successful businessmen. They lost practically all their material assets, their power, wealth, status, and prestige. Most important, they lost their circle of friends and associates. In the American environment, they find it very difficult to adapt themselves culturally and linguistically. Having been educated under the French system, they do not speak English and, at their age, it is usually quite difficult to learn a new language. Consequently, their circle of friends here is limited, and some are socially isolated from their peers. They are of retirement age or close to it, and, because of their linguistic handicap, they do not work or have activities to keep themselves busy. In Vietnam, they lived a relatively comfortable upper-class life, reassured that if anything happened to their fortune, their children would support them for the rest of their lives. In this country, they have neither their own wealth nor the support of their children, who can barely make their own living. They have to accept welfare benefits which, in their view, make them beggars of the state. Unhappy about their present situation, they, understandably, live in the past.

Most likely, the group that can best adapt itself to this society is the one in which the entire family is together and which can provide a network of mutual support. Families composed of three generations provide the strongest support. There may be tension, however, when the parents cannot meet the grandparents' expectations for financial support and moral reverence. The situation of families with school-age children tends to be fairly good. In Vietnam, entrance to public schools was highly competitive and private schools were either very expensive or inferior to public ones. But in the United States, the children have the same educational opportunities available to all.

Housing presents a problem for the large Vietnamese families. Consequently, families tend to be spread out, depriving the Vietnamese of mutual support systems.

Although those who came to the United States in family groups may have mutual moral support, the men who came here alone, leaving their families behind, seem to be more vulnerable to mental health problems. In most cases, they were in the military and left Vietnam thinking that their absence from their families and country would only be temporary. Some of these men have since established second households in the United States, which has created legal problems. Others, because of their linguistic and economic situation, or by preference, are living alone, suffering guilt for having deserted their families and worrying about the welfare of their loved ones. These men exhibit a greater tendency toward alcoholism than does the general refugee population. Other men, believing that their separation from their families would only be temporary, sent their families to the United States, expecting to join them at a later date, but so far, they have not been able to do so. The wives who came to the United States with their children now face the difficult task of raising them alone. Because of the Confucianist concept that the education of women should be limited to training them to become good housewives, the majority of these women have few skills to help them earn a living here. Also, because their world was limited to the home, they had no need to learn English. For all these reasons, a high percentage of these women are on welfare.

Some women who worked in Vietnam had the support of the extended family and/or servants to care for their children and their homes. They now find it difficult to cope with jobs, child rearing, and other household responsibilities. These are generally women from the more privileged class who had the benefits of higher education and never had to concern themselves with domestic chores.

Since April 1975, some parents in Vietnam have held the belief that there is no future for their children in the homeland. Consequently, they are sending them abroad with relatives or friends. These unaccompanied children pose legal problems with regard to adoption and may face ethnic identity problems as they grow up.

The Hmong from Laos
Bruce Thowpaou Bliatout

The Hmong people originated in the lands of southern China. They have traditionally resisted integration into the societies of surrounding people. Pressure under the Manchu government toward incorporation resulted in migration southward into the hills of Laos, Thailand, and Vietnam. In each of these countries the Hmong are a minority ethnic group with a culture and language of their own. In the news media they have been commonly referred to as the Meo people, but Hmong is the preferred name.

During the recent Indochina war many Hmong tribesmen fought with the American army against the Communist-backed Pathet Lao. Because of their involvement in the American war effort, thousands of Hmong fled their Laotian homeland when Laos fell to a Communist regime. The Hmong have now been relocated all over the world. There are about seven thousand in the United States, and even more in France.

In Laos the Hmong people grew rice and corn on hillsides which were cultivated by the old method of slash and burn. New fields had to be cleared periodically. This meant that the Hmong would decide to move their villages (consisting of five to twenty people) about every three years. While men cleared the fields, women tended the vegetable gardens and looked after pigs and chickens. Men, women, and children worked jointly in planting and harvesting.

In Laos the Hmong grew opium and sold it freely until this was outlawed in 1971. In exchange for opium they acquired silver which, in turn, was pounded into necklaces to display the family's wealth. As the most important trading medium, silver played an important part in the exchange of goods. To compensate the family of his bride at the time of marriage, a man had to accumulate two to four silver bars. When opium growing became illegal, the Hmong experienced economic difficulties. They did not feel responsible for other peoples' addiction to the drug, as very few Hmong used opium, except in old age or as a remedy for illness.

The Hmong practice a mixture of ancestor worship and placation of nature spirits. Unhappy ancestral spirits as well as nature spirits can cause sickness and death, and all spirits must be pleased by offerings and sacrifices. There are religious specialists who can communicate with the supernatural and who are asked by people in the community to intervene with the spirits in cases of disputes or where protection against evil spirits is desired. Some Hmong have been converted to Christianity in Laos, and refugees in the United States have turned to Western religions.

Among the Hmong in the rural hillside areas of Laos, a traditional lifestyle continued despite some adaptation to aspects of modern life. Dress, marriage customs, and family life kept a traditional character. Because schools were located far away in the lowland towns, relatively few Hmong children were able to attend. The war years, however, exposed many Hmong to change. Men were recruited into army service, leaving women, children, and the elderly to struggle for subsistence. Many families also lost their homes during bombings and had to find shelter in the towns. So for most Hmong the decade prior to arrival in Hawaii brought considerable upheaval.

Arrival in Hawaii

The first Hmong refugees to reach Honolulu came at the end of 1975, with the bulk of the refugees arriving in 1976. At present, one or two families a month continue to trickle in as they find sponsors or are processed out of the Thai camps. The greatest population of Hmong in Hawaii has been close to a thousand people, decreasing to six hundred despite the trickle of newcomers.

The Hmong brought their culture to Hawaii and have retained much of it, since acculturation is a slow process. Most of the adult men have only primary education and the women have even less. In this male-dominated society, the women are completely submissive to their husbands' will. Women were sold out of their clan at the time of marriage and entered their husband's clan for the rest of their lives. Clans cling together for economic and social support. The typical Hmong family is a large extended one incorporating the mother and father, and sons and sons' wives, along with their children. If children of the same clan should become orphaned, these children will be taken in. In Hawaii and throughout the United States, this custom has persisted. Therefore, families are very large. Family planning practices have not been well accepted, so families continue to grow.

During the resettlement process, many Hmong families were split up. Nuclear families were resettled by social agencies throughout the United States, and as soon as is possible, extended families try to reunite. Since job opportunities for the Hmong in Hawaii have been somewhat limited, many have chosen to leave for the mainland, where they have family and hope for better job opportunities.

Most of the Hmong live in the Kalihi, Makiki, and Kapahulu areas of Honolulu; only three Hmong families have settled in Hilo. Most of the heads of households have found employment, but are doing menial labor at minimum wage. About half the women are employed, either as domestic help or as seamstresses. The children are going to public schools and have learned English very quickly. The adults have been slower to learn English, despite going to evening adult classes. Families in Hawaii average about five children per family and often include one or more grandparents.

Resettlement Problems

The first problem the Hmong people faced was adapting to Western life. They faced a huge culture shock because the differences between lifestyles were so great. Many of the people had never used an electrical appliance before, nor had they used a modern bathroom, or lived in a house with a carpet. Most came with unrealistic expectations.

When the Hmong were in the refugee camps and thought of resettling in the United States, they did not realize the size of their new country. They felt that they would be resettled in one large group, rather like an Indian reservation. None of the older ones realized that they would be living in a city surrounded by strangers, or that they would eventually have to become assimilated into American society. They had the idea they would find some field to have a farm and live as they had done in Laos.

At first, even the idea of attending adult education classes was distressing to the old, who felt they could not learn anything as they had never been to a class in their lives. They were not happy when they learned about American housing standards and could not understand why a house or an apartment with two bedrooms was not suitable for a family of ten. In Laos the whole family shared a bedroom, and they have continued to do so in Hawaii, much to the distress of their American sponsors.

Because of their low income, many Hmong are living in modest dwellings in lower socioeconomic areas. Some have found their neighbors very unfriendly, and a few have even been beaten or threatened. Also, the Hmong feel insecure because their homes are somewhat scattered; they cannot see each other as often as they would like.

The Hmong people have not yet adapted to the new American culture. They need to learn more about modern life, particularly sanitary personal habits. At the same time, they are very independent and have the will to remain autonomous. None feel that they want to give up being Hmong, and until they are able to resolve this ambivalent feeling of keeping their own identity in a new culture, the Hmong will face psychological problems.

The Hmong's resettlement and emotional problems are intensified for those who lack the ability to communicate in English. Job interviews are difficult, and maintaining good work relations after obtaining a job is more difficult; even shopping and finding entertainment is a problem. Many have learned English fairly well, but local idioms and humor are beyond the scope of the Hmong's understanding. There is a constant strain on anyone forced daily to try to talk and think in an unfamiliar language. Housewives have difficulty in the markets because they cannot read any of the labels, and some of the older women cannot even read the price tags. Among those who can speak English, many cannot write it well, which makes filling out any kind of form, from a welfare application to a request for car insurance, almost impossible. Any notice that comes in the mail is subject to the wildest guesses or to indifference. Teachers' notes via children to parents requesting money or permission for excursions, are ignored.

Another problem that causes unhappiness is the lack of entertainment. There are no movies the Hmong can understand, they have no literature of their own to read, and it is not in their culture to eat out (nor can they afford it). They also have more free time on their hands than they did in Laos. Here they work an average of forty hours a week, whereas in Laos twelve out of thirteen days were worked from dawn to dusk. So in Hawaii the Hmong people fill the time with going to see each other. And although in many ways this is good, there is a detrimental side in that in these visits people continue to speak only Hmong among themselves; thus their English does not improve. Also, since it is a small community with few distractions, their close association with each other gives rise to petty gossip and cliquish fights and disagreements.

There has been resistance to the reeducation process among the Hmong when something one has learned goes against traditional beliefs. For example, women learn at school that they should have equal rights in the home. When they express this to their husbands, family dissension results. Another point of dissension is dress and makeup. In Laos "good" Hmong girls did not wear makeup, nor did they wear shorts or backless tops. In Hawaii their peers do, and so they want to follow suit. This again causes family dissension.

Education has undermined the line of authority in the home. In Laos the father or grandfather was the final authority. But as the young ones in Hawaii become more educated they tend to feel they know better how to cope with various situations. So they override the authority of age, causing great disruption in family relations.

One of the biggest emotional problems the Hmong face is the loss of status in the community. In Laos status is as important as being rich. A village headman may have very little money, but is nonetheless very respected in his community. Many of the Hmong refugees had a high status in their home village in Laos. The head of the household either was a military officer of high rank, or was a village official. Some were merchants of high standing, or came from wealthy families. Now that they are refugees, they are at the bottom of the social structure. What bothers them even more is that people no longer respect them within the Hawaii Hmong society itself. In Laos these men would be catered to, and their orders followed immediately. Here people pay less and less attention to them as the young ones start to go their own ways.

In Hmong life nothing is more important than having many relatives. The family provides, in part, social as well as psychological security. In Hmong society no one wants to marry an orphan because it is felt that such a person has no family to help them. Almost everyone lives in an extended-family situation.

When families were separated, with some members in Thailand and Laos and others in the United States, a great deal of mental anguish occurred. For some of the older ones, this put all other thoughts out of their minds, and they now complain that they miss having their whole family together. Besides, they fear for their relatives' safety, and feel deprived of the social security of a large family. In Laos the bigger your family and the more sons you have, the greater respect your family commands.

The most severe disruption of family relations has been in the husband-wife relationship. Until the Hmong came to live in the United States, polygamy was an accepted practice. Women were told from the time of birth that they must obey their husbands, stay at home, cook, care for the home, and never complain. Now that many are working and earning an income for the family, they feel that they deserve more rights. Even housewives are affected by their education and feel that caring for their home and children is work also, and that they too deserve to attend parties, go to movies, and so on, something that the men often do exclusively. This has led to an increase in marital disharmony, and wife-beating has become a problem in the Hmong community.

Child-parent relationships also have suffered disruption. In Laos children were subservient to their parents, showing them every outward respect. They did as they were told and rarely answered back. In Hawaii the children have learned to talk back to their parents. They have found that their parents are ignorant of many of the things they are learning at school and, therefore, have lost respect for the parents. This has placed a strain on family relations that causes many Hmong to experience mental distress.

Since the Hmong people are such a tiny minority in Hawaii, few local people are even aware of their existence, grouping them automatically with the Laotians. It must be stressed that the Hmong people have a strong sense of identity and are proud to be a separate ethnic group. They form a cohesive, but not exclusive, community.

Approaches for Mental Health Counseling

The Hmong do not understand the term *mental health*. To Hmong people, a person is either "crazy," or he is not. A crazy person is like a village idiot who is unkempt and babbles incoherently, or else is inexplicably violent. The Hmong do not understand that family happiness, job adjustment, and personal happiness are aspects of mental health. Because of this black-and-white concept of being crazy, there is great stigma attached to admitting that a family member is experiencing mental health problems. Therefore, many Hmong will not seek help even when they know something is wrong. Families will discourage admitting the need of counseling for fear they will lose face.

A way to encourage more people to seek counseling is to make help easily accessible, without identifying it as mental health counseling. A mental health counseling program could be disguised as an educational program, or a family relations program, and so on. In this way a Hmong refugee will feel more comfortable with the idea and will be more willing to participate. His peers will not look down on him, and he will feel no stigma.

In Laos when the Hmong encounter family, emotional, monetary, or other problems which become too large to handle within the family, the village headman is asked to judge the case. In Hawaii the Hmong people seem to miss this function of the headman the most. They need some person (or persons) to whom they can speak fluently about their problems. They will only feel comfortable telling their problems in their native language. Also, persons from their own culture will understand the nuances of problems that may be obscure to a Westerner.

In other words, the Hmong need other Hmong who are trained to work as paraprofessionals or professionals in the field of mental health. They should be called counselors or community workers, so that the clients will feel they are not seeking help for mental illness, but are just seeking help in general. A professional counselor's role could thus be parallel to that of the village headman in the homeland. The paraprofessionals can help with minor problems and refer larger problems to professionals. Certain major problems may need to be referred to a psychiatrist, but a Hmong counselor could accompany the patient and function as a translator and aide.

References

America: Still the promised land. *U.S. News and World Report,* July 9, 1979.

Bliatout, Bruce. Problems of acculturation of the Laotians in Hawaii. Honolulu: Refugees of Indochina Culture Education Program, Institute of Behavioral Sciences. 1979

Deming, Angus; Copeland, Jeff B.; Buckley, Jerry; and Coppola, Vincent. Home of the brave. *Newsweek,* July 2, 1979.

Fitzgerald, Frances. *Fire in the lake: The Vietnamese and the Americans in Vietnam.* Boston: Little, Brown and Co., 1972.

Kavanagh, Kathryn. Indochinese refugees in Hawaii. Unpublished manuscript. 1979.

Liem, Nguyen Dang. Educational, professional training, health and mental health needs of Indochinese refugees in Hawaii. Unpublished manuscript, 1977.

———. The Vietnamese adjustment in Hawaii. Presented at the Hmong, Lao and Vietnamese Culture Festival. Honolulu, June 28, 1979.

Nguyen, An Thi. The Vietnamese way of life. Presented at the Hmong, Lao and Vietnamese Culture Festival. Honolulu, June 28, 1979.

Nguyen, Chouc. Research paper on the resettlement of Vietnamese refugees in the State of Hawaii. Unpublished manuscript. Honolulu: Vietnamese and Indochinese Volunteer Assistance, 1977.

Sananikone, Prany. Lao adjustment in Hawaii. Presented at the Hmong, Lao and Vietnamese Culture Festival. Honolulu, June 28, 1979.

CHAPTER 12

Toward an Interethnic Society

John F. McDermott, Jr.

You have been introduced to a parade of ethnic groups, each one examined in some detail and with their differences highlighted. At this point, it is appropriate to attempt to synthesize the factors which have contributed to the integration or, at least, the overlap of these groups in this society, that is, to seek out the glue which has held them together. It has been said that if Hawaii's people are not a mixed people, they are at least a mixing people (Hormann, 1972). True mixing has been very gradual, however, and has accelerated only relatively recently as reflected in intermarriage statistics, as well as in the results of more subjective observations of social and occupational interactions among the various ethnic groups. For many years, instead of mixing, there was more of a "pendulum effect" among groups that were dominant, even though none of the groups could claim a majority of the population.

But even during that time assimilation and accommodation were occurring. *Assimilation* in this context refers to the incorporation of the values of a new group by the dominant existing group so that it fits into the existing social network, while *accommodation* suggests movement in the other direction, that is, a new individual or group adapting to the existing or dominant group values by changing in order to continue to live with them. These phenomena are enhanced in a constantly interacting society on a small group of islands. For example, the islands were insulated and isolated for years following the arrival of the first Caucasians, except for the addition of Oriental values which gradually and almost imperceptibly became part of the values of the enlarging population. The fact that the newcomers to

Hawaii were Oriental, identified as coming from "shame" cultures, furthered harmonious living more effectively than would have immigrants from traditional European "guilt" cultures. This is because shame is a group phenomenon and depends upon both ingroups and outgroups for its effectiveness in modulating and controlling behavior. The Orientals, even though imported as a working class for the plantations, had the same achievement values as the Caucasians. Education was believed by them to be the best way to move up in the social hierarchy and was sought almost immediately. Thus, differences were accompanied by similarities which were often hidden or disguised. Perhaps these factors—assimilation, accommodation, limited space, hidden similarities, and complementary differences—account for the success of a multiethnic society, as well as for "island fever," a syndrome felt and expressed in various ways by those who visit or settle in Hawaii for short periods of time. Those who express this "fever" seem to feel confined living so closely with others, the very ingredient that has forced the "others" to live together in relative harmony.

But in order to discuss the phenomenon of the erosion of strong ethnic boundaries, which otherwise serve as barriers and foster ethnocentricity, it is important to review the peculiar historical circumstances and the other sociological, as well as psychological, factors involved. These are predictive when considering current trends and the future of Hawaii's society.

Historical Background

Consider the mainland United States. A European Caucasian minority settled there in relative isolation from the native Americans and dealt with them, after an initial period, primarily through confrontation and domination. They then imported another nonwhite (black) population, as a slave class, and doomed it to live out an inferior role. Only very recently have changed circumstances produced progress toward black self-esteem, but polarity as well as highly differentiated black and white identities, were perhaps necessary for a time.

In Hawaii, by contrast, a white minority was welcomed by a dark majority because the former were believed to have special meaning for their culture and to possess great power which could be incorporated into the existing culture. Incorporating and bringing together were strong Hawaiian values. Indeed, intermarriage occurred almost immediately between Caucasian and Hawaiian upper class (the host culture) and served to break down the taboo of interracial marriage (usually last to go). The Hawaiians looked to Europe and Western countries for the means to progress, but unfortunately, this, as well as their emphasis on coexistence at almost any price, proved their downfall. The pendulum swung inevitably from the Hawaiians, as the dominant ethnic group, to the Caucasians, who looked upon the Hawaiian with a paternal condescension.

The Hawaiians had paid little attention to skin color prior to the short-lived revolution and civil war of the nineteenth century. After the fall of the monarchy it was too late; Hawaiians only then awoke to their loss and were told to "look to the skin" and vote for dark rather than white. Yet, the mainland term *half-caste* did not take in Hawaii; rather the Hawaiian term *hapa-haole,* with a very different implication and meaning, has become common. It connotes intermarriage from the host population's perspective and is a symbol of the first important milestone in the creation of Hawaii's interethnic society—interracial marriage. In addition to intermarriage, which produced a mixed ruling class, other racial groups were soon added in serial succession so that the two groups, Caucasian and Hawaiian, did not have a prolonged period in which to grapple with each other for dominance. Instead, a multiple culture developed and mutiple ways of life were forced upon Hawaii, which muted the creation of a bipolar society. Beaglehole (1937) noted that the flare-up of tension between Hawaiian and Western Caucasian around Liliuokalani burnt itself out; it is probable that the flood of immigrant plantation labor which poured into Hawaii in the latter part of the nineteenth and first decade of the twentieth century tended to throw the Caucasian together with the Hawaiian in such a fashion that it was preferable to forget the antagonisms that had been aroused to such a fiery pitch during the revolutionary years. In other words, Beaglehole ascribed to Caucasians and Hawaiians together an original hierarchy which frowned on mixed marriages with immigrant groups, especially Chinese and Japanese. It was only later, as these groups began to succeed financially and professionally, educationally and politically, that attitudes changed. Now intermarriage is at least the statistical norm.

Perhaps the second milestone toward the creation of an interethnic society was the development of a common language, pidgin. Gavin Daws (1968) has pointed out that interactions between ingroups and outgroups developed subtly over many years in the islands. Only on the plantations and in the armed forces was everything in the open, with occupation and rank displayed for all to see. But there were great differences among the Chinese; among the Japanese who wanted themselves distinguished from the Okinawan minority; among the Koreans who did not wish to be mistaken as either Chinese or Japanese; and among the late-arriving Filipinos who had their own divisions of languages and dialects. So, as Daws points out, everyone living in Hawaii had to become a skillful player of a game in which not one but several stereotypes needed to be kept in mind, and had to develop a talent for manipulating stereotypes that few other Americans had. This was demonstrated every day in conversation. From the welter of languages and dialects spoken in the islands an expressive pidgin emerged; for the sake of communication the island dweller made a point of using the correct version whenever speaking to someone who looked different. The laboring classes developed a sort of cosmopolitan pidgin and way of life among themselves, and the Caucasians took the language up because it got better results. The term *pidgin culture* was used by Hormann (1972) to describe the way of life which emerged in the plantation communities, on the playgrounds of local schools, and in urban working class areas among persons of different ethnic backgrounds. Pidgin was a way in which a young man could court a girl with an ancestry different from his own, and a dialect in which the children would be reared. To this base were added an appreciation for foods from many countries, participation in new forms of recreation and family life, and even beliefs and superstitions, especially regarding illness. Hormann describes the paradox of this pidgin culture: it is so cosmopolitan, so tolerant, so urbane—yet at the same time, so provincial. In any event, it was an important means by which the people of Hawaii moved toward becoming one people, even though each group remained differentiated from the others and exhibited, at times, extreme insularity toward the world. A new "mixed" ethnic group, began to emerge, with only quasi-ethnocentrism. The Asian cultures retained focal points of their identity—ceremonies, temples, language schools—but otherwise began to absorb new influences. Some believe this allowed a peaceful, gradual merging of individual ethnic identity with a common one. For if you are allowed to maintain your own identity, you are then free to give it up.

This informal interdependence between people, symbolized in

language reflecting a subtle merging of the ethnic values of different subgroups, leads us to the consideration of a third milestone, the public school system. It has been a significant factor in the mixing of Hawaii's people, who have been placed on succeeding rungs of the hierarchical ladder as each migrant labor group arrives in the islands. In a sociological study of Hawaii, Lawrence Fuchs (1961) pointed out that the public school system planted "the seeds of educational liberalism that would one day destroy Hawaii's oligarchy." According to Wright (1972), the sugar planters who ruled Hawaii were confronted with a situation far more complex than that created by the southerners in the United States; the multiracial population of Hawaii probably had no parallel elsewhere on the earth. In spite of repressive and even ruthless work methods, the oligarchy of sugar planters believed in progressive educational methods. Wallace Rider Farrington was one of the *kama'āina* elite who, on the one hand, spoke firmly for Big Five control of the islands, but nevertheless, on the other hand, was a strong proponent of universal education and better educational institutions. Indeed, as Fuchs noted, "The teachers of the 1920s and 1930s were the godparents of modern Hawaii." Thus, while there was early *suppression* of the developmental stage of adolescence, which in modern societies is a moratorium for education rather than a direct move to adulthood by commencing work at puberty (as happens in agricultural societies), this suppression gave way to a *promotion* of adolescence through the educational system. With the opportunity to absorb new influences came the maturity, both individual and collective, that permitted the emergence of a quiet rebellion among the young students, for example, the *nisei.* Through education they "grew up" and achieved an independence they did not have before. The conflicts inherent in this educational liberalism —illustrated by the maintenance of English Standard schools which prohibited pidgin (earlier seen as an important factor in the integration of the races)—were major at the time, but minor in historical perspective. Thus, the promotion of universal education by the dominant social group was a third major step toward the internal adjustment of our present society.

Psychological Factors

In addition to these sociohistorical phenomena, there are certain psychological factors that operate in an island culture and among multiple ethnic groups. When people interact every day they must be able to read each other's proclivities and emotional states. For example, keeping promises may be important to people from one subculture and not to those from another; conflicts may result. People from one subculture may not be able to tolerate anger, while accepting a wide expression of other emotions; individuals in another group may be encouraged to suppress all emotional expression. Thus, learning to "read" nonverbal and other cues is critical in avoiding conflict. Those who develop this perceptual ability are likely to be more successful in this society than those who do not.

This may be the point at which mention can be made of the tensions in Hawaii, for it would be naive to suggest that Hawaii is a melting pot of interracial harmony. Many of these tensions are related to social class as much as to race. The Orientals, who could not advance beyond certain white collar jobs a generation ago, are being replaced in this respect by Caucasians who now find themselves in a similar squeeze as the drive for racial balance in executive and supervisory positions accelerates. Tension often exists between these groups, the old and the new, and it can be intraracial as well as interracial. Within one ethnic group, the Filipino, tension and violence seem to exist between those already settled and the newcomers—clearly, a new generation of immigrants being resented by their predecessors.

The influx of Caucasian newcomers from the mainland appears to be a principal determining factor in the future of Hawaii's interethnic value system, for they bring American "individualism" with them. These individuals come to Hawaii to assume roles in companies, and in the transportation and communication industries in particular. They either adapt to the existing culture or attempt to change it; they either stay or leave, but they are increasing in number.

"Locals" may discriminate against mainland Caucasians under an assumption based on past stereotypes: Caucasians are rich just because they are Caucasians. Certainly the increasing number of crimes in which locals choose tourists as victims has this envy and anger in it. The term "local" can mean born in Hawaii or, if more loosely used, graduated from a local high school, especially a public high school. The other group, the *malihini*, are newcomer Caucasians from the mainland. It is the latter's tolerance and their ability to adapt that determine whether they stay in the islands or return to the mainland where they were members of the dominant group. Hawaii may never arrive at James Michener's vision of an entire population of golden men, but it seems to be moving toward a population comprising 50 percent Caucasians and 50 percent "mixed" (a merging of Caucasian, Japanese, Chinese, Filipino, Hawaiian, and others) (Simpich, 1973).

Intermarriage, along with in-migration from the mainland, appears to be the key factor in the future of the delicate balance needed for harmonious interethnic relations. In 1975 the *Honolulu Star-Bulletin* (December 15) reported: "More than one-fourth of Hawaii's residents are of mixed race, mostly part-Hawaiian." A report by Schmitt and Kawaguchi (1977) noted that the largest ethnic groups in Hawaii were Caucasian (27.7 percent), Japanese (26.6 percent), part-Hawaiian (16.4 percent), and Filipino (10.2 percent). As rates of intermarriage accelerate gradually, it seems clear that the resulting interaction among many ethnic groups will continue to contribute more to an erosion of ethnic boundaries than to the fostering of ethnocentricity (Simpich, 1973).

The loosening of ethnic boundaries is a distinct phenomenon throughout the entire island community. Accommodation to each other by the various groups and a considerable blending of cultures are widely acknowledged and are reflected in each of the chapters in this book. The boundaries between groups have become soft instead of hard, often overlapping rather than sharply defined. In this process, however, no group has totally surrendered the core of its traditional cultural identity. If we scan the descriptions of the various ethnic groups for core traditional elements that continue to have significance today, we may find a basis for expectations of the future.

In all groups, except perhaps the Caucasian, the extended family plays a central role. There is an emphasis on the family as the key social unit, and on family cohesion, family interdependence, and loyalty to the family as central guiding values. The individual is seen as part of a larger network, and duties and obligations, as well as much of the sense of personal security, derive from that context.

Caucasians, too, value the family, but they face the world as individuals. This is a basic difference between one group in Hawaii and all the others. It overrides other distinctions and similarities and seems to be unaffected by the accommodations that groups make to each other and to the society in which they live. The importance of the extended family is a value shared and transmitted by most of the groups in Hawaii, and it continues to affect styles of working and social relations in general.

There is no indication that Caucasian individualism will replace the emphasis in the other ethnic groups on the extended family as a valued source of identity, security, and mutual support. This is true despite the obvious signs of Americanization displayed by all of them, such as middle-class orientation and consumption patterns. Although Hawaii is commonly described as having a blended culture, the differences between its component groups are recognized as a desirable aspect of the total blend. The people of Hawaii have learned to appreciate its different elements, its different cultural traditions, its ethnic pluralism.

This concluding observation does not postulate any value judgment about individualism versus the family network—that one is superior to the other or is more favorable for the adjustment and well-being of the people involved. It simply notes that the individual seen as a systemic part of his or her family network is a common factor binding Hawaii's ethnic groups together—with the exception of the Caucasians. Interdependence among these groups will be reinforced by the increasing rate of intermarriage, and will be balanced against the in-migration of Caucasians from the mainland. We can only surmise that this may serve to retain a notion, however vague, that West is West and the Rest is the Rest.

References

Beaglehole, Ernest. *Some modern Hawaiians.* Honolulu: University of Hawaii Research Publication, no. 19, 1937.

Daws, A. Gavan. *Shoal of time: A history of the Hawaiian islands.* New York: Macmillan, 1968.

Fuchs, Lawrence H. *Hawaii Pono: A social history.* New York: Harcourt, Brace and World, 1961.

Hormann, Bernhard L. Hawaii's mixing people. In Noel P. Gist and Anthony G. Dworking (eds.), *The blending of races.* New York: Wiley and Sons, 1972.

Schmitt, Robert, and Kawaguchi, Paul. *Population characteristics of Hawaii, 1976.* Honolulu: Dept. of Health, Research & Statistics Office Report, no. 9, October 1977.

Simpich, Fredrick. *Anatomy of Hawaii.* New York: Avon Books, 1973.

Honolulu Star-Bulletin, December 15, 1975.

Wright, Theon. *The disenchanted isles: The story of the second revolution in Hawaii.* New York: Dial Press, 1972.

Contributors

BRUCE THOWPAOU BLIATOUT, M.S., M.P.H (Tropical Medicine)
Project director of Refugees of Indochina Cultural Education Project, The
Institute of Behavioral Sciences, Inc., Honolulu, Hawaii

JOHN R. BOND, PH.D. (Psychology)
Associate Clinical Professor of Psychiatry (Psychology), John A. Burns
School of Medicine, University of Hawaii

EUGENE W. CARVALHO, M.D.
Resident, University of Hawaii Affiliated Hospitals Psychiatric Residency
Training Program

WALTER F. CHAR, M.D.
Professor of Psychiatry, John A. Burns School of Medicine, University of
Hawaii

SOON-HYUNG CHUNG, M.D.
Psychiatric consultant, Mental Health Team for Courts and Corrections,
State of Hawaii; Clinical Instructor of Psychiatry, John A. Burns School of
Medicine, University of Hawaii

SHEILA FORMAN, PH.D. (Social Psychology)
Program director of Community Resource Development, Mental Health
Association of Hawaii

YOUNG SOOK KIM HARVEY, PH.D. (Anthropology)
Associate Professor of Anthropology, Chaminade University; Clinical
Associate Professor of Psychiatry, John A. Burns School of Medicine,
University of Hawaii

JING HSU, M.D.
Assistant Professor of Psychiatry, John A. Burns School of Medicine,
University of Hawaii

SATORU IZUTSU, PH.D.
Professor of Public Health, School of Public Health, University of Hawaii; Professor of Psychiatry, John A. Burns School of Medicine, University of Hawaii

DEAN F. KEHMEIER, M.D.
Resident, University of Hawaii Integrated Pathology Residency Program

WILLIAM P. LEBRA, PH.D. (Anthropology)
Professor of Anthropology, University of Hawaii

NGUYEN DANG LIEM, PH.D. (Linguistics)
Professor of Indopacific Languages, University of Hawaii

KWONG-YEN LUM, M.D.
Associate Professor of Psychiatry, John A. Burns School of Medicine, University of Hawaii

THOMAS W. MARETZKI, PH.D. (Anthropology)
Professor of Anthropology and Psychiatry, John A. Burns School of Medicine, University of Hawaii

RICHARD A. MARKOFF, M.D.
Associate Professor of Psychiatry, John A. Burns School of Medicine, University of Hawaii

JOHN F. MCDERMOTT, JR., M.D.
Professor and Chairman of Psychiatry, John A. Burns School of Medicine, University of Hawaii

DANILO E. PONCE, M.D.
Associate Professor of Psychiatry, John A. Burns School of Medicine, University of Hawaii

TERENCE A. ROGERS, PH.D. (Physiology)
Dean, John A. Burns School of Medicine, University of Hawaii

CHERYL TACK, M.A. (Anthropology)
Social work experience with Indochina refugees in the states of Washington and Hawaii

WEN-SHING TSENG, M.D.
Professor of Psychiatry, John A. Burns School of Medicine, University of Hawaii

BENJAMIN B. C. YOUNG, M.D.
Associate Dean of Student Affairs and Assistant Professor of Psychiatry, John A. Burns School of Medicine, University of Hawaii

Index

accommodation, 225, 231. *See also* acculturation
acculturation: Caucasian, 39, 51; Chinese, 54–55, 56, 61, 70–71; Filipino, 177–178; Hmong, 219, 220–223; Japanese, 78, 85, 88, 92, 93; Korean, 142, 145–146; Samoan, 197; Vietnamese, 216–217
ACLU. *See* American Civil Liberties Union
aggression: Caucasian, 49; Chinese, 64, 67–68; Filipino, 162, 230; Hawaiian, 19; Japanese, 97; local, 230; Okinawan, 116, 126; Portuguese, 108–109; Samoan, 187, 194, 196
aiga (Samoan extended family), 185–187, 189, 192. *See also* extended family
AJA (American of Japanese Ancestry). *See* Japanese
alcoholism: Caucasian, 45, 48, 50; Chinese, 65–66; Hawaiian, 19; Japanese, 97; Korean, 145, 147, 149; Okinawan, 129; Vietnamese, 217
ali'i ("ruling class"), 5, 8, 9
aloha, 11–12, 13–14, 41
altruism, 177
Alu Like, 23
American Board of Commissioners for Foreign Missions, 7
American Civil Liberties Union (ACLU), 176
American Samoa, 184

Americanism, 35, 55, 78, 232
amor propio ("self-esteem"), 161
Ariyoshi, George, 176
assimilation, 2, 225. *See also under various ethnic groups*

behavior, 1, 2–3, 4, 197
benevolent societies, 22, 70, 104, 122, 139, 164–165, 177
Big Five (Caucasian companies), 35, 36, 78–79
Buddhism, 75, 207–208, 214
Burns, John A., 37, 87

Caucasians: class structure, 30; compared to other ethnic groups, 43–44; contemporary situation of, 37–41, 230–231; cultural style of, 41–45, 230; traditional culture of, 28–31; as dominant group, 3, 29–31, 33–36, 41, 48, 78–79, 106, 226–227, 229; as ethnic group, 25–26; ethnocentric bias of, 26–27, 32, 35, 39; immigration of, 26–28, 36, 37–39, 41, 101, 230–231; in the recent past, 31–37; individualism of, 41, 46, 230, 231–232; in-migration of, 37–39, 40, 41, 230–231, 232; mental health problems of, 45–50; psychological characteristics of, 42–45, 50; stereotypes of, 41–45; therapeutic approaches to, 50–51. See also *haole; kama'aina; malihini;* military; retirees; young Caucasians
Central Union Church, 31